New Casebooks

JUDE THE OBSCURE

THOMAS HARDY

Edited by
PENNY BOUMELHA

First published in Great Britain 2000 by
MACMILLAN PRESS LTD
Houndmills, Basingstoke, Hampshire RG21 6XS and London
Companies and representatives throughout the world

A catalogue record for this book is available from the British Library.

ISBN 0–333–55135–4 hardcover
ISBN 0–333–55136–2 paperback

First published in the United States of America 2000 by
ST. MARTIN'S PRESS, INC.,
Scholarly and Reference Division,
175 Fifth Avenue, New York, N.Y. 10010

ISBN 0–312–22701–9

Library of Congress Cataloging-in-Publication Data
Jude the obscure, Thomas Hardy / edited by Penny Boumelha.
p.   cm. — (New casebooks)
Includes bibliographical references and index.
ISBN 0–312–22701–9 (cloth)
1. Hardy, Thomas, 1840–1928. Jude the obscure.   I. Boumelha,
Penny.   II. Series.
PR4746.J83   1999
823'.8—dc21   99–15876
                                                        CIP

Selection, editorial matter and Introduction © Penny Boumelha 2000

This book is printed on paper suitable for recycling and made from fully managed and sustained forest sources.

10   9   8   7   6
09   08   07   06   05   04

Printed in Hong Kong

Contents

Acknowledgements

The editor and publishers wish to thank the following for permission to use copyright material:

Maria DiBattista, for material from *First Love: The Affections of Modern Fiction* (1991), pp. 101–9, by permission of the University of Chicago Press; Penny Boumelha, for material from *Thomas Hardy and Women: Sexual Ideology and Narrative Form* (1982), pp. 135–56, by permission of Harvester Wheatsheaf and the University of Wisconsin Press; Christine Brooke-Rose, for material from *Stories, Theories and Things* (1991), pp. 103–22, by permission of Cambridge University Press; Richard Dellamora, for 'Male Relations in Thomas Hardy's *Jude the Obscure*', *Papers on Language and Literature*, 27:4 (1991). Copyright © 1991 by the Board of Trustees, Southern Illinois University, by permission of *Papers on Language and Literature*; Tim Dolin, for 'Jude Fawley and the New Man', by permission of the author; Marjorie Garson, for material from *Hardy's Fables of Integrity: Woman, Body, Text* (1991), pp. 152–78. Copyright © 1991 Majorie Garson, by permission of Oxford University Press; John Goode, for material from *Thomas Hardy: The Offensive Truth* (1988), pp. 138–60, by permission of Blackwell Publishers; Patricia Ingham, for 'Introduction' to Thomas Hardy, *Jude the Obscure*, World Classics edition (1985), pp. xi–xxii. Copyright © 1985 Patricia Ingham, by permission of Oxford University Press; Carla L. Peterson, for material from *The Determined Reader: Gender and Culture in the Novel from Napoleon to Victoria* (1986), pp. 207–26. Copyright © 1986 by Rutgers, the State University of New Jersey, by permission of Rutgers University Press; Ramón Saldívar, for 'Jude the Obscure: Reading and the Spirit of the Law', *ELH*, 50:3 (1983), 607–25, by permission of the Johns Hopkins University Press.

Every effort has been made to trace the copyright holders but if any have been inadvertently overlooked the publishers will be pleased to make the necessary arrangement at the first opportunity.

General Editors' Preface

The purpose of this series of New Casebooks is to reveal some of the ways in which contemporary criticism has changed our understanding of commonly studied texts and writers and, indeed, of the nature of criticism itself. Central to the series is a concern with modern critical theory and its effect on current approaches to the study of literature. Each New Casebook editor has been asked to select a sequence of essays which will introduce the reader to the new critical approaches to the text or texts being discussed in the volume and also illuminate the rich interchange between critical theory and critical practice that characterises so much current writing about literature.

In this focus on modern critical thinking and practice New Casebooks aim not only to inform but also to stimulate, with volumes seeking to reflect both the controversy and the excitement of current criticism. Because much of this criticism is difficult and often employs an unfamiliar critical language, editors have been asked to give the reader as much help as they feel is appropriate, but without simplifying the essays or the issues they raise. Again, editors have been asked to supply a list of further reading which will enable readers to follow up issues raised by the essays in the volume.

The project of New Casebooks, then, is to bring together in an illuminating way those critics who best illustrate the ways in which contemporary criticism has established new methods of analysing texts and who have reinvigorated the important debate about how we 'read' literature. The hope is, of course, that New Casebooks will not only open up this debate to a wider audience, but will also encourage students to extend their own ideas, and think afresh about their responses to the texts they are studying.

John Peck and Martin Coyle
University of Wales, Cardiff

Introduction

PENNY BOUMELHA

I

Jude the Obscure has been described by Terry Eagleton as an 'unacceptable text'.[1] It has always been so, though the nature of its unacceptability has taken a number of forms in the just over a hundred years since its first publication. For its first readers, the matter was relatively simple; most were confident that the novel was an affront to prevailing opinions and moralities. Hardy's forays into unconventionality in his two previous novels, *The Woodlanders* and *Tess of the d'Urbervilles,* had caused a degree of public excitement, but they had done little to prepare his audience for *Jude,* and nothing could have prepared him, in turn, for the furore that greeted its publication. 'Jude the Obscene', one reviewer named it, and others called its author 'Hardy the Degenerate' or 'Hardy as a Decadent'. Its sexual plot was condemned as 'dirt, drivel and damnation', as 'filth and defilement' and 'night-soil'. For some reviewers, like the conservative novelist Margaret Oliphant, it marked Hardy's membership of the 'Anti-Marriage League' in its head-on confrontation with prevailing sexual mores and its disrespectful portrayal of womanhood. For a few of a more progressive cast, like the sexologist Havelock Ellis, it was 'the natural outcome of Mr Hardy's development', exemplifying the 'audacity, purity and sincerity' of an artist engaged with issues of morality beyond mere social etiquette. Either way, it was seen as a challenging and radical novel and, needless to say, it was a best-seller.[2]

It is not only the sexual plot that has made the novel 'unacceptable' to some, nor even the defiant bitterness and the excoriating ironies of its assault on cherished British institutions such as the universities and the church. Both were intensified by the novel's refusal to abide by the canons of good taste, with its scenes of pig-killing, child murder and suicide, and sexual repulsion. The sense that *Jude* is somehow generically excessive, too flamboyant in its melodrama for the sombreness of its theme, troubles a number of later critics.

The more recent rise to prominence of largely socially oriented critical modes would seem to offer the novel a chance to come into its own, as the balance of critical attention has shifted away from morality to a set of issues informed by politics in the broader sense. Remarkably, though, the sense of challenge survives into contemporary responses, and the novel has lost little of its power to provoke. For many modern readers, *Jude* remains discomforting in the ideological ambivalences that resist accommodation in a smooth or uniform critical reading. While it makes a courageous case for the equality of its heroine with its hero, for example, it also shows the tenacity of types and plots that cast the woman as instrumental in the story of the man rather than as subject of her own story. While it has been read as a fiercely committed socialist polemic, it is at the same time a novel utterly without any sense of collective action or class solidarity, intently focused on the unfulfilled claims of its exceptional individual.

Jude the Obscure, then, is a novel whose scandalous challenge to its reader lies not in its plot of illicit sexuality or its lack of respect for social institutions, but in the resistance it offers to any given position of reading. It is a novel that draws a good deal of power from its emotional coherence, but which cannot be made to fit neatly into any set of arguments, views or generic conventions. This is surely one of the principal reasons why it continues to draw the attention of readers (and, more recently, of filmgoers) to its unsettling parable of iconoclasm defeated.

II

This collection of essays aims to take up the range of issues that will arise in most contemporary experiences of reading *Jude the Obscure*. First, there are the questions concerning Jude's thwarted educational ambitions and the associated issues of class. Then, there is the novel's representation of the shifting relations among the four central characters, Jude and Sue, Arabella and Phillotson, with the associated issues of gender and sexuality. Finally, central for many readers are the connections to be established between a critical portrayal of English society in the late nineteenth century and the prominence of literary and cultural allusions, with the associated issues of genre, textuality and representation. These questions, which might broadly be described as those of a political or social criticism, now seem in a way the obvious ones to ask of the novel, no doubt partly because they chime in so closely with our current preoccupations. One of the reasons why *Jude* has provoked so much recent attention, however, is that these have by no means always appeared the central concerns of Hardy's work, as even a glance at the history of Hardy criticism will show. Many earlier critics were much more exercised by other matters, such as Hardy's supposed pessimism and its relation to his agnosticism in matters of religion, or the role of fate and coincidence in the lives of the characters, or the possibilities for creating a tragic hero within the novel form.[3] When Hardy criticism largely preoccupied itself with matters of this kind, *Jude the Obscure* took on a particular significance from its status in Hardy's career as a novelist, as his last major work of fiction. It is the only one of his more widely read novels to be set very largely outside the delimited rural communities of his fictional Wessex, and it is also the one most clearly suffused by anger and resentment at contemporary social arrangements and their effects on people's lives. From this perspective, the novel seemed like a defiantly bitter farewell to the gently nostalgic, bleakly pessimistic evocation of life in the English countryside that criticism tended, for many years, to construct as the 'essential Hardy' (a version of Hardy that still underlies his apparently secure place in the heritage industry so central to current representations of Englishness).[4]

My experience of identifying suitable pieces for inclusion in this collection parallels that reported by Peter Widdowson in his companion New Casebook on *Tess of the d'Urbervilles*:[5] I have found that there was such a significant change in the direction of Hardy studies in the early 1980s that accounts of *Jude the Obscure* written before and after 1980 seem to stand on either side of a gulf. A sense of the novel's challenging nature may be shared, but their methodological differences are enormous. The sharp change of direction is, of course, largely a product or a manifestation of the emergence around this time of a much greater emphasis upon theory in criticism, and of the attempt to formulate a more systematic understanding of the processes in which readers or critics are engaged.

This has revitalised Hardy studies, as it has reinvigorated literary study in general. Before passing on to the more contemporary accounts of the novel exemplified in this collection, I should like briefly to sketch in the background of critical orthodoxy against which they have developed.

Much of the earlier Hardy criticism, even as late as the 1970s, was fundamentally concerned with one or both of two lines of argument. First, there was the project of constructing from the novels a world-view which could be attributed to the author as an originating intention. Secondly, there was an aesthetic evaluation which, all too often, resulted rather unsatisfactorily in an implication that the 'major' works are only 'major' somehow *despite* this world-view, perceived as unduly gloomy. The emergence in the criticism of a very clear hierarchy of 'major' and 'minor' novels shows how great has been the selectivity on the basis of a set of criteria that are only rarely articulated. There was one particularly noticeable difficulty with this. The wish to construct Hardy the novelist as a sincere but slightly clumsy analyst of character-centred human tragedy means that only certain aspects of his writing were valued or discussed in detail. His famous self-description as a novelist 'of Character and Environment'[6] was often interpreted in such a way as to exclude from the idea of the human environment such matters as, for example, the social determinations of class and gender, in favour of weather and topography. The Hardy emerging from this critical perspective is above all a practitioner of rural realism, chronicling the vanishing of rural life and its traditions under the onslaught of encroaching urban growth and the supposed sophistication and rootlessness of the townees. His central characters are construed as tragically flawed (like Michael Henchard in *The Mayor of Casterbridge*), as passive victims of the human predicament on a 'blighted star'[7] (like Tess Durbeyfield in *Tess of the d'Urbervilles*), or as stoic stalwarts doomed by progress (like Giles Winterborne in *The Woodlanders*). Behind them, in this view, stands a host of minor characters, quirky and amusing embodiments of sly rustic innocence. His plots have been ruthlessly mined, by such critics, for instances of malign fate, disastrous coincidence, or nature blindly pursuing its impersonal ends at ironic odds with human needs and desires. The moods of his novels are characterised as grim pessimism alternating with a kind of heavy-handed pawky humour.

Yet it is notable that a good deal of what is evident in Hardy's writing, and is the focus of more recent critical scrutiny, had to be omitted or denigrated in order to make even the 'major' novels fit squarely into this critical categorisation. There is, for example, his elaborate and foregrounded plotting, often stigmatised as melodramatic and coincidence-ridden. There is his allusive and self-conscious writing style, often interpreted as showing the heavy-handedness of an insecure autodidact. There are the abrupt shifts of narrative voice and perspective, occasionally seen as symptoms of an uncertain grasp of technique. There is his sometimes audacious mixing and juxtaposition of diverse generic conventions, too easily read as a failure always to recognise his true calling as a rural realist. Above all, the insistent presence in his novels of an intensely historical and even materialist grasp of the social discourses that meet in such ideas as 'character' and 'environment' received scant attention.

As with any such brief, even caricatured, overview of a particular trend, I am of course at risk here of passing over in silence some fine earlier work. There are intelligent, subtle and rewarding accounts of Hardy's fiction by (among others) John Bayley, J. Hillis Miller, Roy Morrell and Penelope Vigar, and the list of Further Reading at the end of this volume directs my reader toward them. Importantly, too, I should not wish to appear to be making any general suggestion that what is more recent is inevitably better. I do not believe this to be the case, though I do regard the intellectual transformations of the period around 1980 as having produced a criticism so different in kind from much of what preceded it that it is sometimes hard to think across such a radical break. For the most part, the intervention of critical theory in writing about Hardy has been beneficial, and has productively shifted the principal areas of concern. With a less evaluative and more properly analytic understanding of the critical process has come a shift in attention towards precisely those elements that do not seem to settle easily into the mould of the rural realist. Where there *has* been a continuity between the older and newer critical versions of *Jude the Obscure*, however, has been in the more or less unspoken consensus that it is an intransigently *social* novel. Whereas some others of Hardy's novels have been recast in the light of social and political concerns, *Jude* has been less drastically transformed. Among the newer critical methodologies, it remains the case that it is very much more likely to be discussed from a feminist or a Marxist viewpoint than in the framework of a less directly socially oriented critical theory such as deconstruction. In fact, most of the interesting and challenging work in *Jude the*

Obscure in the last fifteen years or so has engaged head-on if not exclusively with the issues of gender and/or class, as I hope this *New Casebook* exemplifies.

III

I want now to comment on the essays in this collection, and to some extent on the current or recent work of which they are broadly representative. It is important to realise, though, that critical theories cannot always be kept neatly separated in their different boxes; of the pieces that follow, for example, Marjorie Garson's (essay 9) might as easily be seen as an example of feminist or of psychoanalytic criticism, or John Goode's (essay 5) as fitting perfectly well into definitions both of Marxist and of post-structuralist analysis. With this point in mind, I shall not discuss these essays by allocating them to particular theoretical-critical schools or allegiances but rather in terms of their approaches to those central concerns of *Jude the Obscure* that I have already identified above: that is, class and the educational theme, gender and sexuality, and representation.

The volume of writing on issues of class in Hardy's fiction overall has not been especially great, although much attention has been paid to the complex of feelings attributed to Hardy in relation to his own class position and transition, from the son of a Dorset builder to the successful, wealthy author and friend of the famous. His education, and the fact that he never attended a university, have also attracted much comment. There has been less attention to connecting these aspects of his life with more specifically textual issues concerning class. Pre-eminent in this area, both in influence and in insight, is the chapter by Raymond Williams in his important book of 1970, *The English Novel from Dickens to Lawrence*. Williams significantly identifies in Hardy's writing what might be called an anxiety of voice, a shifting or doubleness of tone and style between those of the experienced countryman and the educated observer:

> The tension is not between rural and urban, in the ordinary senses, nor between an abstracted intuition and an abstracted intelligence. The tension, rather, is in his own position, his own lived history, within a general process of change which could come clear and alive in him because it was not only general but in every detail of his feeling observation and writing immediate and particular.[8]

In this argument, then, Hardy's personal history is made to be exemplary of a larger shift within English culture and society, and William's persuasive and subtle establishment of connections between this shift and the detail of the writing has impressed itself upon a good deal of subsequent criticism.

A later account of class issues, more influenced by poststructuralism, can be found in George Wotton's *Thomas Hardy: Towards a Materialist Criticism* (1985), which brings together a Marxist reading of the novels and analysis of the critical and cultural constructions that have dominated discussion of Hardy. Similarly, Peter Widdowson's *Hardy in History* (1989) draws on the sociological tradition of Marxist criticism to set up its account of the effects of prevailing critical traditions on interpretative commentary. Dealing in more detail with *Jude the Obscure* in particular is Terry Eagleton's Introduction to the Macmillan New Wessex edition of the novel (1975), which takes as its main focus the class-based nature of the Victorian and modern education systems in Britain.[9] Of the essays collected here, those most directed, in their different ways, toward class issues are those by Ingham (essay 1), Boumelha (essay 3), and Goode (essay 5). My own essay (3) is discussed below; here, I will point out only that it is concerned with the novel's exploration of contemporary social structures, by means of its central couple situated at the meeting-point of ideologies and oppressions, class and gender.

John Goode's extended and sometimes difficult discussion of the nature of Jude's obscurity and of the ways in which the novel might be called radical (essay 5) inflects its Marxism through poststructuralist concerns with textuality and epistemology. Taking as his title ('Hardy's fist') part of a famous rhetorical question by Hardy's friend and contemporary Edmund Gosse – 'What has Providence done to Mr Hardy that he should rise up in the arable land of Wessex and shake his fist at his Creator?'[10] – Goode begins by identifying in the novel a certain challenging combativeness in its mode of address to its reader. *Jude* is, he says, from the first 'conceived as an intervention';[11] it is a novel taking up a committed position in relation to significant controversies of the late nineteenth century. Goode goes on to explore the limits of the novel's radicalism by focusing on its allusive and parodic relation to those debates. The various dimensions of the novel – the realist, the mythic, the melodramatic – all serve in their different registers to enact its engagement with 'the ideological couple of late capitalism',[12] education and the family, which constructs and positions Jude's sense of self. Knowledge and sex, embodied in the text at once as the main character's two desires and as the narrative discourses representing education and the family, both represent the possibility of an escape from the self for Jude, but their interaction keeps him imprisoned in place as the novel's structure replays its series of settings and plots.

Patricia Ingham (essay 1) considers some very similar issues. Her Introduction to the novel provides a subtle and textually attentive way of understanding its allusiveness in the context of the stratifications of class and gender which render Jude's educational project a hopelessly naïve one. For Goode's ideological couple of education and the family, Ingham substitutes at the core of the novel three of the most important areas of social debate and change at this period: access to education, women's roles, and the decline of Christianity. She points out that there has been a tendency for critics to identify too intensely and simplistically with Jude, taking on in their readings his own aspiration to education and consequently sharing the bitterness of his rejection. In her own reading, the character's educational aims are more ambivalently presented in the text, as at once self-delusion and disguised ambition for social advancement. 'Obscure', she points out, refers to Jude's social failure, and not to a thwarted love of learning. The frequent allusions to the representatives of high culture, and in particular to Oxford learning, take on an ironic tone from their very irrelevance to the dilemmas faced by Jude and Sue; a Christminster education would have done nothing to provide a resolution to the questions about social organisation posed by the novel. For Ingham, these ambivalences and ironies give *Jude the Obscure* a subversive power beyond that available to a story of failed ambition; it remains, for her, 'the most powerful indictment of the sexual and class oppression of its time'.[13]

IV

In the essays by Goode and Ingham discussed above, questions of class have been moved out of the context of composition (that is, to put it rather crudely, from the author's biography) to the context of representation and the question of reading. A rather similar refocusing can be detected in approaches to gender and sexuality in *Jude*. These are issues that have long been of interest to Hardy criticism, and indeed to his first readers. From the outset, his fiction was associated in particular with central female characters and their fates. In his essay on *Jude*, Havelock Ellis claims:

> The real and permanent interest in Mr Hardy's books is not his claim to be the exponent of Wessex – a claim which has been more than abundantly recognised – but his intense preoccupation with the mysteries of women's hearts.[14]

Hardy's later novels were written in the period of what is now called 'first-wave feminism', and he was soon enlisted on one side or the other of the debates about New Women, alternatives to marriage, sexual morality, and sex education which flourished in the latter part of the nineteenth century as vigorously as do their modern equivalents in our own time. For the feminist Clementina Black, for instance, writing in 1892, Hardy was certainly an ally, 'one of that brave and clear-sighted minority' who are prepared to consider a woman's moral worth as more than her chastity. For Elizabeth Chapman, on the other hand, he exemplifies (in the title of her essay of 1897) 'The Disparagement of Women in Literature':

> I do not think it would be very wide of the mark to describe the abstract being masquerading in Mr Hardy's work as woman as a compound three-parts animal and one-part fay; or, as one might put it, with *Jude the Obscure* fresh in one's memory, three-parts Arabella and one part Sue.[15]

Right from the first, then, the involvement of gender issues in Hardy's texts has been at once acknowledged and contentious, as has the prominence of sex in his plotting.

In the earlier criticism, what seemed most at stake was the creation of his male and/or female characters, and the degree of sympathy with which they and their plights are drawn. Whether or not Hardy liked women was long considered a matter worth attention, and indeed the particular relation between the male author and the female character continues to be an issue within criticism. Perhaps surprisingly, one of the earliest attempts to move the debate away from the author came in D. H. Lawrence's waywardly brilliant 'Study of Thomas Hardy'. This is clearly a recasting of Hardy's novels as they would have been had Lawrence written them, rather than an analysis. It is particularly interesting, though, in the centrality it gives to sexuality in the novel, and in the unusually sympathetic view he takes of Arabella as a kind of principle of the 'primary female', 'reckless and unconstrained', as opposed to Sue, 'the production of the long selection by man of the woman in whom the female is subordinated to the male principle'.[16] Lawrence's account of a Sue Bridehead whose sexual coldness causes the downfall of Jude was for some time highly influential. It took the advent of feminism, with a more theorised understanding of gender, representation and ideology, to restore Sue to critical attention. Among landmark studies of this kind, Mary Jacobus's exploration of how different the novel looks when attention is once shifted from its male to its female central character, 'Sue the Obscure', was excellently supported by Patricia Ingham's demonstration from manuscript sources and emendations that Sue Bridehead was from the first central to the novel's exploration of oppression. In the same vein, John Goode was the first to conduct a critical analysis of the novel in its similarity to and its radical difference from the New Woman fiction of the 1890s.[17]

Since then, questions of gender have been very widely seen as intrinsic both to the novel's radicalism and to the sense of bitter defeat that pervades it. Central to the argument of several of the essays here (including those discussed above) is an exploration of the relationship between class and gender in the novel, especially as focused in the relation between the educational and sexual plots. In her study of reader-protagonists in the nineteenth-century novel, Carla Peterson (essay 4) draws on both the mythic and the realist dimension of *Jude* to pose the educational plot as one of the numerous modes of likeness or complementarity between the protagonists. It is not only Jude who reads and seeks to understand his life in the light of learning; Sue's self-education demonstrates a parallel attempt to situate herself in the cultural mainstream. Interestingly, while Jude's exclusion from that cultural and educational mainstream on the basis of his class has regularly been seen as a tragic injustice, Sue's parallel consignment to self-education on the grounds of her gender still largely goes unremarked.

Richard Dellamora's account of the interweaving of the educational and sexual themes takes a rather different course. Taking its methodological example from feminist criticism of nineteenth-century texts by women, Dellamora's book *Masculine Desire* is focused on representations of masculinity in writing by men:

> My discussion depends on attempts to ascertain masculine experience during the period, experience not only of men who appear recognisably

'homosexual' but of a wider and more varied range of men. For my purposes, these are men who were engaged in the production of revisionary masculine discourses ... that attempt to enlarge masculine capacities for relationships while respecting the boundaries of conventional middle-class patterns of career, including marriage.[18]

In this context, the essay by Dellamora reprinted here (7) explores relationships among the men in the novel. Where Jude and Phillotson have often been cast simply as sexual rivals for Sue, Dellamora discovers what might be called a plot of desire between the two men. The role of male bonding, mentoring and homosociality in relation to the history of men's education becomes central. Dellamora points out that it is Phillotson, and not Sue, whom Jude initially pursues to Christminster, and draws attention to those other men in the novel – from physician Vilbert to the composer Jude visits – who are cast as potential, but failed, mentors. In this context, the novel's focus on the isolation of Jude and Sue becomes newly evident. Jude's relationships with other men (and particularly with other working-class men) are shown as destructive, while Sue Bridehead's combination of intellectual iconoclasm and sexual outlawry means that she has effectively no form of relationship with other women; the two are trapped within the focus on the life of the heterosexual couple.

A crucial shift in contemporary gender-based analysis of *Jude the Obscure* (and, indeed of fiction in general) is to be found reflected in this collection. It is the movement away from character-centred criticism and the representation of male and female characters into a recognition of the role of gender in matters of narrative structure and generic affiliation. My essay (Boumelha, essay 3) is concerned in part with the form of the novel, and especially in relation to the double contexts of 1890s New Woman fiction and of Hardy's own earlier generic experimentation. New Woman fiction, by and large, was written and understood as deliberately controversial, focused on the analysis of particular problems faced by women, and especially upon the domain of sexual relationship. *Jude*, obviously , was seen to fit fairly well into this category, except that it obstinately places Jude equally at its centre. I argue that this is because it is Hardy's final version of a 'double tragedy',[19] in which the woman's sexual tragedy and the man's intellectual or social tragedy for the first time merge into a single, shared plot. The notable stress on the likeness of the two highlights this merging. At the same time, though, the novel takes its episodic form from its hero, with an inevitable distancing of Sue, who is often apprehended through the responses and interpretations of Jude. The result is to de-naturalise the representation of the woman; the reader is forced to recognise the partiality of the text and to attend to the construction of the feminine through the consciousness of the male.

Marjorie Garson (essay 9) starts from a rather similar point: that the structure and the narrative impulse of the novel take their shape from Jude's wanting. The book from which this essay is taken, *Hardy's Fables of Integrity*, has a particular concern with the anxieties Garson detects in Hardy's writing about the integrity of the body; she points out the frequency with which he dwells on the fear of dissolution, on scenes of bodily fragmentation, on clothing, and on grotesques such as gargoyles. These anxieties about wholeness, she suggests, are especially acutely realised in the roles played by women in relation to men. It is for this reason that the plot of *Jude the Obscure* seems to turn obsessively around the same fundamental episode: Jude's desire is thwarted by the intervention of a woman, associated with dismemberment or destruction. Looking at the structural function of the characters rather than at the characterisations themselves, Garson is able to demonstrate the way in which the functional identity of Sue and Arabella seems to confer upon them at once the power of what comes to seem a sexual destiny and a level of collusion among them which is never present in the actual relationship represented. In the patterning of the novel's structure and narrative energy upon Jude's desires and their thwarting, and in the construction of the female characters to correspond to characteristically masculine fears of dismemberment, dissolution and disillusion, Garson finds a scapegoating of the women in a mythic subtext forged from a private obsession.

Similarly focused upon the mythic dimension to the narrative is Maria DiBattista's account of *Jude* (essay 8). The essay is taken from her book *First Love*,[20] in which she interprets narratives of first love as a form of mythicising of the primal. Chronological priority and emotional precedence, she suggests, lie at the core of the anxieties of Hardy's plots and male protagonists: 'This fear of first occurrences governs the love story of *Jude the Obscure* and gives Hardy's familial and folk plot a startling anthropological clarity.'[21] Whereas Garson's *Jude* traced the development of what might be called a private myth into a narrative structure, DiBattista's version of myth finds an archaic anthropological narrative of defloration in the novel's triangulation of relationships. In an interesting reversal of the logic by which Sue is commonly seen to represent the disruptive force of modernity, she is here seen to be the bearer of the archaic. Her surname, Bridehead, is only one indication of the fact that she is a figure of both virginity and defloration. The sense of doom that hangs over the family, the site of Jude and Sue's first meeting at the Spot of the Martyrdoms, and her association with the pagan all combine to invoke the archaic taboo of virginity, foreshadowing the disaster that will follow from consummation of their relationship. DiBattista's account of the novel is centrally focused upon issues of gender and sexuality, though its critical allegiances are clearly to anthropology rather than to feminist scholarship.

Tim Dolin (essay 10) brings together gender criticism and narrative theory in an investigation of the novel's form which could be said to find in the plot the story of the novel's writing. For Dolin, *Jude the Obscure* constitutes an interrogation of a narrative form that might be seen as intrinsically masculine, the English *Bildungsroman* or 'novel of development'. This is a narrative form predicated upon individual aspiration and its social ratification, and as such is commonly the vehicle for stories of success: ambition rewarded, class transition achieved, social recognition accorded. In Hardy's version, Dolin proposes, the form is tested in a way that both probes the ideological starting-points and undermines stable definitions of masculinity. Driven from place to place by the restless pursuit of dream and desire, Jude is simultaneously displaced from one narrative structure of masculinity after another, as the plots of spiritual journey, individual vocation, marriage, and sacrifice are all invoked and discarded. For Dolin, Jude's literal vagrancy comes to equate to a kind of narrative homelessness as the coherence and sequence of familiar nineteenth-century novel forms are continually denied him.

The major developments within gender-focused criticism of *Jude the Obscure*, then, have invoked increasing sophistication in the approach to masculinity and femininity, not as direct reflections of the real experience of people in the world, but as powerful ideological constructions that exercise real pressure upon the possibility of such experience. The study of forms of masculinity has been among the more recent developments. Where once it was tacitly presumed that gender was the preserve of female critics as of female characters, the increasing influence of studies of masculinity and of gay studies has extended the possibilities, enabling critics to analyse the ways in which forms of masculinity, too, are social discourses.

V

The third main area of recent critical concern I have identified in *Jude the Obscure* is that of textuality and representation. It will be evident that that concern has in some sense pervaded most of the essays discussed above. Of course, it has always played some part in responses to Hardy's novels; studies of his narrative technique and style have of necessity raised questions of this kind. In particular, the sometimes contradictory generic allegiances and the notable allusiveness of *Jude* have drawn critical attention to that dimension of the novel that makes implicit claims about the status of fiction and the relation of what might be called 'high' or 'official' culture to the more popular cultural form of the novel. Its frequent invocations of classical myth and the Bible, for example, can be seen as a form of subtle commentary upon the conventions of heroism and the relation to them of the novel's own 'obscure' (because isolated, rural and working-class) hero. Among useful discussions of such aspects of *Jude* can be counted Bayley's account of the Shelleyan themes and references, Giordano's positing of the novel as 'anti-*Bildungsroman*', Sutherland's consideration of the significant presences and withheld names of the ghosts of noted Oxford intellectuals who haunt the text, and, somewhat earlier, the general attentiveness to matters of form and style of Ian Gregor and Albert J. Guerard.[22]

With poststructuralism and deconstruction, however, there has developed a higher degree of self-consciousness in criticism focused on the textuality and language of works of fiction, and two examples of such theoretically alert criticism are included here. The essay by Christine Brooke-Rose (essay 6) is taken from the collection *Stories, Theories and Things*,[23] whose title confirms its writer's multiple focus: on the particularities of narrative texts ('Stories'), on the aims and status of the interpretative act ('Theories'), and on the way in which representation relates to experience of the world ('Things'). Brooke-Rose has combined fiction, theory and teaching in her own work, and is concerned with those interactions within her writing also. She takes her theoretical starting-points in linguistics and in the narratological version of structuralism, but, keen to do justice as she sees it to individual literary creativity as well as to the analytic armoury of the critic, her response to those starting-points is as sceptical as it is well informed. In her account of *Jude the Obscure*, she identifies knowledge as a key element both of the novel's thematic concerns and of its narrative practices. Intellectual knowledge; carnal knowledge; secrecy and revelation; the sources (such as books, common sense, superstition or religion, self-analysis and the expertise of the artisan) from which knowledge might be sought or found: all, in her account, contribute powerfully to the dilemmas, the histories and the fates of the central characters. At the same time, the novel is ostentatiously manipulative in its handling of narrative point of view, forcing the reader to recognise the ways in which textual knowledge is shared, withheld or communicated. A variety of episodes and techniques – the use of the figure of an imagined observer, the withholding of the names of the Oxford worthies, the blurring of narrational commentary and character's thought – serve to make the standpoint of narrative observation unusually evident and to enforce a self-consciousness in the position of the reader.

Ramón Saldívar (essay 2) similarly sees Hardy's relation to his reader as being at the core of the novel and of its interest for critical analysis. In a sometimes demanding and certainly complex essay, Saldívar sets out to explore the tensions and ambiguities between the narrative and figurative dimensions of the novel – between what might be called, taking up the novel's own terms, the 'letter' and the 'spirit'. Focusing on the importance both of literal processes of writing – exchanges of letters, stonecarving of texts, mastery of alphabets – and of metaphors of translation and language-learning, Saldívar represents Jude in the world of the novel as a kind of reader learning to test and correct his own practices of reading. In this argument, the illusions that the novel so painfully shatters in its hero result from Jude's taking too literally the idea of the 'law of transmutation' that he once imagines to exist, by which 'a rule, prescription, or clue of the nature of a secret cipher'[24] would enable him effortlessly to move between languages or, by extension, between his desires and the world. This examination of the figure of the reader as a problem, a potentially disruptive force, provides the basis for a further analysis of Hardy's suspicious, even on occasion antagonistic, narrative stance toward the novel's implied readership.

In such accounts of *Jude the Obscure*, the persistent linguistic themes and self-consciousness of Hardy's writing, often elsewhere noted in passing, shift toward the core of his work. 'The letter killeth' is the novel's epigraph,[25] and the attempts of its central characters variously to live by the letter of the law or to flout its prescriptions are crucial to its central narrative structures. Those modes of criticism starting explicitly in a theorised understanding of language have brought a fresh urgency and sophistication to the analysis of such evident textual self-consciousness. In the process, they have also notably increased the complexity critics locate in Hardy's writing, so that it is seen to join an analysis of its own textual status and a commentary upon its narrative forms to the plots and concerns noticed elsewhere. Like all significant works of fiction, *Jude the Obscure* yields the story of its own writing.

VI

From whichever of these critical modes it is approached (and, of course, other ascendant critical modes will join or displace them), *Jude the Obscure* continues currently to draw the attention of both professional and other readers. In part, this is due to its challenging exploration of the most characteristic arenas in which self-realisation is sought (education, work, and relationship) and its demonstration that they too are permeated by social discourses and structures that block the avenues to imagined individual fulfilment: "'You shan't learn!" ... "You shan't labour!" ... "You shan't love!"'[26] The myth of individual transcedence – that the one who cares the most, or wishes the most intensely, or works the hardest, or has the most talent, depending upon the particular variant of the ideology, will inevitably achieve their goals – is one of the most cherished narrative structures by which we seek to live, as much in the late twentieth century as it was in the late nineteenth. *Jude* provides a most unsettling, because unsentimental, argument for its illusoriness. At the same time, part of the novel's sometimes startling air of modernity comes too from its blurring of the most common gendered versions of the myth: male transcedence is achieved through education or vocation, female transcedence through marriage and motherhood. The utter misery and failure in which each of these ends in *Jude the Obscure* is, undeniably, emotionally bleak, but there is a certain intellectual exhilaration to be derived from its refusal either simply to replicate those gendered structures as if they were somehow natural, or to generalise across them as if they had no social effectivity. Finally, the way in which the novel combines some of the most traditional of popular narrative forms (the hero's life represented as a journey, for example) with a high level of sophisticated and self-conscious reflection upon its status as representation challenges some prevailing assumptions about the distinctiveness and relative value of popular and high cultures. The sexual unorthodoxy and godless universe of *Jude the Obscure* may have lost their power to shock, but the novel continues to provoke and unsettle.

NOTES

1. Terry Eagleton, 'Liberality and Order: The Criticism of John Bayley', *New Left Review*, 110 (1978), 39.

2. The hostile reception given to *Jude the Obscure* is described in Robert Gittings, *The Older Hardy* (London, 1978), pp. 79–80. For contemporary reviews, including those cited here, see Graham Clarke (ed.), *Thomas Hardy: Critical Assessments* (Mountfield, Sussex, 1993), vol. 1, pp. 229–93, and R. G. Cox (ed.), *Thomas Hardy: The Critical Heritage* (London, 1970), pp. 249–315.

3. For example, see respectively, Norman Holland, Jr, '*Jude the Obscure*: Hardy's Symbolic Indictment of Christianity', *Nineteenth-Century Fiction*, 9 (1954), 50–61; William H. Marshall, *The World of the Victorian Novel* (South Brunswick and New York, 1967), pp. 404–24; Arthur Mizener, *The Sense of Life in the Modern Novel* (London, 1965), pp. 55–77; or Dale Kramer, *Thomas Hardy: The Forms of Tragedy* (Detroit, 1975), pp. 136–65.

4. For a discussion of 'heritage' Hardy, see Peter Widdowson, *Hardy in History: A Study in Literary Sociology* (London, 1989), pp. 5–6, 55–72.

5. Peter Widdowson (ed.) *Tess of the d'Urbervilles/Thomas Hardy*, New Casebooks (London, 1992), pp. 3–4.

6. Hardy divided the Wessex edition of his novels into categories: I. Novels of Character and Environment (including *Jude the Obscure*); II. Romances and Fantasies; III. Novels of Ingenuity; and IV. Mixed Novels. See his 'General Preface' to the 1912 Wessex edition of Works, in Vol. 1: *Tess of the d'Urbervilles*. Also reprinted in each volume of the New Wessex edition of his novels.

7. Thomas Hardy, *Tess of the d'Urbervilles: A Pure Woman*. Introduction by P. N. Furbank, New Wessex edn (London, 1975), p. 58.

8. Raymond Williams, *The English Novel from Dickens to Lawrence* (New York, 1970), pp. 111–12.

9. George Wotton, *Thomas Hardy: Towards a Materialist Criticism* (Dublin, 1985); Peter Widdowson, *Hardy in History: A Study in Literary Sociology* (London, 1989); Terry Eagleton, 'Introduction', in

Thomas Hardy, *Jude the Obscure*, New Wessex edn (London, 1975), pp. 13–23.

10. Edmund Gosse, Review, *Cosmopolis* (Jan., 1896), republished in *Thomas Hardy: Critical Assessments*, ed. Graham Clarke (Mountfield, Sussex, 1993), Vol. 1, p. 258.

11. See p. 98 below.

12. Ibid.

13. See p. 30 below.

14. Havelock Ellis, 'Concerning *Jude the Obscure*', *Savoy*, 6 (1896), 35–49; reprinted in Graham Clarke (ed.), *Thomas Hardy: Critical Assessments* (Mountfield, Sussex, 1993), vol. 3, pp. 93–4.

15. Clementina Black, review of *Tess of the d'Urbervilles*, *Illustrated London News* (9 Jan. 1892), 50; Elizabeth Rachael Chapman, *Marriage Questions in Modern Fiction, and Other Essays on Kindred Subjects* (London, 1897), p. 80.

16. D. H. Lawrence, 'Study of Thomas Hardy', in *Phoenix: The Posthumous Papers of D. H. Lawrence*, ed. Edward D. McDonald (London, 1936, reprinted 1961), pp. 493–4, 496.

17. Mary Jacobus, 'Sue the Obscure', *Essays in Criticism*, 25 (1975), 304–28; Patricia Ingham, 'The Evolution of *Jude the Obscure*', *Review of English Studies*, 27 (1976), 27–37, 159–69; John Goode, 'Sue Bridehead and the New Woman', in *Women Writing and Writing About Women*, ed. Mary Jacobus (London, 1979), pp. 100–13.

18. Richard Dellamora, *Masculine Desire: The Sexual Politics of Victorian Aestheticism* (Chapel Hill, NC, 1990), p. 5.

19. See p. 000 below.

20. Maria A. DiBattista, *First Love: The Affections of Modern Fiction* (Chicago, 1991).

21. See p. 170 below

22. John Bayley, *An Essay on Hardy* (Cambridge, 1978), pp. 191–218; Frank R. Giordano, Jr, '*Jude the Obscure* and the *Bildungsroman*', *Studies in the Novel*, 4 (1972), 580–91; John Sutherland, 'A Note on the Teasing Narrator in *Jude the Obscure*', *English Literature in Transition*, 17 (1974), 159–62; Ian Gregor, *The Great Web: The Form of Hardy's Major Fiction* (London, 1974), pp. 207–33; and Albert J. Guerard, *Thomas Hardy: The Novels and Stories* (Cambridge, MA, 1949).

23. Christine Brooke-Rose, *Stories, Theories and Things* (Cambridge, 1991).

24. Thomas Hardy, *Jude the Obscure*. Introduction by Terry Eagleton, with notes by P. N. Furbank, New Wessex edn (London, 1975), p. 54.

25. Ibid., title page and p. 393.

26. Ibid., p. 347.

1

Jude the Obscure

PATRICIA INGHAM

After the crude irony of the first printed title, *The Simpletons*, its lurid replacement *Hearts Insurgent*, and the weakly descriptive suggestion *The Recalcitrants*, *Jude the Obscure* seems satisfactorily precise and untheatrical. But its asymmetry has the effect of over-emphasising the male protagonist; and the apparent protest at his fate has drawn attention to the parallels with Hardy's own life. Editors have felt documentation of the autobiographical element was essential: Jude as Hardy, Sue as Mary Hardy–Emma Gifford–Florence Henniker all in one, and many details to be spelled out, even if they do not include a fictitious son by his cousin Tryphena to represent Little Father Time. This evidence is produced partly to refute Hardy's typically devious denial that there is 'a scrap of personal detail in it'.[1]

But Hardy's obfuscations are often oblique truths and perhaps he was right to throw the critic off that particular scent. In relation to the novel such information is trivial; it tells the biographer nothing he does not know already and critically it is a distraction. It diverts attention from the profounder sense in which *Jude* relates to its own time by engaging with three major forces in late Victorian society. These are the middle-class stranglehold on access to the most prestigious university education and on its content; the awareness of women that the self-estimates and roles forced on them by a partriarchal society were not the only possible ones; and the unresolved tension evoked by an established Christianity which for many had lost rational justification, but which was still socially and imaginatively powerful.

Such a schema is crudely sociological and reductive, whereas the novel itself struggles to express essentially hostile attitudes to these forces, which reach the reader as the 'series of seemings' that Hardy refers to in his original Preface. Only the surface symmetry of the story matches the simplicity of the schematised outline: Jude's hopeful and despairing visits to Christminster; Jude and Sue both unsuitably married, divorced, and captured in the same marriage trap again; the contrast of 'flesh and spirit' represented by Arabella and Sue, appealing to the two sides of Jude's nature; Arabella's child killing Sue's children; Jude liberated by grief, Sue subjugated by it. This symmetrical and stylised design runs through the details of the work: in the double seduction by Arabella, the double reference to Samson, Sue praying to Venus and Apollo, then prostrate on the floor of the 'ritual church', St Silas, a black heap contrasting with the white heap she made when she leapt from Phillotson's bedroom window. But the design is merely a grid superimposed with a specious neatness on a presentation of turbulent contradictory views of the three subjects. The epigraph to the whole novel, 'The letter killeth', would make a better title, its meaning refracted by each of the three themes. The incompleteness of the quotation is vital: in no part of the story does 'the spirit' give life.

The account of failed academic hopes has, unlike the sexual story, often been read simplistically, particularly when taken as a reflection of Hardy's own university hopes thwarted by poverty and lack of influence. But the autobiography must have been unexpectedly self-critical, since the narrator makes clear from the start the delusory nature of the boy's quest. Visually it is uncertain whether at first he really sees Christminster at all or merely the city 'miraged in the peculiar atmosphere', 'hardly recognisable save by the eye of faith'. And at his last view before going there he is not sure of anything about the city except that it 'had seemed to be visible'. He fosters this visual sham on his first night in the city, when passing 'objects out of harmony with its general expression' he allows his eyes to 'slip over them as if he did not see them'. He imagines alleys 'apparently never trodden now by the foot of man' whose 'very existence seemed to be forgotten'. The accounts he has of the place come from unreliable and vague witnesses: the carter recounting a report, the witch-like old woman.

Although as a child he recognises (or thinks he does) a 'city of light' where 'the tree of knowledge grows', and which is a 'ship manned by scholarship and religion', the object of Jude's adult ambition is oddly ambiguous. The learning which he so painfully acquired and proudly lists until brought back to earth by a slap from a pig's penis is already at this stage inextricable for him from religion or scholarship as a profession, with salary attached. In the early stages the narrator speaks of him as a 'prospective D. D. Professor, Bishop, or what not', and fellowships were the entrance to both scholarly and ecclesiastical preferment.[2] For Jude to become an undergraduate and then a graduate is to appropriate middle-class culture and status in one, a fact he is startlingly aware of. This is why when he meets Arabella he is exultantly listing his achievements in Classics and Mathematics, those requirements for access to the 'liberal education' which Oxford defended vehemently for most of the nineteenth century as superior to and subsuming vocational subjects.[3] They open the professional gates to Jude, or so he thinks: '"These things are only a beginning ... I'll be D. D. before I have done! ..." And then he continued to dream, and thought that he might even become a bishop by leading a pure, energetic, wise, Christian life. And what an example he would set! If his income were £5,000 a year, he would give away £4,500 in one form or another, and live sumptuously (for him) on the remainder!'

Rejected by the colleges, he passes on to self-delusion, as the narrator makes clear, when he talks to the curate, Highbridge, about his failure, 'dwelling with an unconscious bias less on the intellectual and ambitious side of his dream, and more upon the theological': '"I don't regret the collapse of my university hopes one jot ... I *don't care for social success any more* ... I bitterly regret the Church, and the loss of my chance of being her ordained minister."' (My italics.)

Rather disconcertingly for the reader, the narrator, whose sympathy with Jude has been acute so far, now berates him for 'mundane ambition masquerading in a surplice' and rebukes him for that social unrest, that desire for upward mobility, which from the 1870s had been an explicit reason for Oxford in particular holding back the spread of adult education to the working class in order to protect 'the overcrowded professions'. The narrator's volte-face sets the future pattern. He may condemn Jude sometimes but elsewhere, for instance in Jude's speech to the crowd at Christminster, he will support his attempt to 'reshape' his course and rise into another class. The very title of the novel (in its final form) is a protest not at Jude's exclusion from the university nor at his thwarted scholarship but at his social failure. The odd emphasis thrown on the adjective by the archaic phrasing suggests that, for some self-evident reason, he ought not to have remained in the 'obscurity' of the working class.

Not only this, but Sue continues to assert rather melodramatically that Jude is one of the very men with a passion for learning that 'Christminster was intended for ... But you are elbowed off the pavements by millionaires' sons.' Long after his academic efforts have become nominal, both of them cling to this idea. He even still hopes for acceptance before they return to the city for the last time: 'I love the place – although I know how it hates all men like me – the so-called Self-taught, – how it scorns our laboured acquisitions ... Perhaps it will soon wake up, and be generous ...'. So Jude is seen equally forcefully as being and as not being the pure seeker after learning.

Despite his delusions about Christminster, both Jude and the narrator are seized of the desirability of the learning that the university offers, and even Sue speaks of some qualified 'respect' for the place 'on the intellectual side'. What Christminster offers manifests itself in the web of allusion and quotation that enmeshes the novel: in the epigraphs, in the Christminster voices, and everywhere in the text.

Comments on this material that spell out references have overlooked its overriding importance as a cruel and varying witness to its own alienation from the lives with which it is interwoven. The very epigraphs relating to Sue and Jude, those bland emblems (at first reading) of the action in each section, dissolve before the reader's eyes into something different. Jude's dealings with Arabella at Marygreen seem aptly summarised by the quotation from Esdras: 'Yea, many there be that have run out of their wits for women ...'. But the point of the original context of the passage is that, though this may be true, truth is stronger than wine, the king, or women – a passionate assertion forlornly unrelated to the story of Jude's life. The two quotations introducing the Christminster section seem to capture the emergent optimism of Jude now embarking on his academic course – 'Save his own soul, he hath no star' – and the joy of his incipient love for Sue – 'Nearness led to awareness ... love grew with time'. Both fragments are torn out of context: Swinburne's eulogy on self-reliance is woefully inapt for Jude; and Ovid is beginning not a joyous love-affair but the tragic story of the doomed lovers, Pyramus and Thisbe.

Even more cruelly irrelevant are the snatches from Sappho and The Book of Esther. 'There was no other girl, O bridegroom, like her!' fixes Jude's growing delight in Sue at Melchester; but what Sappho in context was promising the bridegroom was that erotic joy, the gift of Aphrodite, that Sue, for all her formal worship of the goddess whose image she buys, painfully fails to deliver. Similarly, her final collapse into abject religiosity seems epitomised by the sentence describing Esther: 'And she humbled her body greatly, and all the places of her joy she filled with her torn hair'. But in the original account Esther's penitence is part of a calculated plan which triumphantly achieves the salvation of the Jews from slaughter, while Sue's brings nothing but suffering and death. The epigraphs are mockeries of what they appear to be: not formal and precise summaries linking neatly to each section but statements in an ambiguous and hostile relationship to the text.

Within the novel other allusions relate in the same oblique way. The most extended attempt to annex Christminster learning appears in the voices of the spectres haunting the city that Jude imagines on his first night there. The emptiness of assumed appropriation is evidenced by the fact that many of them are merely indirectly described and remain lifelessly unevocative; those quoted are not named but periphrastically alluded to also. The reader as well as Jude is assumed to be an initiate who can supply the names: Peel as he makes a passionate plea for the repeal of the Corn Laws; Gibbon ironically wondering at the pagan indifference to Christian miracles; Arnold eulogising Oxford; Newman defining faith; Addison lamenting mortality. The reader encounters, despite the coherence of individual passages, an incoherent totality: a boy's anthology of purple passages, 'learning' perhaps in a literal sense, 'touchstones', a kaleidoscope.

For the rest, as the traditional learning reaches the reader through Jude and the narrator it is even more fragmented, useless, and irrelevant to his dilemmas. Jude as a boy innocently misapplies allusions, which rebound ironically. He imagines in the distant glow of Christminster the form of Phillotson (originally Sue) like one of the three in Nebuchadnezzar's furnace; but the story's hope of salvation by God is not fulfilled for either the schoolteacher or the two who join him in that furnace. Later the boy prays to Phoebus and Diana for the happiness and prosperity he is never to know in what was originally a children's joyous festival prayer. He sees Christminster as a 'heavenly Jerusalem', to which he goes full of the hope he derives from an optimistic phrase taken from Spinoza, whose pervading belief was in an indifferent Providence.

Later Jude deliberately misapplies quotations in a perverse way, wrenching them to appropriateness. Exulting in the prospect of Christminster, he claims to be her beloved son, using the words describing God's manifestation at Christ's baptism. For the biblical injunction to persist in patience unto seventy times seven, he substitutes his desire to persist in being tempted by Sue, and it is from her love that he refuses to be divided, in the words St Paul used for separation from God. As he grows disillusioned the perverseness becomes more conscious: exiled by society's condemnation of their unmarried state, he twists St Paul's words about 'wronging no man' and makes this the reason for their being persecuted; when Sue leaves his bed he deliberately invokes the rending of the veil of the temple at Christ's death. What is irrelevant he will make apt by perverting it.

What Jude only learns of life's cruelty the narrator knows from the start; he is already aware of the ironic irrelevance of the literary text. The boy Jude's hopeful radiance illustrates 'the flattering fancy that heaven lies about them in their infancy!' Just before the shattering of Jude's academic hopes, he spells out the 'inexplicable' Greek sounds which translated give St Paul's passionate declaration of faith in a loving and sustaining God. When Jude, already married, rapturously watches Sue in the cathedral, the narrator quotes only the apparently taunting opening of the Psalm that is being sung, 'Where withal shall a young man cleanse his way', not its context of trusting faith. The trick is repeated when the organist of the chapel next to the children's death-house is heard playing the Psalm 'Truly God is loving unto Israel'.

But it is not only the irrelevance and ironic futility of Christian belief which is the point; frequently secular allusions do no more in their fragmented form than encapsulate what Jude and the narrator already know – that pain, injustice, and disillusionment are commonplace. When Jude's scheme for entry to Christminster bursts like an 'irridescent soap-bubble' his thought 'was akin to Heine's':

Above the youth's inspired and flashing eyes
I see the motley mocking Fool's cap rise!

When he abandons principles for Sue he sees himself rejecting Browning's 'soldier-saints'. His views on the chains of marriage are expressed by the trite lines from Thomas Campbell about 'fetter'd love'. There is a laboured and inexplicit comparison between the Fawley family and the houses of Atreus and Jeroboam. A quotation from the *Agamemnon* appropriate to the children's death, 'Things are as they are ...', is given the same embarrassingly superficial and applied quality by Sue's question 'Who said that?' Each of them, but particularly Jude, has grasped only strands from his reading. He once thought that in order to learn Greek and Latin he had only to master a code; the same weakness is evident in his control over what he has read. It has not become his own; its fullness can be withheld from him by others who will not pass on its secret; for a tutor he has only marginal glosses. In the end he possesses only the letter, and 'the letter killeth' here too in a sense that seems not intended by the novel's epigraph. Through the narrator Hardy presents Jude as the true scholar, but the text tells a different and probably truer story of the 'Self-taught' among whom Jude consciously numbers himself.

Hardy intended 'the letter killeth' to refer explicitly to marriage,[4] in particular Sue's return to legal marriage with Phillotson. Many unorthodox views on women and marriage had already been expressed in the New Woman fiction: the nobility of upper-class women offering a free union in place of marriage to respectable suitors; the horrors of sexual relationships without love; the syphilitic consequences of the double standard; the appalling effects of girls' ignorance of marriage. Hardy's treatment stands to this as *Hamlet* to the revenge play. Sue and Jude's relationship springs into complex life because they are both victims of contemporary oppression: Jude through class, Sue through sex. They have other affinities but this goes deepest and is the reason why their claims to two-in-oneness are not absurd, despite the strong hostility that threads through the relationship on both sides. Hardy denied the novel was an attack on marriage laws and was right to discard this superficial reading; but his assertion in the 1912 postscript that 'the general drift' in relation to such laws was that 'the civil law should only be the enunciation of the law of nature' is more problematic. It is at least a strange remark to make of a novel which begins with a painful demonstration of the cruelty and irrationality of that law as demonstrated by the boy and the earthworms. Nor did Hardy find the morality simpler when handling the natural law in relation to man and woman.

The idea of a contrast between legalistic and natural marriage is partly expanded by the narrator in his comment on Arabella's and Jude's first marriage vow 'to believe, feel, and desire' for the rest of their lives precisely as they had done for the preceding weeks: 'What was as remarkable as the undertaking itself was the fact that nobody seemed at all surprised at what they swore'. Sue, looking closer, sees her loveless marriage to Phillotson as part of 'the barbarous customs and superstitions of the times that we have the unhappiness to live in', because 'for a man and a woman to live on intimate terms when one feels as I do is adultery, in any circumstances'. This is the marriage of 'the letter' which she and Jude, sickened by Arabella, reject. Yet, once freed by divorce, what they propose instead is not an Owenite sexual freedom where only passion justifies the act, but a marriage-like monogamy. There is already a joint inconsistency here. The horror of being licensed to love and be loved on the premises is powerfully evoked for the reader, and yet the narrative implies the very promise that the couple and the narrator shudder at: that they will always think and feel precisely as they do now.

Desire cannot be added to this narrational promise, because what is meant by a natural marriage is further complicated by Sue. Paradoxically, when breaking free from her husband she claims with Jude a right to a totally non-sexual bond and to a non-marital sexual relationship. Given women's position at the time it is easy to see why both claims needed to be made; and in a lesser novel the claims would refer to different men. Here the contradiction produces an individual dilemma which captures the complications of the woman's position most forcibly.[5] This is presumably why the text is ambivalent about whether Sue feels desire even for Jude. There are passages which encourage the reader to think that she does not. Locked into this most feminist of all Victorian novels is a strange fragment of the orthodoxy exalting female chastity or at least virginity: '"I seduced you ... You were a distinct type – a refined creature, intended by Nature to be left intact. But I couldn't leave you alone!"' On the other hand, the 1912 edition contains carefully inserted references to suggest warmth in Sue: they kiss 'long and close', she admits that she 'didn't dislike' him to kiss her, tells him 'I do love you', and just before going to Phillotson's bed admits to having 'loved' Jude 'grossly'. Arabella, closing the novel, suggests that Sue never found peace except in Jude's arms, but how reliable a witness is she? Like Lockwood at the end of *Wuthering Heights*, she is the last person to read relationships aright. The novel can be read as showing that Sue felt desire or as showing that she did not, since at the very end she says: '"I wanted to let it stop there, and go on always as mere lovers ... Women could: men can't ... we ought to have lived in mental communion, and no more."'

On Jude's side a further contradiction appears. Although he is a victim of legalistic marriage and speaks violently against it, he behaves finally in their version of 'Nature's own marriage' as the law told a nineteenth-century husband he might do: he enforces his 'conjugal rights', not by force, but by blackmail. Having agreed to live celibately with Sue he uses Arabella's return to force her into sexual relations:

> 'If she were yours it would be different!'
>   'Or if you were.'
> 'Very well then – if I must I must. Since you will have it so, I agree! I will be. Only I didn't mean to.'

The slide into the orthodox view which makes male desire paramount passes unnoticed and by the narrator's sleight-of-hand it is next morning and Jude is arranging to marry her. Such shifts characterise Hardy's attempts to break free of the orthodoxies of the day, attempts backed by passionate feelings, cutting across rational arguments, and in which an apparent success is always followed by regression. The novel enacts the struggle with all its inconsistencies.

The pains of a 'natural marriage' in a society that goes in for the other kind are felt; the pleasures are not so easily grasped. Like the fruits of learning they prove evasive. The joyless pain evoked by Sue and Jude's relationship is not cancelled or even dented by Sue's strained assertion at the Great Wessex Agricultural Show as they saunter around the flowers, unable to evoke even a spark of pleasure in Little Father Time: '"We have returned to a Greek joyousness, and have blinded ourselves to sickness and sorrow, and have forgotten what twenty-five centuries have taught the race since their time … "' Again, it is only Arabella who reads an enduring idyll into this scene. The joy is looked forward to and back on, but is never actually there. When Sue returns after the children's deaths to 'the letter' of civil marriage which kills, what it kills remains undefinable.

By this time the rejection and oppression that both experience have taken on gradually a single distinct form. As Jude's hostility to the forces of rejection increases it focuses not on Christminster but on the Church, which has overarched the novel from the time of his dreams of success as a clergyman:

> His … sudden antipathy to ecclesiastical work … which had risen in him when suffering under a smarting sense of misconception

remained ... [and] would not allow him to seek a living out of those who would disapprove of his ways ... hardly a shred of the beliefs with which he had first gone up to Christminster now remaining with him.

Christminster, that hothouse which grew clergymen like radishes, has rejected him; Christians have ostracised him and Sue; the Church has administered the marriage of the letter. It has gradually become the symbol of all that oppresses. Jude thinks that he is free of it after the children's death; but it is precisely then that its imaginative power grips Sue, the instinctive worshipper whether of Venus or the Galilean. Her earlier vague sense that the world resembled 'a stanza or melody composed in a dream' was 'now exchanged for a sense of Jude and herself fleeing from a persecutor', the God of the Old Testament – the 'ancient wrath'. That bass accompaniment in the references to Job, in the Psalms in the cathedral, and at the deaths of the children, now becomes dominant. The narrator, like Jude, is terrified by the crippling power of the guilt that the 'ritual church' can induce in Sue, who finally stops her ears against Jude's human voice and returns to Phillotson's bed. Christianity in the form it takes in their lives is the killing letter. Hardy evidently meant this to be one of the novel's contrasts which he interwove through the story between Greek pagan joy and the life-denying force of the pale Galilean. But by a final and confounding contradiction there also is woven through the text the image of Christ as suffering human being; Jude, Sue, even Phillotson, are seen as His incarnations. The pointless and extreme suffering, which in Hardy's world is the paradigm experience, is refracted through the many Christ images. When Phillotson's pupils desert him as he is leaving Marygreen, the narrator equates them with the cowardly disciples at Christ's trial. Sue sees herself and Jude driven from Kennetbridge to Christminster as Jesus sent from one hostile judge, Caiaphas, to another, Pilate. The falseness of Jude's sense that he is favoured like God's 'beloved son' is hinted at by the narrator associating him with Calvary, by his own realisation that Sue is able to 'crucify' him, and when she separates herself from him, by a cry for the rending of the veil of the temple that took place at the time of that other Cruxifixion. Finally, the text subverts itself: its attack on the Church draws power from acceptance of a central Christian image. The imaginative attraction of the creed is still felt, just as it was by Hardy himself.

The three strands in the story are really one. The mental and physical struggles against oppression in all three aspects are the same in their nature and outcome: Jude's infatuation for Christminster reappears long after he has broken free of it; Sue who prided herself on her rationality embraces irrational guilt and legalistic marriage; and the hatred of the Church shows as its other face a powerful sense of affinity with its founder.

Despite, or perhaps because of, these contradictions the novel remains the most powerful indictment of the sexual and class oppression of its time. The pandemonium it evoked was appropriate. This focused on the sexual story, but beneath the charges that it was 'the most indecent novel ever written' there is a sense of deeper panic. And rightly: Hardy was struggling towards, and sometimes momentarily achieved, beliefs subversive of the whole of established society. He felt a deep desire to 'break up the present pernicious conventions in respect of manners, customs, religion, illegitimacy, the stereotyped household'.[6] Contemporary society recognised a revolutionary when it saw one.

From Thomas Hardy, *Jude the Obscure*, The World's Classics (Oxford, 1985), pp. xi–xxii.

NOTES

[This essay is Patricia Ingham's introduction to her edition of *Jude the Obscure*, published in 1985. Interestingly, and unusually, she bases some of her editorial practices on her principles of literary theory. In a prefatory Note on the Text, she traces the history of the novel's composition, pointing out the large number of variations, emendations by Hardy and alterations by others which confront the editor of the novel. Rejecting the notion of authorial intention as an overarching principle, she produces a composite text, drawing primarily on Hardy's last major revisions for the 1912 Wessex edition, but also using variations from the manuscript and from other editions where appropriate.

In her critical introduction, reprinted here, Ingham analyses the novel's educational, marital and religious plots, concluding that 'the three strands in the story are really one'. In each case, the novel identifies a source of powerful social oppression, and details the struggles of its protagonists against the oppression. The novel, she contends, is subversive in ways extending far beyond the superficial sexual indecencies of its plot: 'Hardy was struggling towards, and sometimes momentarily achieved, beliefs subversive of the whole of established society'.

All quotations in the text are from Ingham's own World's Classics edition (Oxford, 1985). Ed.

1. Florence Emily Hardy, *The Later Years of Thomas Hardy: 1892–1928* (London, 1930), p. 196.

2. A. J. Engel, *From Clergyman to Don: The Rise of the Academic Profession in Nineteenth-Century Oxford* (Oxford, 1983), pp. 286–7.

3. Stuart Marriott, *A Backstairs to a Degree: Demands For an Open University in Late Victorian England* (Leeds, 1981), pp. 67 ff.

4. William R. Goetz, 'The Felicity and Infelicity of Marriage in *Jude the Obscure*', *Nineteenth-Century Fiction*, 38 (1983), 189–213.

5. Penny Boumelha, *Thomas Hardy and Women: Sexual Ideology and Narrative Form* (Sussex, 1982), p. 143. [Reprinted in this volume – see pp. 53–74. Ed.]

6. Thomas Hardy, *The Collected Letters of Thomas Hardy*, ed. Richard Little Purdy and Michael Millgate (Oxford, 1978–1988), vol. iii, p. 238.

2

Jude the Obscure: Reading and the Spirit of the Law

RAMÓN SALDÍVAR

> The letter killeth, but the spirit giveth life.
> (II Corinthians)

Concern for the nature and response of an author's audience is, in some respects, one of the original tasks of literary criticism. Over the past decade, however, attempts to incorporate rhetorical, linguistic, and cognitive theories into literary criticism have led to the development of a hefty bibliography on the nature of the reader's role in the communication network of author, text, and reader. These reader-oriented studies stress, from their various perspectives, that the reader, as much as any character, contributes to the shaping of the novel's fictive world through his interpretive actions.[1]

The value of this recent emphasis on the reader's role in fiction and of 'reception history' in general could very well be tested by a text such as the author's 'Postscript' to *Jude the Obscure*. There, the reading public is accused of 'curing'[2] the novelist of all desire to write prose fiction. In this case Hardy would seem to have us question the reader's role in the *destruction* of texts, for in no uncertain terms, it is the reader, in his incapacity to read, who is the problem. Since we cannot read his meaning properly, even when there has been no 'mincing of words' in its enunciation, complains Hardy, he will spare himself and the reader by simply ceasing to write novels.[3]

Yet readers often find this and Hardy's later comment that he expected *Jude the Obscure* to be read as 'a moral work' (p. ix) somewhat

32

disingenuous. We can hardly imagine, after the reception of *Tess* and after his attempt to cancel his contract with Harper & Brothers for *Jude*, that Hardy would not have anticipated the 'shocked criticisms' (p. ix) that the publication of the novel evoked. In fact, when Hardy announces in the 'Preface to the First Edition' that the novel will 'deal unaffectedly with the fret and fever, derision and disaster, that may press in the wake of the strongest passion known to humanity' (p. viii), and then denies that 'there is anything in the handling to which exception can be taken' (p. viii), he raises the very real possibility that the novel will be misread.

And it was misread. Angry reviewers and a solemn bishop saw in it, among other things, a cynical attack on the sacrament and institution of marriage. In a letter of November 1895 to Edmund Gosse, Hardy continued to express his concern for the proper reading of his novel by indicating that *Jude* was not merely 'a manifesto on "the marriage question" (although, of course, it involves it)', but was more the story of the tragic result of two marriages because of 'a doom or curse of hereditary temperament peculiar to the family of the parties'.[4] The fact is, of course, as critics have convincingly argued, that the novel *is* concerned with the marriage laws in more than just a casual way.[5] And Hardy himself points out that the plot of *Jude* is 'geometrically constructed'[6] around the marital realignments of the four principal characters. They repeatedly change their relationships through their alternately prospective and retrospective visions of one another and of the options society and nature allow them.

Poised between a desire for natural freedom and the need for a stabilising social order, Hardy's characters try to act within their 'geometrically constructed' system of marital and symbolic associations to accommodate their desires and needs. Hardy is clear about this. He tells us that *Jude the Obscure* dramatises the sociological effect of the Victorian failure to reconcile the antithetical realms of culture and nature: 'The marriage laws [are] used ... to show that, in Diderot's words, the civil law should be only the enunciation of the law of nature' ('Postcript', p. x). But the difficulty of reading *Jude* properly may well stem from the fact that the novel is more than a realistic analysis of the historical condition of marriage in late Victorian England. I would like to suggest that the ambiguous status of the act of reading in the author's prefatory statements is only an indicator of a more radical investigation concerning reading and interpretation. By considering the interplay between 'natural' and 'civil' law, and by examining the nature of Hardy's 'geometrically constructed' plot, we will be able to reflect on the possible relation of these issues to the apparent ease with which, according to Hardy, the novel can be misread. A reading of *Jude* that attempts to account for this cluster of formal and thematic elements can, I think, provide a new perspective on Hardy's conception of the realistic novel.

A first difficulty in understanding the novel is thematic and stems from the portrayal in the text itself of numerous cases of misreading. From the beginning, for instance, Jude sees in Christminster and its university the image of an attainable ideal world. His desire for this ideal vision involves a rejection of reality. For his own sporadically controlled, partially understood world, he substitutes the image of a unified, stable, and understandable one. Beguiled by his desire for order, the young Jude thus turns initially to language study both as a means of entering university life and as a possible course of stability. The narrator tells us:

> Ever since his first ecstasy or vision of Christminster and its possibilities, Jude had meditated much and curiously on the probable sort of process that was involved in turning the expressions of one language into those of another. He concluded that a grammar of the required tongue would contain, primarily, a rule, prescription, or clue of the nature of a secret cipher which, once known, would enable him, by merely applying it, to change at will all words of his own speech into those of the foreign one. ... Thus he assumed that the words of the required language were always to be found somewhere latent in the words of the given language by those who had the art to uncover them, such art being furnished by the books aforesaid.
>
> (I.iv.30–1)

Jude feels betrayed, consequently, when in his attempt to learn Latin he finds that 'there was no law of transmutation, as in his innocence he had supposed' (p. 31). Jude's desired 'law of transmutation', the 'secret cipher' to a system of translation, could exist only if a prior permanent code existed to allow a free substitution of signifiers for one autonomous signified. The metaphor of translation at this early point in the novel is doubly interesting. It both reveals Jude's desire for a serenely immobile text whose content might be transported without harm into the element of another language, and alludes to the relation Hardy establishes in the 'Postscript' of 1912 between civil and natural law, making one the 'enunciation' (p. x) of the other. These will continue to be decisive issues throughout the novel. At this point, Jude has no doubt that the voice of nature can, indeed, be read and translated, for when he 'address[es] the breeze caressingly', it seems to respond: 'Suddenly there came along this wind something towards him – a message ... calling to him, "We are happy here"'(I.iii.22). By imposing single terms on the disparate variety of experience, we come to know and control our environment. Early on, however, Jude intuits that language is not a fixed system through which meaning can be 'transmuted' from one system to another. Yet this is precisely the insight that Jude refuses to apply to his other readings of the world around him.

As he proceeds into the countryside, where the markings that hint at the limitations already imposed on his life stand to be deciphered, Jude's readings continue: 'The only marks on the uniformity of the scene were a rick of last year's produce ... and the path ... by which he had come. ... [To] every clod and stone there really attached associations enough and to spare – echoes of songs ... of spoken words, and of sturdy deeds' (I.ii.10). History, echoing across the generations, seems to focus on Jude at the bottom of 'this vast concave' field (I.ii.9), but he does not yet understand its voice. The substance of this discourse latent in the countryside is the essential dimension of the tradition into which he has been born. These 'marks' and 'associations' in the landscape of Wessex are 'signs' inscribed by the force motivating all events, which Hardy was in *The Dynasts* to name the 'Immanent Will'. Thus, long before his birth, long before the story of his family has been inscribed, this tradition has already traced the pattern of behaviour within which are ordered the possible changes and exchanges that will occur in Jude's short life. Each crucial event in Jude's life seems to invite the reader to interpret Jude's actions as an attempted reading of the role ascribed to him in some determining book of fate.

Initially, the young orphan Jude seems to see the schoolmaster, Phillotson, as an embodiment of his controlling 'dreams' (I.iii.20), and as a symbolic substitute for the absent 'real' father.[7] Accordingly, when Phillotson leaves Marygreen, Jude replaces him with an ideal representation. Jude reads that ideal presence into the natural landscape of Wessex as Christminster, 'that ecclesiastical romance in stone' (I.v.36):

> Through the solid barrier of cold cretaceous upland to the northward he was always beholding a gorgeous city – the fancied place he likened to the new Jerusalem. ... And the city acquired a tangibility, a

permanence, a hold on his life, mainly from the one nucleus of fact that the man for whose knowledge and purposes he had so much reverence was actually living there.

(I.iii.20)

In this ecstatic vision, Christminster, whose mark is 'a halo or glow-fog' (I.iii.21), seems to send that 'message' (I.iii.22) I mentioned earlier, but it is a message that must be translated from natural to human terms with all the inherent errors of language and its 'figures' (I.iii.25). In a moment of revelation, George Eliot's narrator in *Adam Bede* comments that 'Nature has her language, and she is not unveracious; but we don't know all the intricacies of her syntax just yet, and in a hasty reading we may happen to extract the very opposite of her real meaning'.[8] Now, as Jude attempts to learn the 'syntax' of nature's 'message', Christminster, through Phillotson, becomes the organising centre of his life: 'It had been the yearning of his heart to find something to anchor on, to cling to – for some place which he could call admirable. Should he find that place in this city if he could get there?' (I.iii.24). The phrasing of his question in the rhetorical mode produces a grammatical structure that implies the existence of freedom of choice, when in fact, the pattern of choices has already been established for Jude by his own propensity for misreading. As he answers the questions posed in indirect discourse, beguiled by the transformation his mind has imposed on the scene through figurative language, Jude takes literally his own metaphors of the 'new Jerusalem', 'the city of light', and 'the castle, manned by scholarship and religion' (I.iii.24–5).

Sue Bridehead is also presented in the metaphoric language that names Christminster. Jude has seen, for example, 'the photograph of [her] pretty girlish face, in a broad hat, with radiating folds under the brim like the rays of a halo' (II.i.90). In fact, the metaphoric process by which Sue will later replace Christminster and Phillotson in Jude's dreams has been facilitated by the nature of Jude's language long before he is even conscious of Sue: earlier, he had become 'so romantically attached to Christminster that, like a young lover alluding to his mistress, he felt bashful at mentioning its name' (I.iii.22). The transfer from Phillotson, to Christminster, and finally to Sue as metaphors of that sustaining vision is thus a simple, determined step. Jude's false reading of Sue at a chapel in Christminster as being 'ensphered by the same harmonies as those which floated into his ears' leads him to conclude that he has 'at last found anchorage for his thoughts' (II.iii.107). When Jude finally meets Sue, he approaches her cautiously and speaks to her as he has spoken of Christminster, 'with the bashfulness of a lover' (II.iv.117). At each step in the evolution of his story, his controlling dream is a fiction that he imposes on wayward circumstances.[9]

From the beginning then, the object of desire is not 'real' in any sense, but is a 'phantasmal' (II.ii.97) creation of Jude's own mind, as are the 'ghosts' that haunt Christminster. For Jude, however, the ghosts of his desires disappearing into the 'obscure alleys' (II.i.92) of Christminster are as real as Arabella's 'disappearance into space' (II.i.92). Constituting himself as a whole subject by an identification with another who repeatedly disappears, 'A hungry soul in pursuit of a full soul' (III.x.233), Jude is accordingly threatened by the possibility of disappearing too: 'Jude began to be impressed with the isolation of his own personality, as with a self-spectre ... seeming thus almost his own ghost' (II.i.92). Phillotson, Christminster, Arabella, and most strikingly, Sue, thus become the figures of an ideal paradise, which is fundamentally inaccessible, in so far as it is one more metaphor in a structuring system of substitutions and exchanges of phantasmal dreams. The displacement of desire among the various characters points out the existence of a symbolic order, which creates the idea of autonomy when, in fact, the characters exist determined by their propensity for interpretive error.

As an exegetic scholar, 'divining rather than beholding the spirit' of his texts (I.v.34), Jude can never resist the temptation to read deep meanings, the 'assemblage of concurring and converging probabilities' of 'truths', into a scene (II.i.95). Yet it is less 'absolute certitude' (II.i.95) that lies hidden beneath the manifest content of human experience in the novel than it is a mystified, but nonetheless threatening, organisation of that content. When Jude thereafter looks into Sue's 'untranslatable eyes' (II.ii.104) and immediately begins to interpret her character, he is only repeating the established pattern of error. Despite the difference in the agency that produces it, Jude manifests again the desire for that earlier 'law of transmutation'. Here, Sue's eyes reveal a text to be translated; but, as with the Greek and Latin grammars, no master code exists to guarantee the authority of Jude's translation. The rules governing the metonymic transfer, the figure Latin rhetoric calls *transmutio*, belong to the same illusion of a metaphysics of presence in the word, and to the same hallucination of a language determined on the basis of a verbal representation.[10] Just as language is constituted through repetition, so too does Jude's life acquire a narratable consistency. But the symbolic 'inscription' of Jude's desires upon the surface of Wessex as he travels its roads from Christminster to Shaston, to Aldbrickham and back again, constitutes only the provisional creation of meaning through a process of deferment. As Jude's dreams are transmuted from Arabella to Christminster, and to Sue, the fantasy of stability creates an apparently meaningful and readable text. It is always only in retrospect, however, that Jude's perceptions of those illusions of totality and stability can be organised and lived as an aesthetically coherent *meaning*.

But it is more the inner tensions produced by the characters' shifting relations that shape the action than haphazard or indifferent circumstance. And it is not entirely coincidental that the act of reading surfaces again to indicate these changes in connection with the constant letters that reaffirm the importance of writings, signs, inscription, and marks in the lives of these characters.[11] Altogether there are at least thirty-two letters indicated or implied in the novel, ranging from one-line suicide notes ('*Done because we are too menny*') to full-sized 'carefully considered epistle[s]' (VI.iv.433), directly or indirectly narrated, delivered or not delivered. The numerous instances of inscriptions and carvings reinforce the importance of the 'letter' in the text as the emblem for the force of illusion.

The first of these letters between Jude and Sue had simply called for their initial meeting, but it was 'one of those documents which, simple and commonplace in themselves, are seen retrospectively to have been pregnant with impassioned consequences' (II.iv.115–16). By the time Sue is engaged to Phillotson, Jude is receiving sudden 'passionate' letters (III.i.153) from her that seem to close the psychic distance between them in a way that they can never quite imitate in person. '"It is very odd –"' Jude says at one point, '"That you are often not so nice in your real presence as you are in your letters!"' '"Does it really seem so to you?"' asks Sue, who then replies, '"Well, that's strange; but I feel just the same about you, Jude"' (III.vi.197). A letter is a medium that effectively separates the writer from the effects of the message, while the message received is often one created by the reader himself. Even in their coldest tones, Sue's letters, while banishing Jude, nevertheless constantly summon him to her by the very fact that they establish a link of communication between them. Similarly, Phillotson's letter relinquishing Sue paradoxically begins re-establishing his hold on her; for the 'shadowy third' (IV.v.288), like the substantial couple, is always primarily constituted by this act of communication.

Moreover, when Sue writes a letter, she simultaneously removes and retains her absence and distance. This simultaneity of absence and presence is primarily an outcome of written discourse and is indicative of Jude's more general mystification concerning the existence of a stabilising meaning. Sue is an eminently desirable woman, but she also becomes a sign in Jude's mind for an absent source of meaning. Accordingly, the act of writing becomes a bolster for the illusion of presence and wholeness within a discourse that appears innocent and transparent. Sue's letter can never replace her, but, conversely, her 'real presence' is never identical with the original self promised in the letter. The written word does not allow access to the thing in itself, but always creates a copy, a simulacrum of it that sometimes moves the reader of the word more strongly than can the actual presence of the represented thing. Thus, the curious result is that the graphic sign, rather than the actual presence, of the desired becomes the cause of emotive energy. For Jude, the desire for this originary 'anchoring point' becomes an indispensable illusion situated in the syntax of a dream without origin.

The intersubjective complex that structures the novel *Jude the Obscure* offers us some version of the following schema:

(1)   dreams that fail – Jude, Phillotson, Sue;
(2)   marriages that fail – Jude and Arabella; Sue and Phillotson; Jude and Sue; Arabella and Cartlett; both sets of parents; the legendary ancestor (mentioned in V.iv.340);
(3)   returns to original failures – Jude and Arabella at Christminster; Sue and Phillotson at Marygreen.

We began, remember, with Jude and Arabella at Marygreen, and with Sue and Phillotson at Christminster. The intervening movements in the plot that lead to the present renewal of the characters' former relations thus trace the pattern that characterises the narrative structure. It is a *chiasmus*, the cross-shaped substitution of properties: the original couples are reunited, but in reverse locales. Hardy had referred to this structure more obliquely as the 'geometric construction' behind his novel. Elsewhere he calls it the 'quadrille' that puts in motion the opposing qualities of the four main characters. But it turns out that the very process of 'construction' that the characters' actions enact is really one more reversal of earlier misguided 'constructions'. Would it not follow then that this new turn should restore the characters to their 'proper' places? That is, if Jude and Sue have been improperly associated at Christminster, might we not recover a measure of truth by simply restoring her to Phillotson at Marygreen? Since this structure of reversal is not only at work on the thematic level of the story, within the marital relationships among the characters, but also animates the greater structure of the narrative, the plot itself, the deconstruction of its pattern has significant implications for the novel's concept of a readable, constructive, integrating process in general.

Jude's idea of a synthetic 'anchoring point' of semantic stability originates as the effect of a prior requirement, namely, the requirement that the elements of that synthesis can themselves be permanently fixed in relation to stable qualities. Failing to integrate the ideal and the real with Sue, Jude is no more likely to do so with Arabella. Sue's situation with Phillotson and Jude is even more complex, for the two are versions of the same in different registers. Further reversals, consequently, promise only continued instability. And, I would say, it makes little difference in this novel whether one calls the trope governing the structure of the narrative metaphor, metonymy, chiasmus, or simply a 'geometric construction', for from the first, the characters' roles have been inscribed in the determining contextual system defined by the marriage laws.

In the Victorian novel marriage is pre-eminently the foundation of social stability. As a quasi-contractual agreement, it sets up the participants as a centre for other integrating relationships. These relationships are not simply necessary for society; they constitute it. And that larger social and historical life, the world of symbolic relationships, forms in dialectical turn the structure that orders individual behaviour in Hardy's novels. In a moment of pure poetic insight Sue comments on the nature of those relations:

> I have been thinking ... that the social moulds civilisation fits us into have no more relation to our actual shapes than the conventional shapes of the constellations have to the real star-patterns. I am called Mrs Richard Phillotson, living a calm wedded life with my counterpart of that name. But I am not really Mrs Richard Phillotson, but a woman tossed about, all alone, with aberrant passions, and unaccountable antipathies.
>
> (IV.i.246–7)

With remarkable clarity Sue recognises that the social woman is a representation, transposed and supplemented by desire, of her real self. But the relation between her natural and social selves is like the relation between 'real star-patterns' and traditional interpretations of the 'conventional' constellation shapes, like that between a referent and its linguistic sign – that is, *aesthetic* and hence *arbitrary*. The concept of the self is the product of an aberrant substitution of rhetorical properties. Sue here clearly understands that this rhetorical operation is at best a metaphorical, interpretive act – one that is necessarily open to a variety of figural misreadings.

We have seen that the law that regulates marriage ties in this novel superimposes the kingdom of *culture* on that of *nature*.[12] Following its dictates, Jude artificially imposes a vision of organic totality (figured at different times by Phillotson, Christminster, Sue, etc.) onto nature and accords it a moral and epistemological privilege. In contrast, the narrator's ironic comments show Jude's substitutions and realignments within the marriage system and within the pattern of metaphors for his vision of an 'anchoring point' to be purely formal, analogous only by contingency, and hence without privilege. When the value of those associations is questioned, when the notion of Sue as the representation of Jude's dreams is made problematic, the possibility of a simple relation between signified and signifier is also questioned.

That formerly unquestioned assumption is the original moment of illusion that the narrative demystifies. The narrator reveals to us that Jude's and Sue's notion of a privileged system of law is an hypothesis, or a fictional construct (a *doxa*), that makes the orderly conduct of human affairs possible. It is not a 'true' and irrefutable axiom based on knowledge (an *episteme*).[13] Their tendency, as revealed by the metaphorical rhetoric of their desires, is always to abide by the lawful order of 'natural' logic and unity: "'It is,'" Sue says at one point, "'none of the natural tragedies of love that's love's usual tragedy in civilised life, but a tragedy artificially manufactured for people who in a natural state would find relief in parting!'" (IV.ii.258). But if the order of 'natural' law is itself a hypothetical construct rather than a 'natural' occurrence in the world, then there is no necessary reason to suppose that it can, in fact, provide 'relief'. And it is Sue once again, who, after the tragic deaths of their children, perceives that possibility when she says to Jude:

> 'We said ... that we would make a virtue of joy. I said it was Nature's intention, Nature's law and *raison d'être* that we should be joyful in what instincts she afforded us – instincts which civilisation had taken upon itself to thwart. ... And now Fate has given us this stab in the back for being such fools as to take Nature at her word!'
>
> (VI.ii.408–9)

Jude, who likes to think of himself 'as an order-loving man' of an 'unbiased nature' (IV.ii.252), can only stand by helplessly as he hears Sue destroy the basis of their 'natural' marriage.[14]

Hardy's novel situates itself explicitly within the context of the marriage laws that establish Victorian society. It portrays, as Hardy tells us, the attempted translation of the law of nature into civil terms. The characters, however, cannot legitimately perform this translation without confusing the names of two such divergent semantic fields as those covered by 'natural law' and 'civil law'. Confusion arises because the terms designate contextual properties, patterns of integration and disintegration, and not absolute concepts. In Hardy's Wessex, the 'law of nature' designates a state of relational integration that precedes in degree the stage of 'civil law' since civil law only 'enunciates' what is already present in nature to be read. The undoing of a system of relations codified in 'civil law' will always reveal, consequently, a more fragmented stage that can be called 'natural'. This prior stage does not possess moral or epistemological priority over the system that is being undone.[15] But Jude always does assign it priority.

Remembering that 'his first aspiration – towards academical proficiency – had been checked by a woman, and that his second aspiration – toward apostleship – had also been checked by a woman', Jude asks himself ungallantly "'Is it ... that the women are to blame; or is it the artificial system of things, under which the normal sex-impulses are turned into devilish domestic gins and springs to noose and hold back those who want to progress?'" (IV.iii.261). The weight of the second clause of the question makes it simply rhetorical: the women are of course not to blame. Although the 'natural' pattern that Jude and Sue attempt to substitute for the accepted 'civil' one is itself one system of relations among others, they see it as the sole and true order of things and not as an artifice like civil structure. But once the fragmentation of the apparently stable structure of civil law is initiated, endless other versions of 'natural law' might be engendered in a repeating pattern of regression.

The decisive term characterising Jude's and Sue's relationship, 'natural law', thus presents itself to be read as a chiastic pattern also. Natural law deconstructs civil law; but natural law is then itself open to the process of its own analysis. Far from denoting a stable point of homogeneity, where they might enact the mythic integration of their 'one person split in two' (IV.iv.276), the 'natural law' of Hardy's Wessex connotes the impossibility of integration and stability. Any of Hardy's texts that put such polarities as natural and civil law, desire and satisfaction, repetition and stability into play will have to set up the fiction of a synthetic process that will function both as the deconstructive instrument and as the outcome of that deconstruction. For Hardy, dualisms are never absolute. Deconstruction, however, is the process that both reveals the deluded basis of the desire for the synthesis of dualism, and also creates the elements necessary for a new and equally deluded desire for integration. *Jude the Obscure* thus both denies the validity of the metaphor that unites 'natural' and 'civil' law, and elaborates a new metaphor to fulfil the totalising function of the original binary terms. This new metaphor of life as an organic and orderly process now allows the narrative to continue by providing a myth of a future moment when, as Phillotson's friend Gillingham says, Jude and Sue might make 'their union legal ... and all would be well, and decent, and in order' (VI.iv.433). This mythic moment, however, never comes.

It is crucial, then, that the basic conflicts of the novel occur within the 'give and take' of marriage, for it situates the issue directly in the referential contexts of ethics and legality. Civil law, in fact, can be conceived as the emblem of referentiality *par excellence* since its purpose is to codify the rules for proper social intercourse. But to abide by the law, we must be able to read its text; ignorance is after all, in English common law, no excuse. Attempting to read it, Jude concludes that 'we are acting by the letter; and "the letter killeth"!' (VI.viii.469). Jude thus interprets the Pauline dictum, 'The letter killeth but the spirit giveth life', as an injunction against a *literal* reading of the codes governing ethical action. Yet his *figural* reading leads to no spiritual truth either. On the contrary, Jude's illusions result from a figurative language taken literally, as with Sue he takes 'Nature at her word'. For Jude and Sue, then, there is no text present anywhere that is yet to be transmuted, yet to be translated from natural to civil terms. There is no *natural* truth written anywhere that might be read without being somehow altered in the process. The text of associations Jude fabricates around him is already woven of interpretations and differences in which the meaning of dreams and the desire for illusions are unnaturally coupled. Everything in Wessex 'begins' with repetition, with secondary images of a meaning that was never present but whose *signified* presence is reconstituted by the supplementary and belated word of Jude's desires.[16]

I am saying, of course, that the narrative of *Jude the Obscure*, while telling the story of Jude's and Sue's unhappy marriages, also dispels the illusion of a readable truth; that the novel gains its narrative consistency by the repeated undoing of the metaphor of life as organic unity. But the story that tells why figurative denomination is an illusion is itself *readable* and *referential* to the negative truth that Jude never perceives, and the story thus relapses into the very figure it deconstructs. The structure of the narrative as chiasmus, the cross-shaped substitution of properties, also tells, therefore, another story in the form of allegory about the divergence between the literal and figural dimensions of language. That the text reverts to doing what it has claimed to be impossible is not a sign of Hardy's weakness as a novelist, for the error is not with the text, nor with the reader who attempts to understand it. Rather, I would say that with Jude we find that language itself, to the extent that it attempts to be truthful, necessarily misleads us about its own ability to take us outside its own structures in search of meaning.

The myth of a stabilising natural or civil law, then, is actually the representation of our will to make society seem a unified and understandable organism. But Hardy's novel persists in showing society's laws as open to subversion by the actions of the individuals who make up society. In everyday life, there is an ever possible discontinuity between the word of the law, its spirit, and the practice, the letter, of the law. And the necessary failure of the law to enforce its monologic interpretations of the infinite variety of human behaviour can lead to the subversion of the entire relational system. This explains why Jude, by his actions, constantly and unintentionally subverts the Word that he figures in Sue and in his dreams of a university career.

In applying the accepted social law to themselves, Jude and Sue constitute a version of the law, but in applying the general law to their particular situation, they instantaneously alter it. Rather than serving as a source of universal order from which social relations might be stabilised and unified within a social totality, the accepted social law exhibits its inability to constrain the heterogeneity of social relations. The law, then, is always shown to be grammatically structured, since it always engenders only a contingent, contextual meaning. Jude's revolutionary attempt to establish a ground for authentic meaning thus produces an anarchy of mutually exclusive readings of the one piece of language. 'The letter killeth.' This discontinuity between the 'letter' and the 'spirit' of the law, between a literal and a figural reading of its sign, is what constitutes Hardy's break with referentiality. Although the law indicates that 'The letter killeth', Jude finds it impossible to decide what is the *letter* and what the *spirit* of the law. In each reading, whether within a 'natural' or a 'civil' system, the law is transposed, altered, and led to produce the conditions for its own undoing. Like Sue's ambiguous letters, the law is consequently only a promise (which cannot be kept) of a future stability and is never adequate to deal with the instability of the present moment.

The repetitions in the novel put at stake not only the relation between Jude's present actions and his family's history, but also the very readability of the initial text of that history. Everywhere about him, history calls out to be read, but Jude consistently fails to do so properly. Because he cannot read it, his actions are never simply a representation of that past, but are an interpretation that has gone awry. Since the novel is itself a kind of history, it too is open to all the errors of interpretation of which it speaks. Hardy's 'Postscript', which calls attention to the decisive issues of reading and interpretation, must thus be seen in retrospect as an ironic repetition of the situation dramatised in *Jude* concerning the impossibility of authoritative readings, for it accuses the reader of partaking in Jude's error. We cannot read the novel as Jude reads the motto of his life, that is, with the expectation of encountering an ideally sanctioned stable truth.

But how *are* we to read it then? If the notion of representation is to be at all meaningful, we must presuppose the stability of subjects with stable names who are to be represented, and a rapport between the sign and the referent in the language of the representation. Yet both conditions are absent from this text (notoriously so in the allegorical figure of Little Father Time). We can, of course, discern similarities among the characters' various actions. And as we read, attempting, in Hardy's words, 'to give shape and coherence to this series of seemings' (p. viii), we too must rely on Jude's example in constructing an interpretive model. But we cannot accept his model of metaphoric synthesis as an absolute.[17] Jude's model of metaphor (governing the patterns of idealisation and substitution) is erroneous because it believes in its own referential meaning – it believes that the inwardly desired 'anchoring point' can be concretely encountered in the external world as Phillotson, as Christminster, as Arabella, or as Sue. It assumes a world in which literal and figural properties can be isolated, exchanged, and substituted. For the reader and the narrator, metaphoric synthesis persists within the interpretive act, but not as the ground of ultimate reconciliations. Jude himself, however, remains caught in the error of metaphor. But it is an error without which reading could not take place.

We thus find that Hardy's narrative puts the assurance of the truth of the referent into question. But in making this situation thematic, it does allow a meaning, the text, to exist. We are not dealing simply with an *absence* of meaning, for if we were, then that very absence would itself constitute a referent. Instead, as an allegory of the breakdown of the referential system, *Jude the Obscure* continues to refer to its own chiastic operations. This *new* referentiality is one bounded strictly by the margins of textuality. In our courses on the nineteenth-century novel we find it convenient to use *Jude* as a 'transitional' text; it is either the last of the Victorians or the first of the Moderns.[18] Morton Zabel has written, for instance, that Hardy was 'a realist developing towards allegory ... who brought the nineteenth century novel out of its slavery to fact'.[19] This seems to me fine, as far as it goes. But I would add that this allegorical pattern manifests itself in *Jude* primarily through the subversive power of the dialogic word, which refuses to be reduced to the single 'anchoring point' of a transcendent and determining Will, Immanent or otherwise.

As Hardy came to see early on, the function of realistic fiction was to show that '*nothing* is as it appears'.[20] It is no wonder, then, that Hardy's last novel was misread. The suggestive and poetic force of *Jude* arises less from its positive attempt to represent appearance than from its rejection of any vision pretending to convey the totality and complexity of life. Accordingly, in *Jude* Hardy repudiates the notion that fiction can ever be Truth, that it can ever 'reproduc[e] in its entirety the phantasmagoria of experience with infinite and atomic truth, without shadow, relevancy, or subordination'.[21] He dramatises, instead, the recognition that in narrative 'Nothing but the illusion of truth can permanently please, and when the old illusions begin to be penetrated, a more natural magic has to be supplied'.[22] To be realistic, the text must proceed as if its representing systems correspond to those in the world; it must create a new illusion of reference to replace the old of representation.

But this transmutation of illusions modifies the original considerably. Like Sue's 'real presence', perpetually deviating from the ideal figure of Jude's dreams, the letter of the text, '*translat[ing]* the qualities that are already there' in the world,[23] contains after all only the inadequate ciphers of the spirit of meaning, not the 'thing' itself. The deconstruction of the metaphorical model of substitution and translation (operating in Jude's various desires for Christminster, Sue, natural law, etc.) is performed by the rhetorical structure of chiasmus, whose own figural logic both asserts and denies referential authority. From the reader's point of view, the results of each of the figural movements can then be termed 'meanings', but only by forgetting that the resulting sociological, ethical, legal, or thematic categories are undone by the very process that creates them.

It may well be, therefore, that Hardy's final novel does not 'mean'; but it does signify to a redoubtable degree. It signifies the laws of language over which neither Hardy nor his readers can exercise complete control. To read those laws is to undermine their intent. This is why Hardy, like Jude who adds to the textual allegory of Wessex and generates its history while marking its closure, is bound to allegorical narratives: he creates the fiction of an ideal reader while he constructs a narrative about the illusion of privileged readings. On this level of rhetorical self-consciousness, prose fiction is on the verge of becoming poetry.

From *ELH*, 50:3 (1983), 607–25.

NOTES

[An expanded version of this essay was published in Ramón Saldívar, *Figural Language in the Novel: The Flowers of Speech From Cervantes to Joyce* (Princeton, NJ, 1984). In that book, Saldívar makes clear the theoretical starting-points of his critical practices. First, he contends that every literary text is centrally concerned with the question, 'how can this story be told?' In other words, the narrative and linguistic modes of a novel are not extra to and separate from its meaning: 'I would like to propose in contrast a theory of reading which concerns itself in practical terms with the texture and the historical resources of language, as well as with the formal and referential aspects of the work at hand' (p. xiii). Saldívar rejects the long-standing assumption that the role of the critic is to eliminate error and ambiguity from the text under analysis. As others have done, he argues that ambiguity is inherent in and constitutive of language, and is to be specifically analysed by the critic rather than argued away.

In this reading of *Jude*, in which both deconstruction and semiotic theory exercise an influence, Saldívar begins by pointing out the oddly antagonistic tone in which Hardy is apt to address his reader. Reading, he deduces, is posited as a threatening, potentially a destructive, practice. He goes on to look at the attempts of the novel's characters to identify a 'letter of the law' which will stabilise meaning. The novel, he argues, does not simply represent the world as meaningless, which would establish only another form of stability. Instead, it offers 'an allegory of the breakdown of the referential system'.

All quotations in this essay are from the American issue of the Wessex edition (Anniversary Edition, New York, 1920) and are given by part, chapter and page number. Ed.]

1. See, as a sampling, the following studies that stress the need to recognise the reader's role and the process of reading as crucial aspects of the development of meaning in literature: Wayne Booth's *The Rhetoric of Fiction* (Chicago, 1961) is still the most widely influential of these studies. After Booth, the topic develops in several directions. Cf. Martin Price, 'The Fictional Contract', in *Literary Theory and Structure* (New Haven, CT, 1973); Richard Ohmann, 'Speech, Literature and the Space Between', *New Literary History*, 5 (1974), 37–63; Georges Poulet, 'Phenomenology of Reading', *New Literary History*, 1 (1969–70), 58–68; Roland Barthes, *S/Z* (Paris, 1970) and *Le Plaisir du texte* (Paris, 1973); Wolfgang Iser, *The Implied Reader* (Baltimore, MD, 1974), 'Interdeterminacy and the Reader's Response in Prose Fiction', in *Aspects of Narrative*, ed. J. Hillis Miller (New York, 1971), 'The Reading Process: A Phenomenological Approach', *New Literary History*, 3 (1972), 279–99, and most recently, *The Act of Reading* (Baltimore, MD, 1978). See also Hans Robert Jauss, 'Levels of Identification of Hero and Audience', *New Literary History*, 5 (1973–74), 283–317, on the 'aesthetics of reception'. And see the current efforts of language philosphers to apply speech act theory to literary discourse: John R. Searle, 'The Logical Status of Fictional Discourse', *New Literary History*, 4 (1972), 319–32; and Mary Louise Pratt, *Towards a Speech Act Theory of Literary Discourse* (Bloomington, IN, 1977). The most recent and engaging contribution is Paul de Man's 'Reading (Proust)', in *Allegories of Reading* (New Haven, CT, 1980), pp. 57–78.

2. Thomas Hardy, 'Postscript' (added April 1912) to *Jude the Obscure* in *The Writings of Thomas Hardy in Prose and Verse*, The Anniversary Edition (New York, 1920), vol. 3, p. ix.

3. Thomas Hardy, 'Preface to the First Edition' of *Jude the Obscure* (August 1895), p. viii. For a more detailed summary of the reception of Hardy's novel, see R. G. Cox (ed.), *Thomas Hardy: The Critical Heritage* (London and New York, 1970), pp. 249–315; and especially, for its difference from the prevailing response, the review by Edmund Gosse in *Cosmopolis* (January 1896), i, 66–9. Cf. Lawrence Lerner and John Holmstrom (eds), *Thomas Hardy and His Readers* (New York, 1968), pp. 103–52. See also the pertinent discussions in Albert Guerard (ed.), *Thomas Hardy* (New York, 1964); Ian Gregor, *The*

Great Web (London, 1974); Michael Millgate, *Thomas Hardy: His Career as a Novelist* (New York, 1971), pp. 317–35; and J. Hillis Miller, *Thomas Hardy: Distance and Desire* (Cambridge, MA, 1970). See also Florence Emily Hardy, *The Life of Thomas Hardy 1840–1928* (1928 and 1930; reprinted New York, 1962), pp. 262–75, which discusses Hardy's reactions to the negative reception of his novel.

4. Letter to Gosse, cited in Florence Emily Hardy, *The Life of Thomas Hardy 1840–1928* (1928 and 1930; reprinted New York, 1962), p. 271. Hardy writes Gosse to thank him for his favourable review of *Jude*.

5. William R. Rutland, *Thomas Hardy: A Study of His Writings and Their Background* (Oxford, 1938), pp. 250–7.

6. Letter to Gosse, cited in Florence Emily Hardy, *The Life of Thomas Hardy 1840–1928* (1928 and 1930; reprinted New York, 1962), p. 271. Hardy goes on to say: 'I ought not to say *constructed* for beyond a certain point, the characters necessitated it, and I simply let it come'. In a subsequent letter of January 1896, also to Gosse, Hardy elaborates: 'The rectangular lines of the story were not premeditated, but came by chance: except, of course, that the involutions of four lives must necessarily be a sort of quadrille' (p. 273).

7. I use the term in the sense that Jacques Lacan assigns to it in 'The Function of Language in Psychoanalysis', trans. Anthony Wilden in *The Language of the Self* (Baltimore, MD, 1968), and in 'D'une question préliminaire à tout traitement possible de la psychose', *Ecrits II* (Paris, 1970), pp. 43–102. Lacan speaks of the symbolic substitution of a father figure for an absent real procreator. This symbolic construct need not have a procreative function at all; it is sufficient that the symbolic figure stand for a guarantee of social order with which the child might identify. Although Jude's idealisation of Phillotson is shattered at an early stage in the novel, the system of social formulae set up in relation to Phillotson retains its affective force, even after Jude discovers the illusory basis of his beliefs. This process of 'idealisation' is constant throughout the novel and even characterises Jude's relations with Arabella: 'His *idea* of her was the thing of most consequence, not Arabella herself, [Jude] sometimes said laconically' (I.ix.65).

8. George Eliot, *Adam Bede*, Rinehart Editions (New York, 1948), ch. xv, p. 155. In *A Pair of Blue Eyes*, Hardy's narrator makes a similar observation: 'Nature seems to have moods in other than a poetical sense. ... She is read as a person with a curious temper. ... In her unfriendly moments there seems a feline fun in her tricks, begotten by a foretaste of her pleasure in swallowing the victim' (ch. xxii, p. 243). See also Charles May ('*Far From the Madding Crowd* and *The Woodlanders*: Hardy's Grotesque Pastorals', *English Literature in Transition*, 17 [1974], 147–58), who notes that 'Hardy's central vision springs

from the tension between his longing for a ground of meaning and value inherent in the natural world and his hard recognition that no such value or meaning exists there' (p. 150).

9. The problem of interpretation is complicated by the formal pattern of the narrative itself, which often ascribes speeches to Jude through the mode of indirect discourse. The *diegetic* instance, the narrative mode that Plato so deplores in book III of *The Republic*, forces the reader to shift attention from the question of the *meaning* of the characters' linguistic confusions to that of deciding which *voice* is the cause of ambiguity. In the passages discussed above, for example, some can be readily ascribed to Jude (I.iii.20; I.iii.24–5; IV.v.243). Other passages, however, seem to be the narrator's interpretations of Jude's interpretations. This layering of interpreting minds dramatises the difficulty in *Jude* of establishing absolute linguistic reference. Cf. John Sutherland, 'A Note on the Teasing Narrator in *Jude the Obscure*', *English Literature in Transition*, 17 (1974), 159–62.

10. See Jacques Derrida, 'Freud et la scène de écriture', in *L'Ecriture et la différence* (Paris, 1967), p. 316.

11. It is of course appropriate that Jude reads St Paul at several points in the novel since the Pauline text is itself concerned with the issue of a proper reading. Referring to the relationship of the Old Testament to the new, Paul in fact applies the linguistic metaphor of Christ as the Spirit inseparable from the letter of the Bible where it is expressed. As John Freccero pointed out in a seminar on Dante at Yale University in the Fall of 1975, Paul later suggests that the Word of God interprets the hearts of men, turning to stone the hearts of unbelievers, while the Spirit writes upon the fleshy tablets of the faithful. Hardy thus directs our attention to the nature of Jude's spiritual, but apocryphal, word. See also R. P. C. Hanson, *II Corinthians* (London, 1954), p. 39, commenting on II Corinthians 3 and 4, from which, of course, derives the epigraph to *Jude the Obscure*.

12. See Anthony Wilden's discussion of the relationship between social and linguistic systems in *The Language of the Self* (Baltimore, MD, 1968), pp. 253–4.

13. Cf. Friedrich Nietzsche, 'On Truth and Falsehood in an Extra-Moral Sense', in *The Complete Works*, vol. 2, trans. Maximilian A. Mügge (London, 1911), pp. 173–92. See also Hardy's journal entry of 5 August 1980, cited by Florence Emily Hardy in *The Life of Thomas Hardy 1840–1928* (1928 and 1930; reprinted New York, 1962), where he indicates that 'Art is a changing of the actual proportions and order of things. ... Art is a disproportioning – (i.e., distorting, throwing out of proportion) – of realities, to show more clearly the features that matter in these realities, which, if merely copied or reported inventorially, might possibly be observed, but would more probably be overlooked.

Hence "realism" is not Art' (pp. 228–9), and compare with Nietzsche's statements in essay III, section 24 of *On the Genealogy of Morals*, concerning the nature of the interpretive act.

14. See also, among numerous and often contradictory allusions to 'natural' and 'civil' systems of law in Hardy's novel, the following passages: I.xi.80; III.ii.165; III.vii.206; IV.ii.258; V.viii.384; VI.i.396; VI.ii.408–9; and VI.iii.418; in addition to 'Postscript', p. x and the epigraphs to Part First from the Book of Esdras and Part Fourth from Milton's *The Doctrine and Discipline of Divorce*.

15. Paul de Man, in the chapter 'Promises (Social Contract)' of *Allegories of Reading* (New Haven, CT, 1980) points out the relation between textual and legal systems: 'In the description of the structure of political society, the "definition" of a text as the contradictory interference of the grammatical with the figural field emerges in its most systematic form' (p. 270).

16. I use the word 'supplementary' in Derrida's sense in *Of Grammatology*: 'But the supplement ... adds only to replace. It intervenes or insinuates itself *in-the-place-of*; if it fills, it is as if one fills a void. If it represents and makes an image, it is by the anterior default of a presence' (trans. Gayatri Chakravorty Spivak [Baltimore, MD, 1976], p. 145).

17. See Gérard Genette, 'La rhétorique restrainte', and 'Métonymie chez Proust', in *Figures III* (Paris, 1972), pp. 21–40, 41–66, respectively, for instances of the kinds of interpretations that use such a totalising metaphorical model.

18. Irving Howe, *Thomas Hardy* (New York, 1967), argues for a similar reading when he noted that if 'modernist' literature works 'on the premise that there is no secure meaning in the portrayed action, or that while that action can hold our attention and rouse our feelings, we cannot be certain, indeed must remain uncertain, as to the possibilities of meaning', then *Jude the Obscure* 'does not go nearly as far along the path of modernism' as do Kafka's, Joyce's, or Faulkner's novels (p. 144). In my reading, Hardy's refusal to posit the absolute *absence* of meaning, but only its unverifiability, is, in some respects, a more profoundly 'modern' act than would be the simple negation of 'meaning'. See also Lawrence O. Jones, 'Imitation and Expression in Thomas Hardy's Theory of Fiction', *Studies in the Novel*, 7 (1975), 507–25; and J. Hillis Miller, 'Fiction and Repetition: *Tess of the d'Urbervilles*', in *Forms of Modern British Fiction*, ed. Alan Warren Friedman (Austin, TX, 1975), pp. 43–71; and also the discussion by Edward Said in *Beginnings* (New York, 1975), pp. 137–9.

19. Morton Zabel, 'Hardy in Defense of His Art: The Aesthetics of Incongruity', in *Thomas Hardy*, ed. Albert Guerard (New York, 1964), p. 43.

20. Florence Emily Hardy, *The Life of Thomas Hardy 1840–1928* (1928 and 1930; reprinted New York, 1962), Journal entry for 21 December 1885, p. 176.

21. Thomas Hardy, 'The Science of Fiction' (1891), in *Thomas Hardy's Personal Writings*, ed. Harold Orel (Lawrence, KS, 1966), p. 135.

22. Ibid., p. 135.

23. Florence Emily Hardy, *The Life of Thomas Hardy 1840–1928* (1928 and 1930; reprinted New York, 1962), Journal entry for January 1887, p. 185.

3

Jude the Obscure: Sexual Ideology and Narrative Form

PENNY BOUMELHA

Hardy comments in his 1912 Preface to *Jude the Obscure* that an unnamed German reviewer had described Sue Bridehead as 'the first delineation in fiction of ... the woman of the feminist movement – the slight, pale "bachelor" girl – the intellectualised, emancipated bundle of nerves that modern conditions were producing ... '. He adds, 'Whether this assurance is borne out by dates I cannot say' (p. 30). This is a characteristic piece of obfuscation. It is as well to note, first, that Sue is no way representative of any discernible move- ment, although organised feminism had already appeared in fiction, for example, in E. L. Linton's *The Rebel of the Family* (1880), Henry James' *The Bostonians* (1886), and George Gissing's *The Odd Women* (1893), all of which, in any case, predate the publication of *Jude*. Sue belongs not to feminism as such, but to the literary tradition of the New Woman; and here again, she is in no sense a precursor. Hardy certainly knew of at least some of the large number of writers, both new and established, dealing at the same period with just that topic. It is evident from his letters that he was personally acquainted with some of these writers – Sarah Grand and Ménie Muriel Dowie, for instance.[1] He received a letter about *Jude* from George Egerton, and he wrote to the editor of the *Contemporary Review* in 1890 to intro- duce an article about marriage by Mona Caird, remarking that he be- lieved there to be 'nothing heterodox in it'.[2] Hardy had read at least some of the works in question: he thought *The Heavenly Twins* over-praised,[3] and copied extracts from Egerton's *Keynotes* into his note-book.[4] In 1892 he wrote at some length to Millicent Garrett Fawcett about the portrayal of sex in contemporary fiction:

> With regard to your idea of a short story showing how the trifling with the physical element in love leads to corruption: I do not see that much more can be done by fiction in that direction than has been done already. You may say the treatment hitherto has been vague & general only, which is quite true. Possibly on that account nobody has profited greatly by such works. To do the thing well there should be no mincing of matters, & all details should be clear & directly given. This I fear the British public would not stand just now; though, to be sure, we are educating it by degrees.

He adds that he has read a recent novel ostensibly on the subject, Lucas Malet's *The Wages of Sin*, and found it 'not very consequent, as I told the authoress'.[5] He was certainly aware of Grant Allen, probably the most widely read and influential of the 'woman question' writers, whose aspirations to martyrdom and posturings of high moral seriousness led a contemporary to describe him hyper-bolically as '"the Darwinian St Paul"'.[6] Allen's works led to a kind of industry of rebuttal and parody; in the year of the publication of *Jude* alone, his *The Woman Who Did* spawned *The Woman Who Didn't* by 'Victoria Crosse' and *The Woman Who Wouldn't* by 'Lucas Cleeve', while *The British Barbarians, A Hill-Top Novel* pro-voked H. D. Traill's parody, *The Barbarous Britishers. A Tip-Top Novel*. In *The British Barbarians* Allen refers very favourably to *Tess* as a work '"of which every young girl and married woman in England ought to be given a copy"'.[7] Hardy returned the compliment by sending him a dedicated copy of *Jude The Obscure*.[8] There are few similarities between Allen's fiction and Hardy's, but their attacks on marriage have points in common, such as the Owenite idea that unchastity is sex without love, whether within or outside marriage, and the position that marriage as an institution crushes individuality and makes a legal obligation of '"what no human heart can be sure of performing"';[9] further, Grant Allen's 'monopolism', the jealous and exclusive annexation which marks patriotism, prop-erty, capitalism and marriage,[10] bears some relation to Hardy's '"save-your-own-soul-ism"', the common characteristic of possessive parenthood, class-feeling and patriotism, all '"a mean exclusiveness at bottom"' (p. 288).

The New Woman – by no means identical with the feminist, but clearly a relative – had, indeed, become almost a cliché by 1895. One contemporary reviewer remarks of *Jude* that 'If we consider broadly and without prejudice the tone and scope of the book, we cannot but class it with the fiction of Sex and New Woman, so rife of late'.[11] Meanwhile, H. G. Wells, in a review in February 1896, is able to assert confidently that 'It is now the better part of a year ago since the collapse of the "New Woman" fiction began.'[12] Far from being a pioneer, Sue Bridehead comes in company with a crowd of 'intellectualised, emancipated bundle[s] of nerves' (p. 30). This is not, of course, to suggest that she is commonplace. I shall be considering Sue Bridehead in some detail later, but there are significant differences which mark her out from the type of the New Woman and which should at once be pointed out. A contemporary account of the 'new convention in heroines' describes the characteristic New Woman:

> The newest is beautiful, of course, in a large and haughty way. She is icily pure. … She despises the world, and men, and herself, and is superbly unhappy. In spite of her purity she is not very wholesome; she generally has a mission to solve the problems of existence, and on her erratic path through life she is helped by no sense of humour.[13]

This is a caricature, but those features which are being exaggerated and distorted remain clearly identifiable. Sue Bridehead, with all her hesitations, evasions and tentativeness, has none of this messianic sense of purpose which distinguishes her contemporaries, and in fact she consistently refuses to speak for women as a group, posing herself always as a special case. A further difference is made more evident by this description, from the same source, of the hero with whom the free union is to be contracted:

> He is always a young man of excellent birth, connected with the peerage, and has literary or artistic tastes. He has had a reckless past, but it has done him no harm. … He is all passion, and coolness, and experience, and gentlemanly conduct.[14]

As this quotation suggests, the New Woman and the free union are, in 1890s fiction, firmly rooted in the upper middle class; the social hazards to which these women are exposed are of the nature of being ostracised by the wives of bishops. The marryings and unmarryings of working-class characters are more characteristically seen in the brutal and condescending stories of writers such as Henry Nevinson or Arthur Morrison.[15] *Jude the Obscure* is unique in its siting of Jude and Sue at the conjuncture of class and sexual oppression.

Nevertheless, the novel was certainly perceived by its contemporary readers as being part of a trend, and, despite Hardy's disclaimers of writing about the marriage question,[16] his sense of participating in a continuing debate is evident in, for example, the argument of Phillotson and Gillingham over '"domestic disintegration"' and the collapse of the family as the social unit (p. 247), or in this rather didactic interchange after a discussion of marriage:

> 'Still, Sue, it is no worse for the woman than for the man. That's what some women fail to see, and instead of protesting against the conditions they protest against the man, the other victim ...'
> 'Yes – some are like that, instead of uniting with the man against the common enemy, coercion.'
>
> (pp. 299–300)

It seems that, with the advent of 'Ibsenity' and the problem play, the marriage question and the New Woman novel, Hardy was able for the first time in a major work to place the examination of sexual relationships openly at the centre of his novel, and to make the tragedy turn on marriage, instead of displacing it with the more traditional materials of tragedy, as he had done earlier. Whatever Hardy's account of the genesis and composition of *Jude*, which he describes in a letter to Florence Henniker as 'the Sue story',[17] there can surely be no doubt now that, as Patricia Ingham has shown, Sue Bridehead and marriage are the very impulse of the novel, not an afterthought.[18]

Nor is this the only area of *Jude*'s contemporaneity. It can be seen as attempting to superimpose the sexual and marital preoccupations of the 1890s upon the intellectual concerns of the 1860s, Hebraism and Hellenism and Mill's liberal individualism.[19] There is obviously some truth in this, though Mill's name is not in itself a sign of being fixed in the past; it is a recurring name on the reading lists of the New Woman, though more often for his *Subjection of Women* (of which Hardy somewhat ambiguously remarks in September 1895 that 'I do not remember ever reading [it]')[20] than for *On Liberty*. At the same time, the novel is very much abreast of contemporary currents of thought. The 'deadly war waged between flesh and spirit' to which Hardy refers in his Preface (p. 27) had taken on a new significance in the latter part of the century, as the Darwinian notion of an extremely complex material world in constant change challenged the hitherto dominant form of the duality by reversing the priorities. The new dualism – materialist, certainly, but often mechanistic – makes physiological organisation the determinant, with consciousness a kind of subsidiary product – an idea which underlies Hardy's image, recurrent in his poetry, of the mind as an evolutionary mistake. Such a privileging of the biological led easily into a scientificism in social theory – in the positivist investigations of the Fabians, for example, in Social Darwinism, and the associated manifestations of the 'science' of eugenics, claimed alike by reactionaries like Max Nordau (*Degeneration*, published in English translation in 1895), radical feminists like the American Victoria Woodhull Martin (editor of *The Humanitarian* [NY] from 1892), and socialists like Edward Aveling. This is the period in which sexuality moves decisively from the area of moral discourse to that of scientific discourse. The relative downgrading of the mind and, hence, of the intellectual surely enters into the 'simple life' philosophy of Edward Carpenter and his associates, as well as giving apparent support to the irrationalism and pessimism of Schopenhauer, for whom (as sometimes for Hardy) human consciousness and the scientific laws of the universe are inherently at odds. The signs of these ideological currents are easily seen in the dominant literary modes of the period, as the three-decker novel gives way to the fleetingly poised moment of the short story, and as the 'scientific' fictions of naturalism become prominent, with their avowedly organicist aim of dissecting a society as though it were precisely analogous with a human body.

This same sense of the ceaseless shiftings and modifications of the apparently stable material world can be related to the ascendancy of the philosophies of relativism and pragmatism, where the petrified social categories of morality and knowledge are felt to be in contradiction with the intricacies and flexibilities of personal experience. *Jude the Obscure* is heavy with this sense: Sue cannot associate her inner life with the Mrs Richard Phillotson she has outwardly become (p. 223); Phillotson's dilemma over Sue is compounded by his feeling that his 'doctrines' and 'principles' are at odds with his 'instincts' (p. 246); and Jude's '"neat stock of fixed opinions"' is torn away from him by his experience, leaving him '"in a chaos of principles"' (pp. 336–7). One of the novel's most painful ironies is the way that the desire for education is undercut by its inadequacy and irrelevance to the experiences of all the central characters. The tension between 'private' experience and the cold, superficial generalisations of the public language which alone is available to articulate that experience comes to dominate the novel. '"I can't explain'" becomes a kind of motto – a variant on one of the senses of the novel's epigraph, 'the letter killeth' – and is used by both Sue and Jude, particularly in relation to sex (Sue's half-hearted attempts to give Little Father Time the truth about the expected child; Jude's failure to account to Sue for his casual night with Arabella), highlighting the irreconcilability of individual sexual experience and its public discourses, whether scientific or moral. Sue and Jude take divergent paths with regard to language and the literary culture. Sue moves into silence; in her two last appearances, she stops her ears to avoid hearing Jude, and clenches her teeth to avoid addressing Phillotson. Jude, however, moves into a kind of sardonic or parodic quotation in which the language of culture becomes a commentary on his own life in a quite original way – the anthem 'Truly God is living unto Israel', the last quotation from Job with its choric, amen-like punctuations of 'Hurrah!'. The two are caught at the point where their courses diverge in an exchange which appears only in the serial text: when they overhear two clergymen discussing the eastward position for altars Jude exclaims '"What a satire their talk is on our importance to the world!"', and Sue replies, '"What a satire our experience is on their subject!"'[21] These two processes of distancing from language and literary culture are mimicked in the form of the novel and its place in Hardy's work. The end of *Jude* is a most sardonic imposition of the twin conventions of novel closures, the happy marriage and the death of the hero, and offers by way of apparent summing-up Arabella's reinstatement of the romanticised truisms of a love as strong as death and the two lovers as halves of a single whole.[22] *Jude* is also Hardy's last novel, and so is followed, in this respect, by silence.

Jude the Obscure is Hardy's final double tragedy. In his previous versions of the double tragedy of a man and of a woman, the woman's tragedy has resulted from her sexual nature, while the man's has been more involved with intellectual ideals and ideological pressures. There has been a polarity of nature and culture which has meant that the protagonists have rivalled one another for the centre of the novel, pulling it in different directions and making it hard for him to use marital or sexual relationship as the crucial point of the divergence. In *Jude*, however, Hardy gives for the first time an intellectual component to the tragedy of the woman – Sue's breakdown from an original, incisive intellect to the compulsive reiteration of the principles of conduct of a mid-Victorian marriage manual – and, to the man's, a sexual component which resides not in simple mismatching, but in the very fact of his sexuality. There is no sense that Jude and Sue inhabit different ideological structures as there is in the cases of Clym and Eustacia, or even Angel and Tess. Indeed, for all the emphasis on the 'enigma' of Sue's logic and motivation, there is an equal stress – and this is something new in Hardy – on her similarity to Jude. The fact of their cousinship, besides contravening the exogamy rule and so adding an incestuous *frisson* to their sense of an impending and hereditary doom, serves to highlight their similarities;[23] there are episodes which quite openly draw attention to this, either by careful counterpointing of plot (Jude, in his distress, spending the night at Sue's lodging, balanced by Sue, in hers, spending a night in Jude's room) or by means of images such as that of Sue's appearance in Jude's clothes as a kind of double. Again, the discussion between the two after Jude's impulsive visit to the hymn-writer turned wine-merchant points up their own sense of sameness between them; and Phillotson justifies his action in letting Sue go partly in terms of "'the extraordinary sympathy, or similarity, between the pair. He is her cousin, which perhaps accounts for some of it. They seem to be one person split in two!'" (p. 245). Their lives follow a very similar course. Both make a mistaken marriage as a result of sexual vulnerability, as is evident in an interesting MS revision: when Jude, on his first outing with Arabella, visits an inn, he sees on the wall a painting of Samson and Delilah, a clear symbol of his male sexuality under threat; but the picture had originally been a painting of Susannah and the Elders, a symbol of female sexuality under threat, which corresponds very closely to the roles of Sue and Phillotson (MS f. 44). Both Sue and Jude escape these first marriages, become parents, lose their jobs, their children, and their lover. Yet Sue is destroyed, while Jude is even at the end able to talk of dying "'game'" (p. 394). Jude offers explanations for this phenomenon – 'The blow of her bereavement seemed to have destroyed her reasoning faculty' (p. 368) – and raises questions about it – "'What I can't understand in you is your extraordinary blindness now to your old logic. Is it peculiar to you, or is it common to woman? Is a woman a thinking unit at all, or a fraction always wanting its integer?'" (p. 359). Sue's actions and reactions are constantly faced, whether by Jude, by the narrator, or by Sue herself, with this alternative: either she must be peculiar, or she must be representative of her sex.[24] It is worth noting, in passing, that this alternative is one which certain critical readings continue to enforce upon the text; a recent example can be found in John Lucas' argument that 'we need more in the way of women than the novel actually gives us' in order to judge whether Sue is to be seen as a 'pathological case' or as a 'representative woman'.[25] This apart, it is noticeable that Sue's life follows almost exactly the course of the 'after-years' marked out for the female sex in the earlier and notorious passage about the 'inexorable laws of nature' and the 'penalty of the sex': that is, 'injustice, loneliness, child-bearing, and bereavement' (pp. 160–1). It seems to me that Sue is to be seen as a representative of her sex in this sense alone, that her sexuality is the decisive element in her collapse. It has become a critical reflex to refer to Sue Bridehead as sexless or frigid, whether as an accusation of her, in the Lawrentian tradition, or as an accusation of Hardy, as in Kate Millett.[26] There is much in the literature of the New Woman that appears to support such an assumption: their concern with the double-standard, for instance, takes almost invariably the form of a demand for male chastity, and some of the more successful problem novels, such as Sarah Grand's *The Heavenly Twins*, turn on the terrible injuries wreaked on women by libidinous and venereally-diseased husbands. *Jude* itself provides some evidence for this argument also, in Sue's rather absurd wish '"that Eve had not fallen, so that ... some harmless mode of vegetation might have peopled Paradise"' (p. 241), or in the numerous revisions in which Hardy removes expressions referring to Sue's warmth and spontaneity and substitutes references to her reserve or coolness. In one scene, for instance, her reply to Jude's worries that he may have offended her reads thus in the serial text: '"Oh, no, no! You said enough to let me know what had caused it. I have never had the least doubt of your worthiness, dear, dear Jude! How glad I am you have come!"' In the first edition, however, she is considerably less affectionate and spontaneous: '"O, I have tried not to! You said enough to let me know what had caused it. I hope I shall never have any doubt of your worthiness, my poor Jude! And I am glad you have come!"'. As she comes to meet Jude, the serial text runs: 'She had come forward so impulsively that Jude felt sure a moment later that she had half-unconsciously expected him to kiss her.' The revised text, on the other hand, reads: 'She had come forward prettily; but Jude felt that she had hardly expected him to kiss her.'[27]

It is simplistic, however, to equate such changes with a total absence of sexual feeling, or with frigidity. They should be seen, rather, as her response to the complexities and difficulties of her sexuality and its role in her relationships than as a straightforward denial of it. Hardy subjects Sue's sexuality to some of the same ironies which undercut Diana Warwick's sexual self-possession in George Meredith's *Diana of the Crossways*, and for some of the same reasons. It is intimately connected in both cases with the woman's sense of selfhood, and the reserve is, to quote John Goode, 'not a "defect" of "nature", but ... a necessary stand against being reduced to the "womanly"'.[28] A refusal of the sexual dimension of relationships can seem the only rational response to a dilemma; in revolt against the double bind by which female–male relationships are invariably interpreted as sexual and by which, simultaneously, sexuality is controlled and channelled into a single legalised relationship, Sue is forced into a confused and confusing situation in which she wishes at one and the same time to assert her right to a non-sexual love and her right to a non-marital sexual liaison.[29] It is the conflict of the two contradictory pressures that makes her behaviour so often seem like flirtation. Diana Warwick is a victim of the same dilemma, for her unconventionality and intelligence lead her to despise the taboo placed on friendships with men, and yet any and every sexual advance, whatever the state of her feelings toward the man, is felt as at once an insult, a threat, and an attack. 'The freedom of one's sex' is a double-edged concept.

In the case of Sue Bridehead, her diagnosis of marriage as constraint implies as its apparent corollary the equation of non-marriage and freedom. The myth of the free individual subject leads her to see her life, provided it lies outside sexual coercion, as an affair of personal choices freely made. Telling Jude of her unhappiness, she does not perceive the irony in his repetition of her phrase:

> 'How can a woman be unhappy who has only been married eight weeks to a man she chose freely?'
> 'Chose freely!'
> 'Why do you repeat it?'
>
> (p. 227)

Her tragedy takes in part the form of her gradual confrontation with the fact of her non-freedom, with the knowledge that she is no less constrained and reduced by her denial of her sexuality than by Phillotson's legal or Jude's emotional demands upon it. She must learn that sexuality lies to a large degree outside the control of rationality, will, choice. The serene confidence with which she tells Jude of her sexless liaison with the undergraduate and draws from it the general conclusion that "'no average man – no man short of a sensual savage – will molest a woman by day or night, at home or abroad, unless she invites him'" (p. 167), is a fantasy of freedom and control which she will not willingly surrender. Hardy states in a letter to Edmund Gosse what the novel itself also implies, that it is irrevocable sexual commitment which she fears and abhors, and that she has attempted to retain control of her sexuality by a straightforward restriction of her sexual availability:

> 'One point illustrating this I could not dwell upon: that, though she has children, her intimacies with Jude have never been more than occasional, even when they were living together... , and one of her reasons for fearing the marriage ceremony is that she fears it would be breaking faith with Jude to withhold herself at pleasure, or altogether, after it; though while uncontracted she feels at liberty to yield herself as seldom as she chooses.'
>
> (*Later Years*, p. 42)

The final, ironic twist is that when she can no longer fail to recognise the limitations upon her freedom – the moment is clearly marked for us in her identification of the three commandments of the "'something external'" which ironically mock the Hebraic Ten Commandments (p. 347) – she simply re-makes the equation in reverse, preserving the polar opposition of marriage and non-marriage. In her re-marriage with Phillotson, she subjects herself fully to the legalistic and Hebraic codes of the ideology of marriage.

Sue, then, undergoes an exploration of the limits of a liberationist impulse, the demands of a Millian individualism, not in terms of biological destiny (although, at a time when contraception and abortion were still very limited of access and widely abhorred, the biological 'destiny' of motherhood is a very formidable 'given' indeed), but in terms of the impossibility of the free individual. This is, in a sense, a response to certain feminist and anti-marriage novels of the period, where the conversion of marriage into a civil contract varying in individual circumstances (as in Mona Caird), or the levelling 'up' of the double standard (as in *The Heavenly Twins*), or the replacement of marriage by the free union (as in *The Woman Who Did*), are seen as potential guarantees of the freedom of women; symptoms of the oppression of women are taken for the very structures of that oppression, and a perspective of equal rights is seen as not merely a necessary, but a sufficient programme for liberation.

Nevertheless, there is a very important sense in which Sue is right to equate her refusal of a sexual relationship with her freedom, in that it avoids the surrender to involuntary physiological processes which her pregnancies entail. It is in this respect that women are at the very junction of the 'flesh and spirit'; the point where mind and body are in potential conflict – this is the crucial area of that dominance of the material over the intellectual in the duality which is characteristic of the ideology of the period. It is Sue, and not Jude, who is the primary site of that 'deadly war waged between flesh and spirit' of which Hardy speaks in his Preface (p. 27).[30] In Jude, the two are constantly juxtaposed, the dominance of his sexuality displacing the dominance of his intellectual ambitions and vice-versa in a continuing series. Jude's sexuality is a disruptive force in a way that it has not previously been for Hardy's male characters; there is no question here – except in Jude's tortured self-questioning after the death of his children – of a predatory male sexuality destroying a weaker and more vulnerable female through her sexuality, but rather of a sexual nature in itself disturbing, partly because it is so largely beyond the conscious processes of decision and intention. When Jude first meets Arabella his intentions and wishes are overmastered by his sexual attraction toward her; the phrase used in MS is 'in the authoritative operation of a natural law' (MS f. 36), but this is cancelled and a less scientific phrase finally substituted – 'in commonplace obedience to conjunctive orders from headquarters' (p. 63). It is this episodic 'battle' of Jude's which gives the novel its similarly episodic form, in which there is a repeated pattern of the abrupt confrontation of his inner life with his material situation: his meditation over the well is broken by the strident tones of his aunt (p. 35), his sympathies with the hungry birds are interrupted by Farmer Troutham's clacker (p. 39), and his recitation of his intellectual attainments is answered by the slap of a pig's penis against his ear (p. 61); from this point on, the dons of Christminster temporarily give way to the Donnes of Cresscombe. Jude's attempt to unite the two through his marriage founders with the significant image of Arabella's fingermarks, hot and greasy from lard-making, on the covers of his classic texts. His wavering thereafter between the two women enacts the alteration of dominance within himself. Points of crisis and transition are marked by Jude's personalised *rites de passage*: his burning of his books, auctioning of his furniture, removing his pillow from the double bed, and so on.[31]

Kate Millett argues that Sue is the 'victim of a cultural literary convention (Lily and Rose)' that cannot allow her to have both a mind and sexuality.[32] The very persistence with which Jude attempts to bring Sue to admit her sexuality into their relationship suggests that this is too simple an account of the self-evident contrast of Sue and Arabella. Hardy seems to have been making conscious use of the convention *within* the figure of Sue; her name means 'lily', and there is symbolism in the scene in which Jude playfully forces her into contact with the roses of which she says '"I suppose it is against the rules to touch them"'(p. 308).[33] It is interesting to note, by the way, that in the year of *Jude*'s publication, Hardy was collaborating with Florence Henniker on a story where the heroine's name, Rosalys, seems consciously to draw together the two symbolic traditions.[34]

For Sue, mind and body, intellect and sexuality, are in a complex and disturbing interdependence, given iconic representation in her twin dieties, Apollo and Venus, which she transmutes for Miss Fontover – prefiguring the later collapse of her intellect and repudiation of her sexuality – into the representative of religious orthodoxy, St Peter, and the repentant sexual sinner, St Mary Magdalen. Further, there are the complementary images of Sue as 'a white heap' on the ground after her desperate leap from her bedroom window (p. 242), and as a 'heap of black clothes' on the floor of St Silas after the death of her children (p. 358); as victim of her sexuality and as victim of religious ideology, she is the arena of their conflict. Her intellectual education throughout the novel runs alongside her emotional involvements: the undergraduate who lent her his books and wanted her to be his mistress; Phillotson who gives her chaperoned private lessons in the evenings; and, of course, Jude, with whom she spends much of her time in discussion. But in each case, sexuality is a destructive, divisive force, wrecking the relationship and threatening the precarious balance in Sue's life between her intellectual adventurousness and her sexual reserve. Her relationship with Jude involves her in the involuntary physiological processes of conception, pregnancy and childbirth, and these in turn enforce upon her a financial and emotional dependence on Jude which proves destructive for both of them.

Sue, then, is at the centre of this irreconcilability of 'flesh' and 'spirit'; yet she is constantly distanced from the novel's centre of consciousness by the careful manipulation of points of view. A variety of interpreters interpose between her and the reader – Phillotson, Widow Edlin, even Arabella; but chiefly, of course, Jude.

There is a kind of collusion between him and the narrator, which is most evident in the scene of Jude's first walk round Christminster, when he sees the phantoms of past luminaries of the university; the actual names are withheld from the reader as if to convey the sense of a shared secret between narrator and character. This collusion enables us to follow the movements of Jude's thoughts and actions – the narrator's examination of his consciousness is authoritative. Sue, on the other hand, is, as John Bayley remarks, consistently *exhibited*;[35] she is pictorialised, rendered in a series of visual images which give some accuracy to Vigar's descriptions of the novel as employing a '"snapshot" method'.[36] Sue's consciousness is opaque, filtered as it is through the interpretations of Jude, with all their attendant incomprehensions and distortions; it is this that makes of her actions impulses, of her confused and complex emotions flirtation, and of her motives 'one lovely conundrum' (p. 156).[37] The histories of Jude and Sue are, in some respects, remarkably similar, and yet she is made the instrument of Jude's tragedy, rather than the subject of her own. In a sense the reader's knowledge of her exists only through the perceiving consciousness of Jude, and so it is that after his death, she is not shown at all; Arabella takes on Jude's role of interpreting her to us. The effect of this distancing is to give what is openly a man's picture of a woman; there is no attempt, as there is with Tess Durbeyfield, to make her consciousness and experience transparent, accessible to authoritative explanation and commentary! She is resistant to appropriation by the male narrator, and so the partiality of the novel is not naturalised.

It is often said that Sue's 'frigidity' brings about not only her own tragedy, but also – and in this view more importantly – Jude's.[38] In fact, this tragedy follows upon not merely the sexual consummation of their relationship, but Sue's assimilation, through her parenthood, into a pseudo-marriage. Once she has children, she is forced to live with Jude the economic life of the couple, and gradually to reduce her opposition to marriage to formalism by pretending to marry Jude and adopting his name. It is motherhood – her own humiliation by the respectable wives who hound her and Jude from their work, Little Father Time's taunting by his schoolmates – that convinces her that '"the world and its ways have a certain worth"' (p. 368; this is an insertion in the first edition), and so begins her collapse into '"enslavement to forms"' (p. 405). For the anti-marriage theme of the novel is not entirely concerned with legally or sacramentally defined marriage, though these play a significant role, and it differs again here from most of the contemporary New Woman fiction. In most cases (as in Grant Allen, for example) it is merely the legal aspect that is attacked, while a 'free union' which duplicates the marital relationship in every respect but this is seen as a radical alternative. Even for a radical feminist theorist like Mona Caird, it is the inequality of the terms on which the contract is based that is the root of the problem:

> The injustice of obliging two people, on pain of social ostracism, either to accept the marriage-contract as it stands, or to live apart, is surely self-evident. ... [I]f it were to be decreed that the woman, in order to be legally married, must gouge out her right eye, no sane person would argue that the marriage-contract was perfectly just, simply because the woman was at liberty to remain single if she did not relish the conditions. Yet this argument is used on behalf of the present contract, as if it were really any sounder in the one case than in the other.[39]

Her solution is to propose a more flexible and personalised contractual relationship. Jude and Sue experience the same sense that predetermined social forms, however they may be for other people, cannot suit '"the queer sort of people we are"' (p. 299); they regard themselves unequivocally as the argument from exception, despite various intimations that they are simply precursors of a general change of feeling. It is curious that this argument contradicts the general tendency of the attack on marriage, for if they are exceptional in their relationship, it is in their 'perfect ... reciprocity' (p. 221), their '"extraordinary sympathy, or similarity"' (p. 245). Their Shelleyan vision of themselves as twin souls, two halves of a single whole, is a version of Romanticism which is in conflict with the attack on marriage as enforcing a continuing and exclusive commitment; the same contradiction is apparent in Shelley's *Epipsychidion* itself, an important source for *Jude*.[40] Sue and Jude see themselves as giving freely just this kind and degree of commitment, embodying in a 'purer', because unconstrained, form the very ideal of marriage; indeed, they often talk of their relationship precisely *as* a marriage, and refer to each other as 'husband' and 'wife'. Other relationships of this kind are perceived by them as invariably gross and degrading – the cowed and pregnant bride who marries her seducer '"to escape a nominal shame which was owing to the weakness of her character"', the boozy, pock-marked woman marrying '"for a lifetime"' the convict whom she really wants '"for a few hours"' (pp. 297–8).

Their own relationship, however, they perceived as refined and singled out, its sexuality as merely the symbol of its spirituality. But, in the course of the novel, they are forced to recognise that their relationship is not transcendent of time, place, and material circumstance, as they have tried to make it; their Romantic delusion gives way, leaving Jude cynical, but in Sue's case leading on into the ideology of legalised and sacramental marriage that her experiences have led her to respect. Ironically, it is a debased Romantic version that concludes the book, through Arabella's final statement that "'She's never found peace since she left his arms, and never will again till she's as he is now!'" (p. 413). Sue comes to see in Phillotson her husband in law, as Tess comes to see in Alec her husband in nature; the logic is only apparently opposite, for in both cases it is underpinned by that sense of the irrevocability of commitment which is inculcated by the ideology of marriage. *Jude* illustrates how a relationship conceived by its protagonists as in opposition to marriage cannot help becoming its replica – that it is in the lived texture of the relationship that the oppression resides, and not in the small print of the contract. The 'alternative' relationship proves ultimately no alternative at all, for its material situation presses upon it to shape it into a pre-existing form. Jude and Sue escape none of the oppressions of marriage, but they incur over and above these the penalties reserved for transgressors against it. There is no form for the relationship to take except those named and determined by the very form that they seek to transcend: unless it is marriage, it is adultery or fornication. It is in this sense that Jude comes to see that he too is one of "'that vast band of men shunned by the virtuous – the men called seducers'" (p. 352).

In a sense, then, *Jude the Obscure* offers a challenge to contemporary reformist feminism. It challenges in particular the notion of the home or the love-relationship as a protected zone, beyond the reach of existing material and ideological structures, which could be reformed by individual acts of will and intention. Jude comes finally to see himself and Sue as martyred pioneers: "'Perhaps the world is not illuminated enough for such experiments as ours! Who were we, to think we could act as pioneers!'" (p. 360). They show rather the unimaginable nature of female–male relations as they would exist outside the economic and ideological pressures which wrench the relationship back into predetermined forms of marriage, just as Hardy's novel is wrenched back finally into pre-existing fictional forms; but it is part of the strength of *Jude* that it makes visible the violence of those wrenchings, and gives a sense of the energy which cannot be wholly contained within those forms. The novel points, too, to the crucial role of parenthood, and so of the nuclear family, in enforcing the marital model, for it is when Little Father Time arrives that the relationship is forced to adapt, economically and in appearance, to the conventional marital couple. There are two references, very radical in their time, to the necessity for socialised childcare, though without challenging the existing sex-role division. In the first, Phillotson tells Gillingham that "'I don't see why the woman and the children should not be the unit without the man'" (p. 247); in the serial text, he argues in more detail that "'I don't see why society shouldn't be reorganised on a basis of Matriarchy – the woman and the children being the unit without the man, and the men to support the women and children collectively – not individually, as we do now.'"[41] Later, Jude raises the same question when confronted with the possibility that Arabella's son need not necessarily be also his:

> 'The beggarly question of parentage – what is it, after all? What does it matter, when you come to think of it, whether a child is yours by blood or not? All the little ones of our times are collectively the children of us adults of the time, and entitled to our general care.'
>
> (p. 288)

It is interesting that, although in 1892 Hardy had written to Alice Grenfell that he did not support women's suffrage,[42] by 1906 he had changed his mind, largely on the grounds that women would take on a more progressive role in introducing socialised childcare:

> ... the tendency of the women's vote will be to break up the present pernicious convention in respect of manners, customs, religion, illegitimacy, the stereotyped household (that it must be the unit of society), the father of a woman's child (that it is anybody's business but the woman's own except in cases of disease or insanity).[43]

In the light of this, it is not surprising that, while Sue's sexuality all but destroys her, Arabella's is the very guarantee of her survival. She, neither enigma nor conundrum, is clear-sighted about her means of economic survival, and barters her sexuality accordingly. She runs an ironically parallel course to Sue Bridehead's in her rejection of one husband and finding of another, her (temporary) sublimation of her sexuality into religiosity, her loss of her child, and her eventual return to her first husband. Her education, carried out largely by her workmates, parallels and undercuts the more formalised self-education of both Jude and Sue, forming part of the collision in the novel between 'dogma', 'doctrines', 'principles' – in short, formal education – and 'instincts', 'impulse', 'inclinations' – the complexities and contingencies of personal experience.

Arabella is always connected with both sexuality and fecundity. The scene of her first meeting with Jude, even more overtly symbolic in the texts of the serial and first edition, is suggestive of a literal seduction. In this earlier version, Jude is timorous, picking up the pig's penis with the end of his stick, and averting his eyes while he offers it to Arabella. She responds in this way: 'She, too, looked in another direction and took the piece as though ignorant of what her hand was doing.'[44] In subsequent editions, this is replaced by her 'sway[ing] herself backwards and forwards on her hand' (p. 63). After this, the scene of the actual seduction seems redundant; it continues, however, the emphasis on breasts which frequently accompanies Arabella's appearances in the novel.[45] The egg which she is hatching between her breasts introduces the idea of fertility into the self-evident sexuality of the scene. She is a kind of surrogate mother for the orphan Jude; at his unexpected re-meeting with her in the bar, he reacts as though he had been 'whisked … back to his milk-fed infancy' (p. 217). Yet it is Sue who becomes a mother, not only of her own children, but also of Arabella's son, while Arabella herself, for all the implied multiplicity of her sexual involvements, never plays a maternal role. This is crucial, given the way in which this role precipitates Sue into her '"enslavement to forms"' (p. 405); and there is a hint that it is not simply coincidental that Arabella's sexual 'freedom' is preserved. Before her marriage to Jude, she meets Physician Vilbert; she 'had been gloomy, but before he left her she had grown brighter' (p. 80). Since the idea of obliging Jude to marry her has been her intention from the outset, it is unclear whether she has obtained from the physician a simple piece of advice – pretend to be pregnant – or whether, pregnant in fact, she has got from him some of those '"female pills"' which he had earlier asked the boy Jude to advertise in payment for the grammars he never brings (p. 52). 'Female pills' was at this time a widely-understood euphemism for abortifacients. Arabella, then, is perhaps able to safeguard herself from the consequences of her sexuality, at least in the form of unwanted children, and so to resist some of the more urgent economic and ideological pressures which push women back into nuclear family units.

A. O. J. Cockshut considers *Jude the Obscure* a refutation of contemporary feminist thought, and Sue Bridehead an illustration of Hardy's pessimism about women's attempts to defy the inexorable, 'natural' limitations of their sex; he concludes that 'The attempt to turn Hardy into a feminist is altogether vain'.[46] He is right, I think, in seeing the novel as in conscious dialogue with both feminist and anti-feminist fiction of its time; but his interpretation of the novel's role in this dialogue is, surely, entirely mistaken. Sue's 'breakdown' is not the sign of some gender-determined constitutional weakness of mind or will, but a result of the fact that certain social forces press harder on women in sexual and marital relationships, largely by virtue of the implication of their sexuality in child-bearing. Even among the apparently radical New Woman novelists, there is widespread agreement that motherhood is a divinely – and biologically – appointed mission, providing the widest and purest field for the exercise of the 'innate' moral qualities of the woman. In some anti-feminist novels – such as *A Yellow Aster* – it is the approved agent of the rebellious woman's recuperation into the fold of happy docility. Only Mona Caird[47] and Hardy, among the more widely-read novelists dealing with this issue, draw attention to its coercive role in the reproduction of the nuclear family unit. *Jude the Obscure* poses a radical challenge to contemporary reformist feminist thought in its understanding that the '"something external"' which says '"You shan't love!"' also and at the same time says '"You shan't learn!"' and '"You shan't labour!"' (p. 347).

But it is not only its challenge to the existing social and ideological formations of the period that makes *Jude the Obscure*, in Eagleton's phrase, an 'unacceptable text'.[48] It is a novel that threatens to crack open the powerful ideology of realism as a literary mode, and throws into question the whole enterprise of narrative. 'The letter killeth' – and not only Jude. Tess, too, is destroyed by letters: the text-painter's flaming sign, Joan Durbeyfield's letter of advice, Tess's own misplaced written confession, the various appeals and denunciations and warnings dispatched to Angel in Brazil. It is wholly fitting, then, that Angel should finally track down Tess once more by following the directions of the local postman! Sue Bridehead, on the other hand, is progressively reduced from a challenging articulacy to a tense and painful silence that returns her to the fold of marriage – a conclusion which ironically duplicates the death of Jude. Writing comes increasingly to resemble an instrument of death, for the women in particular. From the fatal 'letter' of fiction, Hardy will turn to the 'letter' of a poetry that memorialises.

From Penny Boumelha, *Thomas Hardy and Women: Sexual Ideology and Narrative Form* (Brighton, 1982), pp. 135–56.

NOTES

[*Thomas Hardy and Women* draws on feminist and Marxist literary theory in offering a reading of Hardy's major novels, in particular, in relation to ideologies of femininity and sexuality in the latter part of the nineteenth century. The book's argument is partly that the Victorian period was not, as was and sometimes still is presumed, a time when sex was simply suppressed and unspeakable, but rather a time when there was enormous public debate over marriage, divorce, prostitution, contraception, the age of consent, and other matters directly related to sex and to female sexuality in particular. In this context, *Jude the Obscure* emerges less as a lonely pioneer of subversion and iconoclasm, and more as a contribution to a widespread dialogue within and beyond fiction.

Here, the ways in which Jude and Sue experience the same problems and dilemmas are counterposed to the way in which their specific experiences are shaped by issues of gender and class. A previously dominant critical presumption that the tragedy of the novel is Jude's, and that it is caused by Sue's frigidity, is challenged, and a different view is offered: that it is specifically the difference of sex that shapes the equally harrowing tragedies of the two central characters. The novel's attack on marriage, detected by its earliest reviewers, is far more radical and thoroughgoing than has sometimes been suggested.

All quotations in this chapter are taken from the New Wessex edition of the novel (London, 1976). Ed.]

1. *One Rare Fine Woman: Thomas Hardy's Letters to Florence Henniker 1893–1922*, ed. Evelyn Hardy and F. B. Pinion (London, 1972), pp. 3, 46.

2. Egerton's letter, dated 22 November 1895, is referred to in *Thomas Hardy's Correspondence at Max Gate: A Descriptive Check List*, ed. Carl J. Weber and Clara Carter Weber (Waterville, Maine, 1968), p. 56. Hardy's letter about Caird is 'To Percy Bunting', 13 January 1890, *Collected Letters of Thomas Hardy: Volume 1, 1840–1892*, ed. R. L. Purdy and Michael Millgate (Oxford, 1978), p. 208.

3. *One Rare Fine Woman: Thomas Hardy's Letters to Florence Henniker 1893–1922*, ed. Evelyn Hardy and F. B. Pinion (London, 1972), p. 8.

4. Gail Cunningham, *The New Woman and the Victorian Novel* (London, 1978), pp. 105–6.

5. 'To Millicent Garrett Fawcett', 14 April 1892, *Collected Letters of Thomas Hardy: Volume 1, 1840–1892*, ed. R. L. Purdy and Michael Millgate (Oxford, 1978), p. 264.

6. William Robertson, *The Novel-Reader's Handbook: A Brief Guide to Recent Novels and Novelists* (Birmingham, 1899), pp. 1–2.

7. Grant Allen, *The British Barbarians: A Hill-Top Novel* (London, 1895), p. 94.

8. Richard Little Purdy, *Thomas Hardy: A Bibliographical Study* (London, 1954), p. 91.

9. Grant Allen, *The Woman Who Did* (London, 1895), p. 41.

10. Ibid., pp. 182–90.

11. Robert Yelverton Tyrrell, '*Jude the Obscure*', *Fortnightly Review*, 65 (1896), 858.

12. [H. G. Wells], '*Jude the Obscure*', *Saturday Review*, 82 (1896), 153.

13. 'Novel Notes', *Bookman*, 6 (1894), 24.

14. Ibid., p. 24.

15. For a representative selection, see *Working Class Stories of the 1890s*, ed. P. J. Keating (London, 1971).

16. E.g. 'To Florence Henniker', 10 November 1895, *One Rare Fine Woman: Thomas Hardy's Letters to Florence Henniker 1893–1922*, ed. Evelyn Hardy and F. B. Pinion (London, 1972), p. 47.

17. *One Rare Fine Woman: Thomas Hardy's Letters to Florence Henniker 1893–1922*, ed. Evelyn Hardy and F. B. Pinion (London, 1972), p. 43.

18. Patricia Ingham, 'The Evolution of *Jude the Obscure*', *Review of English Studies*, 27 (1976), 27–37, 159–69; a decisive refutation of John Paterson's 'The Genesis of *Jude the Obscure*', *Studies in Philology*, 57 (1960), 87–98.

19. Ward Hellstrom reads the novel in terms of Arnold in 'Hardy's Scholar-Gipsy', in *The English Novel in the Nineteenth Century: Essays on the Literary Mediation of Human Values*, ed. George Goodin, Illinois Studies in Language and Literature, no. 63 (Urbana, IL, 1972), pp. 196–213; while William J. Hyde reads in terms of Mill, in 'Theoretical and Practical Unconventionality in *Jude the Obscure*', *Nineteenth-Century Fiction*, 20 (1965), 155–64.

20. *One Rare Fine Woman: Thomas Hardy's Letters to Florence Henniker 1893–1922*, ed. Evelyn Hardy and F. B. Pinion (London, 1972), p. 46.

21. 'Hearts Insurgent', *Harper's New Monthly Magazine*, European edn, 30 (1895), 594.

22. Cf. Alan Friedman, 'Thomas Hardy: "Weddings Be Funerals"', in *The Turn of the Novel* (New York, 1966), pp. 70–1.

23. Cousin, or brother and sister, relationships were widely used in feminist fiction to contrast the treatment and expectations and experiences of sex-differentiated pairs; e.g. in Elizabeth Barrett Browning, *Aurora Leigh* (1856), and Sarah Grand's *The Heavenly Twins* (1893).

24. Cf. John Goode, 'Sue Bridehead and the New Woman', in *Women Writing and Writing About Women*, ed. Mary Jacobus (London, 1979), pp. 100–13.

25. John Lucas, *The Literature of Change: Studies in the Nineteenth-Century Provincial Novel* (Hassocks, Sussex, 1977), pp. 188–91.

26. D. H. Lawrence, 'Study of Thomas Hardy', in *Phoenix: The Posthumous Papers of D. H. Lawrence*, ed. Edward D. McDonald (1936; reprinted London, 1961), pp. 495–510; and Kate Millett, *Sexual Politics* (London, 1971), pp. 130–4.

27. *Harper's New Monthly Magazine*, European edn, 29 (1895), 576; and *Jude the Obscure* (London, 1895), p. 161.

28. John Goode, 'Woman and the Literary Text', in *The Rights and Wrongs of Women*, ed. Juliet Mitchell and Ann Oakley (Harmondsworth, 1976), p. 242.

29. See her comments on p. 186 ('"Their philosophy only recognises relations based on animal desire"') and p. 222 ('"they can't give it continuously to the chamber-officer appointed by the bishop's licence to receive it."').

30. Cf. Geoffrey Thurley, *The Psychology of Hardy's Novels: The Nervous and the Statuesque* (St Lucia, Queensland, 1975), p. 191.

31. Cf. William H. Marshall, *The World of the Victorian Novel* (London, 1967), pp. 404–24.

32. Kate Millett, *Sexual Politics* (London, 1971), p. 133.

33. Cf. Mary Jacobus, 'Sue the Obscure', *Essays in Criticism*, 25 (1975), 304–28.

34. 'The Spectre of the Real', in *In Scarlet and Grey: Stories of Soldiers and Others* (London, 1896), pp. 164–208.

35. John Bayley, *An Essay on Hardy* (Cambridge, 1978), p. 201.

36. Penelope Vigar, *The Novels of Thomas Hardy: Illusion and Reality* (London, 1974), p. 193.

37. Cf. Elizabeth Langland, 'A Perspective of One's Own: Thomas Hardy and the Elusive Sue Bridehead', *Studies in the Novel*, 12 (1980), 12–28.

38. E.g. Shalom Rachman, 'Character and Theme in Hardy's *Jude the Obscure*', *English*, 22, no. 113 (1973), 45–53; and T. B. Tomlinson, *The English Middle-Class Novel* (London, 1976), pp. 121–4.

39. Mona Caird, 'The Future of the Home', in *The Morality of Marriage and Other Essays on the Status and Destiny of Woman* (London, 1897), p. 117.

40. For an interesting account of the Shelleyan motif in the novel, see Michael E. Hassett, 'Compromised Romanticism in *Jude the Obscure*', *Nineteenth-Century Fiction*, 25 (1971), 432–43.

41. *Harper's New Monthly Magazine*, European edn, 30 (1895), 125.

42. 'To Alice Grenfell', 23 April 1892, *Collected Letters of Thomas Hardy: Volume I, 1840–1892*, ed. R. L. Purdy and Michael Millgate (Oxford, 1978), p. 266.

43. 'To Millicent Garrett Fawcett', 30 November 1906, Fawcett Library, London.

44. 'The Simpletons', *Harper's New Monthly Magazine*, European edn, 29 (1894), 80. The serial title was changed to 'Hearts Insurgent' in subsequent instalments.

45. E.g. on pp. 62, 64, 93 and 197.

46. A. O. J. Cockshut, *Man and Woman: A Study of Love and the Novel 1740–1940* (London, 1977), p. 129.

47. See Mona Caird, *The Daughters of Danaus* (London, 1894), pp. 341–2.

48. Terry Eagleton, 'Liberality and Order: The Criticism of John Bayley', *New Left Review*, 110 (1978), 39.

4

Jude the Obscure: The Return of the Pagan

CARLA L. PETERSON

In *Jude the Obscure*, Hardy revived the general debate over the value of book culture and institutionalised forms of learning in Victorian England. In particular, Hardy was concerned with the relationship between Classical and Christian cultures, and returned quite directly to those cultural issues raised by Mme de Staël at the beginning of the century in her Romantic novel *Corinne* – the possible reconciliation of pagan and Christian, Northern and Southern, past and present, male and female in modern European culture. Like George Eliot before him, Hardy saw these cultural tendencies as not only divergent from but also in direct conflict with one another. And, indeed, *Jude the Obscure* can be viewed as a fictional gloss on Matthew Arnold's argument over Hellenism and Hebraism in *Culture and Anarchy*. Hellenism and Hebraism are both ethical and social tendencies that pursue spiritual truths and moral modes of conduct. Hellenism is characterised above all by flexibility and spontaneity, by a straightforward acceptance of the difficulties involved in attaining moral goals, and is invested with a kind of 'aërial ease, clearness, and radiancy' that sheds 'sweetness and light' all around. In contrast, Hebraism is much stricter and more inflexible in its philosophical outlook; it consists of 'energy driving at practice, this paramount sense of the obligation of duty, self-control, and work, this earnestness in going manfully with the best light we have'. Upholding 'strictness of conscience', it views sin as 'something which thwarts and spoils all our efforts', and the frail-ties of the flesh as obstacles to 'right-acting'.[1]

In his essay Arnold traces the oscillating development of these two traditions in Western culture from premature Hellenism to the development of an ethical but stern Hebraism in mankind's early history, to a simultaneous revival of both in the Renaissance, vividly depicted for example in Eliot's *Romola*. The problem, according to Arnold, was that in Victorian England, Hellenism was on the decline and Hebraism in the ascendancy. For, as critics have noted, Arnold's Hebraism is nothing other than his particular interpretation of pre-vailing contemporary English Protestant Nonconformism, which es-poused such negative values as excessive religiosity, commercialism, social individualism, and so on.[2] Arnold's essay thus constituted a call to his fellow citizens to restore Hellenism, but it held out no hope for Mme de Staël's earlier Romantic vision of a future culture that would synthesise pagan and Christian values.

Hardy's own statement defining the major theme of *Jude the Obscure* does indeed focus on the value of book culture and of insti-tutionalised forms of book learning in Victorian England, for, in his own words, the novel 'is concerned first with the labours of a poor student to get a University degree'.[3] But critics have often com-plained that to this issue of book education Hardy added another, incompatible one, that of 'the marriage question', thus creating an irreconcilable double focus in the novel. But if we bear in mind the specifics of Arnold's definition of Hellenism and Hebraism, and the way in which textuality and sexuality are so often linked to one another, the connection between the two themes becomes readily apparent. Cultural concerns inevitably include sexual ones and are often expressed in terms of sex; sexuality may thus function as a metaphor for textuality. Thus Jude's desire to obtain a university education and Sue's attempts at self-education in order that they might both enter into the cultural mainstream of the times may quite naturally be related to issues of sexuality.

Following the pattern set by such earlier Victorian novels as *David Copperfield* and *The Mill on the Floss*, *Jude the Obscure* is highly autobiographical in fact and in spirit.[4] Like Jude, Hardy was born into a lower-class family but had aspirations to becoming a scholar; and while Hardy did receive a formal academic education for several years at a Nonconformist school where he studied French and Latin, he was self-taught in Greek and, in particular, learned on his own to read the Greek New Testament. Like Jude,

Hardy was forced to leave school and acquire a trade, entering into architectural training; and, as an architect, he exhibited, as did Jude, a tremendous sense of historical consciousness. Like Jude, he remained throughout his life quite sensitive about his working-class origins. Like Jude, he underwent a gradual loss of faith and became an agnostic. Finally, like Jude, he was tremendously attracted to his cousin, Tryphenia Sparks, but married another woman, Emma Gifford, out of love, only to watch the marriage slowly disintegrate as each lost any sense of values shared in common. We can appreciate, then, the extent to which *Jude the Obscure* is a projection of Hardy's own concerns.

The orphaned child of divorced parents, Jude feels that his identity, his origin are indeed obscure. Lonely and alienated from his community, he possesses no role models with whom he can identify. His Aunt Drusilla is a brusque, practical woman, with little time or inclination to love Jude, nurture him, and teach him moral values – indeed, she feels that Jude is a tremendous burden and would be better off dead; neither can the community in which Jude lives – the village of Marygreen – compensate for his aunt's moral and spiritual emptiness. A combination of debased Christian culture (Mary) and an alienating natural landscape (green), it is a place that has lost all sense of identity and historical origins. Thus, it has permitted the original church – symbol of Christianity – to be torn down, and in its place 'a tall new building of modern Gothic design, unfamiliar to English eyes, had been erected on a new piece of ground by a certain obliterator of historic records who had run down from London and back in a day' (pp. 11–12); and it has allowed the surrounding natural landscape to be disfigured by 'fresh harrow-lines' that 'seemed to stretch like the channellings in a piece of new corduroy, lending a meanly utilitarian air to the expanse, taking away its gradations, and depriving it of all history beyond that of the few recent months, though to every clod and stone there really attached associations enough and to spare – echoes of songs from ancient harvest-days, of spoken words and of sturdy deeds' (p. 13); it is certainly a nature devoid of God. What Hardy offers us in Marygreen, then, is a community that has cut itself off from its historical roots and lost all sense of cultural origins.

Like the town of Marygreen, Jude too is lost, and this sense of loss is hinted at first of all in the boy's analogy between himself and the birds he is supposed to frighten away from Farmer Troutham's field, who 'seemed, like himself, to be living in a world which did not want them', and whose nests he is always sure to reinstate 'in their original place' (pp. 14, 15). Jude's loss of identity and quest for it are further suggested in his repeated confrontations with his own image. Thus, his staring into the well at the beginning of the novel represents a search for individual and cultural origins, for his own specular image as well as that of Marygreen itself: 'The well into which he was looking was as ancient as the village itself, and from his present position appeared as a long circular perspective ending in a shining disk of quivering water at a distance of a hundred feet down' (p. 11).[5] Jude's later confrontations with his own image in photographs reinforce this notion of his search for a specular image. Jude's quest for image and identity, for the origins of self and culture, lies however chiefly in his book reading.

Jude discovers the world of books through the village school-master, Phillotson, to whom he turns in his isolation as the one mas-culine authority in the village, and whom he romanticises as a father figure. As the father, it is Phillotson who sets up Jude's early expectations of life and establishes his patterns of desire. Because Phillotson is a reader of books, Jude wants to read books. Because Phillotson wants to leave Marygreen, Jude desires to leave. Because Phillotson hopes to go to Christminster and study to become ordained in the church, this dream becomes Jude's dream too. Knowing nothing of life, these desires do not originate in Jude but come to him through the intermediary of Phillotson. Moreover, they are actually verbalised by none other than his Aunt Drusilla who throughout the novel exhibits uncanny ability for divining the truth: '"Why didn't ye get the schoolmaster to take 'ee to Christminster wi' un, and make a scholar of 'ee. ... I'm sure he couldn't ha' took a better one. The boy is crazy for books, that he is"' (pp. 12–13). In Girard's terms, then, Phillotson is Jude's media-tor of desire.[6] And we shall see that all throughout his life Jude will follow in Phillotson's footsteps.

Like Jude, however, Phillotson appears to have no origins; he too is a lonely, rootless individual, an outsider to Marygreen, and so eventually resumes his wanderings. Jude tries then to replace Phillotson the father figure with the itinerant physician Vilbert. But Vilbert, the second representative of culture in the novel, reveals himself to be nothing more than a self-centred quack, indifferent to culture, and interested only in material advancement. Jude is thus forced back on himself to acquire knowledge on his own. Left to his own devices, reading becomes for Jude a secret ritual performed in isolation from society, indeed in the face of societal hostility and violence. For the only time that Jude can study his books is while driving his aunt's cart, which he thus transforms into a private study. Such a method of 'combining work and play' is, however, met with the opposition of the townspeople who deem it 'not altogether a safe proceeding for other travellers', and set the law after him (pp. 28–9).

Jude's private reading involves him first of all in the study of pagan Classical authors, and he reads an impressive list of them – Homer, Hesiod, Thucyidides, Herodotus, Aeschylus, Sophocles, Euripides, Plato, Aristotle, Caesar, Vergil, Horace, Seneca, Livy, Tacitus, and others – with great intensity and joy, but with very little guidance. It finally occurs to Jude one day that such a reading of pagan authors is a highly inappropriate course of study for a young man whose chief intellectual goal is to become an ordained minister in the Church of England; if he is to follow Phillotson to Christminster and study divinity, he must prepare himself by reading Christian authors. And so, with the same intensity with which he had read Classical texts, Jude plunges into the reading of the Greek New Testament and of such Christian authors as Newman, Bishop Ken, John Wesley, Keble, and others. Jude identifies with these Christian authors and desires to emulate them; they become his specular image. But in reading without guidance Jude reads uncritically, distorting his texts in order to make them coincide with his own desires. Thus, he remembers Matthew Arnold's apostrophe of Christminster/Oxford as a '"serene"' city, '"so unravaged by the fierce intellectual life of our century"', forgetting that Arnold later mourned the city as '"the home of lost causes"' (p. 66).

Like Phillotson, Jude fails in his quest to acquire Christian knowledge and thereby spend his life in service to the church. As in his earlier reading of the Latin and Greek grammars that Phillotson had sent him, Jude discovers that no 'laws of transmutation' apply to his current situation. In studying ancient languages as a youngster, he had discovered that no validity existed to the Romantic myth of absolute origins, which he had imagined as an extension of Grimm's law whereby a single 'rule' or 'prescription' would give him 'the clue of the nature of [the] secret cipher' of a foreign language and thus enable him 'to change at will all words of his own speech into those of the foreign one' (p. 26). As a young man, he again realises that there is no validity to his equally Romantic belief that Christminster would open up its halls of learning to a working-class

man. Indeed, Christminster is no city of light and brings Jude no intellectual enlightenment; on the contrary, it plunges him into deeper
and deeper obscurity. Just as Eliot had attacked 'masculine' learning
in *The Mill on the Floss* as a system of education that excludes
women and is irrelevant to the common problems of daily life, so
Hardy here delivers a similar indictment against university education and Christian learning as exemplified by Christminster. This
educational institution is elitist and hypocritical, unfairly excluding
Jude and wrongly convincing him that his quest for knowledge 'had
not been an ethical or theological enthusiasm at all, but a mundane
ambition masquerading in a surplice' (p. 103). It teaches, as Sue so
well perceives, outdated, medieval forms of knowledge, based on
modes of imitation that degrade rather than ennoble the mind.
Thus, the high point of Jude's first stay in Christminster consists of
his drunken recital of the Nicene Creed one night in a tavern. Such
a repetition of religious phrases in Latin no longer suffices to endow
the working-class man with a privileged status; as Jude recognises,
he could just as well be reciting "'the Ratcatcher's Daughter in
double Dutch'" (p. 100). Finally, Christminster's teachings offer
Jude no wisdom that can help him deal with the daily vicissitudes of
life; in particular, Christianity's negative sexual attitudes cannot
help Jude in his problematical relationships with Arabella and Sue.

In thus adopting Phillotson's Christian ideals and following him to
Christminster, Jude betrays his true pagan self. For Jude's earlier
study of Classical authors had struck a responsive chord in him as no
other texts ever had. And nowhere is Jude's love of Classical literature made so evident as in his impassioned declamation one evening,
with the sun going down on one side and the moon rising on the
other, of Horace's 'Carmen Saeculare': 'His mind had become so im-
pregnated with the poem that, in a moment of ... impulsive emotion
... , he stopped the horse, alighted, ... knelt down on the roadside
bank with open book. He turned first to the shiny goddess, who
seemed to look so softly and critically at his doings, then to the
disappearing luminary on the other hand, as he began: "Phoebe
silvarumque potens Diana!"' (p. 29). In striking contrast to the fragmented and debased world of Marygreen, Horace's poem celebrates
the unity and harmony of the Classical world that had successfully
conciliated such opposing forces as nature and culture, sun and
moon, heaven and earth, male and female. More important,
however, Horace's poem is a hymn to the twin gods Phoebus Apollo
and Diana, portrayed by the poet as the chief rulers and protectors of

Roman culture. The importance of these twin deities in relation to Hardy's novel cannot be underestimated for, if read properly, *Jude the Obscure* may be seen as a mythological fable in which Jude and Sue have become modern reincarnations of the twin deities in nineteenth-century Victorian England.

In classical mythology, Apollo is of course a sun god. He also represents culture and knowledge, as he is associated with poetry and music, and with building and architecture as well. He is, as Horace states in his poem 'acceptus ... novem Camenis', 'dear to the muses nine'.[7] More than any other god, then, Apollo testifies to the glory of Classical culture. Furthermore, in Nietzsche's later formulation, Apollo represents the principle of ideal beauty. He is always, even in anger, 'hallowed by beautiful illusion'; he is the 'ruler over the beautiful illusion of the inner world of fantasy'; he embodies the 'dream experience', the search for 'the higher truth, the perfection of these states in contrast to the incompletely intelligible everyday world'; he is, finally, a figure of harmony, a deity who seeks to reconcile opposing and clashing forces.[8] In Hardy's novel Jude appears very much to be an Apollonian figure: he is driven by a desire for enlightenment as provided by culture and knowledge. More than any of the other characters, he is marked by a deep love of poetry and music, as demonstrated, for example, in his passionate emotional response to the little-known hymn 'At the Foot of the Cross'. He is a builder and reveres architectural monuments. And, finally, his life truly represents an Apollonian quest for ideal beauty, 'for the beautiful illusion of the inner world of fantasy' that he hopes to find both in his books and in Sue. In contrast to the French novelists Stendhal and Flaubert, who saw Dionysian excess as the only possible response to the social and political chaos of nineteenth-century France, Hardy, like Matthew Arnold, looked to the Apollonian impulses of Greek culture as the most powerful antidote to Victorian Hebraism.

Indeed, from his very beginnings Jude experiences himself as incomplete, as obscure, and goes in search of that twin who will complement him, of that other who will bring him out of obscurity and into light. He initially, and quite erroneously, turns to Arabella Donne in the hope that she will complete him, but she reveals herself to be opposite to him rather than complementary. Herself a representative of the artificiality and disharmony of modern nature, rather than of the harmonious nature of the Greeks, Arabella is totally scornful of Jude's Apollonian quest for ideal beauty through books. Jude then turns to his cousin Sue Bridehead – first in image and then in actuality – and comes to believe that she is the other for whom he is searching. As critics have observed, Sue is for the most part seen from Jude's point of view, and from this perspective she is consistently depicted in terms of ideality and radiance, as a shining moonlike figure who brightens Jude's dark sun. She is an 'ideality', a 'half visionary form' (pp. 80, 74); more concretely, her photograph offers the portrait of 'a pretty girlish face, in a broad hat with radiating folds under the brim like the rays of a halo' (p. 63); her voice is 'tremulous' but 'silvery' (p. 82).

The moon goddess Diana, as Horace's poem suggests, is a more complex figure than the sun god, Apollo, for, in her association with the moon Diana was seen as representing both chastity and fertility. Through the whiteness and coldness of the moon, Diana symbolised first of all chastity and purity. In addition, as goddess of the hunt, she also represented the virginal aspects of nature. In such a capacity, she lived in isolation from men, surrounded only by her nymphs, enjoying the pleasures of the hunt and severely punishing any male, like Actaeon, who chanced upon her. But Diana was also seen as a goddess of fertility. For, as a moon goddess, she was associated with women's menstrual cycles, and thus with women's capacity to be fertile. Finally, it was also claimed that as the firstborn of the twins, Diana had helped her mother, Leto, give birth to the second-born Apollo.

For the Ancients these two aspects of woman – chastity and fertility – were not perceived as incompatible. According to them, a woman could give herself fully and sexually to a man, become fertile, and yet also remain chaste and virginal. This is because, as Esther Harding has suggested, such concepts are purely symbolic and must be interpreted psychologically, so that virginity comes to 'refer to a *quality*, to a subjective state, a psychological attitude, not to a physiological or external fact'. To the Greeks and Romans then, the virgin was a woman who was able to give herself to a man but who even after 'remained one-in-herself. She was not dependent on the man, she did not cling to him or demand that the relationship should be permanent. She was still her own mistress, a virgin in the ancient, original meaning of the word.'[9] Harding further points out that the moon goddess was dual in yet another, equally natural, way. As the goddess of fertility, she was good, kind, and beneficent, and corresponded to the bright moon. As the goddess of chastity, however, she was cruel, destructive, and evil, as represented by the dark moon.

In *Jude the Obscure* Sue represents Diana in both of her aspects –
she is both chaste and fertile, beneficent and cruel. This duality is
apparent first of all in Sue's name, Susanna Florence Mary
Bridehead. For if Susanna (and Florence as well) means lily, a flower
symbolic of chastity and purity, the name also reminds us of
Susannah in the Bible, the married and fertile woman who successfully overcame the charges of adultery levelled at her by the Elders.
The name Mary can refer to both the Virgin Mary and the sexually
promiscuous Mary Magdelen; and we must of course remember
that the Virgin Mary is both virgin and mother, chaste and fertile.
Finally, as Elizabeth Hardwick has noted, Sue's last name,
Bridehead, combines the chastity of the maidenhead and the fertility
suggested by 'bride'.[10]

More important, Sue's own sexual feelings and experiences are
dual, although the complexities of her sexual attitudes have been
veiled by D. H. Lawrence's narrow, patriarchal interpretation of the
novel.[11] Sue's sexuality is, indeed, ambiguous. Aunt Drusilla states
that as a child, she appeared to be both girl and boy. As an adult
woman, she is alternately sexually reticent and thus 'cruel', and sexually passionate and thus 'beneficent'. Thus Jude refers to her
'curious unconsciousness of gender', and Sue herself speaks of '"a
peculiarity in me. I have no fear of men, as such, nor of their books.
I have mixed with them – one or two of them particularly – almost
as one of their own sex"' (p. 118). Sue is indeed quite reluctant to
have sexual relations with those men with whom she is otherwise
quite close. The case of Phillotson is quite easy to understand, for he
is, by the admission of all the other women in the novel, particularly
the sensible widow Edlin, sexually unattractive. With Jude,
however, Sue does come to feel true sexual passion, and Hardy's
narrator makes this abundantly clear in the second half of the novel,
starting with the kiss at Shaston that becomes the 'turning-point in
Jude's career' (p. 172). Parting from one another, they turn back
for a last look and, in the words of the narrator, 'that look behind
was fatal to the reserve hitherto more or less maintained. They had
quickly run back, and met, and embracing most unpremeditatedly,
kissed close and long' (p. 172). Equally passionate kisses are exchanged when Sue, re-married to Phillotson, returns to see Jude for
the last time and then confesses to the widow Edlin that she loves
him still – '"O, grossly! I cannot tell you more"' – and wishes for
Phillotson's death so that she might return to Jude (pp. 313–14).
The widow Edlin clearly perceives Sue's love for Jude, and so does

Arabella, albeit more reluctantly. Finally, Sue is a fertile woman and is a mother figure. Metaphorically, she is mother to Jude, nurturing him and trying to bring him out of obscurity into light. She is also spiritual mother to Father Time, whom she associates with the god of culture, Apollo, by analogising him to Melpomene, the muse of tragedy. Last, she is of course a biological mother, as her union with Jude results in several children whom Father Time, fulfilling his tragic function, kills.

Such qualities in Sue have often been overlooked in the emphasis of critics on her sexual reticence and consequent 'cruelty' to men. If seen as a Diana figure, however, it becomes evident that Sue's chief desire is to retain that pagan 'one-in-herselfness', necessary to her sense of identity in the patriarchal Hebraic culture of Victorian England, in which a married woman must wholly subordinate herself to her husband and give herself over to the process of childbearing. It is at this point in our analysis of Sue that cultural and sexual issues start to converge in the novel. In Sue's world, Christian marriage laws attempt to take a woman's identity away from her by taking away her name and giving her that of another, indeed by taking her away from herself and giving her to that other: "'my bridegroom chooses me of his own will and pleasure; but I don't choose him. Somebody *gives* me to him, like a she-ass or she-goat, or any other domestic animal'" (p. 136). In such a Christian world view, it is impossible to maintain any pagan sense of 'one-in-herselfness', just as it is impossible to maintain a positive view of female fertility in this same post-Darwinian, post-Malthusian world where men and women no longer live in harmony with themselves or nature. For in this world nature is devoid of God's presence and has been debased by the imprint of technology; individuals have become identityless and rootless wanderers, alienated from their progeny. Sue herself feels oppressed by this world and "'crave[s] to get back to the life of my infancy and its freedom'" (p. 111). But it is Father Time who best represents this debased culture, what Hesiod has called the age of 'the race of iron',

> When babies shall be born with greying hair.
> Father will have no common bond with son,
> Neither will guest with host, nor friend with friend;
> The brother-love of past days will be gone.[12]

Indeed, it is in his overpowering sense of dispossession that Father Time kills himself and Sue's children.

Jude and Sue are, then, modern reincarnations of the twin deities, Apollo and Diana, complementary and necessary to one another for completion. Their sense of twinship, their quest for completion in one another, their desire to function as each other's specular image are expressed by the narrator in both intellectual and sexual terms.[13] Their twinship is intimated first of all in their family situation, in their cousinship and orphanhood. It is also suggested in their love of books. As Aunt Drusilla remarks, both Jude and Sue as children were "'crazy for books'", and both had the same capacity to conjure up visions on the basis of their reading: "'You too, Jude, had the same trick as a child of seeming to see things in the air'" (p. 91). Like Jude, Sue likes to read pagan authors: "'I know most of the Greek and Latin classics through translations, and other books too'" (p. 118). Their twinship is further noted by Jude in his perception of Sue, after she has run away from the Training School at Melchester, as 'a slim and fragile being masquerading as himself' (p. 116), as well as by the narrator, who comments on their 'complete mutual understanding, in which every glance and movement was as effectual as speech for conveying intelligence between them, made them almost the two parts of a single whole' (p. 231). The most important perception of Jude and Sue's twinship comes, however, as critics have noted, from Phillotson, who analogises them to Laon and Cythna, the brother and sister visionary revolutionaries in Shelley's *Laon and Cythna* (1817), an analogy to which we shall shortly return: "'I have been struck with these ... facts; the extraordinary sympathy, or similarity, between the pair. He is her cousin, which perhaps accounts for some of it. They seem to be one person split in two! ... I found from their manner that an extraordinary affinity, or sympathy, entered into their attachment, which somehow took away all flavour of grossness. Their supreme desire is to be together – to share each other's emotions, and fancies, and dreams. ... They remind me of – what are their names – Laon and Cythna'" (pp. 183–5).

Jude and Sue fail in their quest for intellectual and spiritual complementarity, and their failure marks the complete breakdown of Mme de Staël's earlier Romantic belief in the complementarity of pagan and Christian cultures. The progression of Jude and Sue's failure can be traced through their many references to characters, events, and ideas they have come across in their books that mirror their own situation. Failure of male and female complementarity is expressed, for example, in their quoting from selected poems by

Browning, which provide a poetic gloss on their situation: 'The Worst of It' in which a husband holds his own excessive love for his wife responsible for her adultery; 'The Statue and the Bust' in which a man and a married woman fall in love and plan to elope, but betray their own emotional integrity by failing to do so; and 'Too Late' in which, similarly, a man who has been separated from the woman he loves through her marriage to another continues to live in the hopes of one day being able to marry her, only to discover quite suddenly that she has died.

More important, however, the failure of Jude and Sue's quest for complementarity becomes most apparent if one measures their accomplishments against those of Shelley's Laon and Cythna and views Hardy's novel as an ironic revision of Shelley's poem. Shelley portrays Laon and Cythna as brother and sister, and as close to one another as any two mortals can be. Laon describes his sister in the following terms: '"As mine own shadow was this child to me, / A second self, far dearer and more fair."'[14] They grow up together in nature, far away from all human society. Despite their isolation, they are both fully educated and are great lovers of books, for Laon has made sure that his sister receives all the same educational advantages that he has had: thus, with Cythna's 'fairest form, the female mind / Untainted by the poison-clouds which rest / On the dark world, a sacred home did find' (2:35). When Laon and Cythna reach adulthood, they leave their natural home and together fight the patriarchal tyrant, determined to overthrow a cultural system that keeps women in an oppressed state. Initially victorious, they celebrate a new revolutionary culture that is maternal in nature, in which Mother Earth is fully productive, and nature and humankind reproduce abundantly. The perfection of this new culture, and of Laon and Cythna's sympathetic relationship, is symbolised by their blissful lovemaking in a secluded natural place midway through the poem, and by the child that is the fruit of this union. The revolution ultimately fails, the tyrant is restored to his throne, and Laon and Cythna die; but Shelley's hopeful outlook is intimated, as critics have remarked, in the circular movement of the poem. For although Laon has died, his voice, like Cythna's, lives on to tell his story, a story that Cythna interrupts at the point when he is narrating the failure of the revolution to return us to the beginning to tell us her story, which parallels Laon's. Finally, Laon and Cythna's reunion in death suggests an ultimate victory; for at the end of the poem they are seen journeying to the Temple of the Spirit, that same temple to which the narrator and his female companion had journeyed in canto I.[15]

No such Romantic hopefulness prevails in *Jude the Obscure* in which the movement of the narrative suggests Jude and Sue's inexorable progression toward defeat. No such ecstatic union of body or spirit ever occurs between them, and neither do they come to preside over the defeat of patriarchal culture and the triumph of a new revolutionary matriarchal society. The reason for their defeat is suggested in Sue's quote from another of Shelley's poems, *Epipsychidion* (1821), shortly after Phillotson's reference to the two cousins as Laon and Cythna (p. 195). Like Hardy's novel, *Epipsychidion* records a simultaneous search for spiritual communion with ideal beauty and for sexual union with an ideal woman (biographically, Teresa Viviani is Emilia in the poem and not the poet's wife Mary Shelley). In quoting lines from the poem ('There was a Being whom my Spirit oft / Met on its visioned wanderings far aloft'), Sue is suggesting that a parallel exists between Shelley and Jude, between Shelley's quest and Jude's, and that in Emilia she has found her specular image and thus her identity.[16] At the beginning of the poem, Shelley speaks of the relationship between himself and the feminine other (Beauty, Emilia) in the now familiar terms of twinship, brother and sister, Sun and Moon; and the Moon is imaged at this point in the most positive terms:

> Thou Moon beyond the clouds! Thou living Form
> Among the Dead! Thou Star above the Storm!
> Thou Wonder, and thou Beauty, and thou Terror!
> Thou Harmony of Nature's art! Thou Mirror
> In whom, as in the splendour of the Sun,
> All shapes look glorious which thou gazest on![17]

But, later on, as Shelley recapitulates his search for the feminine other, the descriptive images suddenly change and introduce the more negative aspects of the Diana myth. The poet himself becomes Actaeon, torn apart by his own thoughts and falsely seeking salvation in 'the cold chaste Moon' who, instead of delivering him from pain, leads him into a state of anxiety, frustration, and, finally, spiritual death. Salvation only comes to the poet when the Moon is eclipsed by a new vision, one 'Soft as an Incarnation of the Sun'. From a pagan perspective, Shelley's poet has failed to understand the true nature of the moon, the dualities within her of 'soft' and 'ice', 'bright' and 'dark', 'waxing' and 'waning', 'Life' and 'Death' (ll. 273–307).

The pagan values of Horace's poem, Hardy is telling us, cannot survive in nineteenth-century England. The intellectual and sexual equality and complementarity of male and female, sun and moon, suggested in the line 'Phoebe silvarumque potens Diana!' give way under pressure from Hebraic patriarchal culture and, in particular, from Swinburne's 'pale Galilean'. Jude and Sue's failure to achieve complementarity is fully recorded in their reversion to Christian culture and its most important texts. Jude, as we have already seen, had early turned to Christian culture as a youngster in imitation of Phillotson. For a while he briefly attempts to replace Christian book culture with that of sculpture and architecture. For the city of Christminster, Hardy tells us, is like a book that offers its 'architectural pages' to Jude to be read. And Hardy suggests that Jude's proper sphere of learning is not Christian book culture but the world of architecture in which Jude can be both reader and creator. Jude himself feels that the stoneyard in Christminster is 'a centre of effort as worthy as that dignified by the name of scholarly study within the noblest of the colleges' (p. 69). But he then loses this feeling 'under stress of his old idea'. Moreover, Hardy also indicates that in Christminster, architecture has become as corrupted by Christian culture as have books. Christminster can only offer Jude architectural examples of a debased and imitative medievalism whose inauthenticity offers him no spiritual guidance.

Torn between two cultures, Jude gradually loses all sense of balance and harmony, and alternates between two excessive and contradictory modes of behaviour – the Christian on the one hand, and the Dionysian on the other, represented by his increasingly powerful sexual urges and propensity toward intoxication. Indeed, Jude becomes a totally split personality, giving in to the Dionysian impulse of drink and sexual appetite (his return to Arabella) at one moment, and then castigating himself as a Christian sinner at the next, understanding Sue's pagan striving for 'one-in-herselfness' but then attempting to possess her completely in accordance with Christian law. Jude foreswears Christian learning after the kiss at Shaston, burning his copies of Jeremy Taylor, Butler, Doddridge, Paley, Pusey, and Newman, yet he cannot shake off their teachings. 'Under stress of his old idea' or, as Sue thinks, under 'the strange operation of a simple-minded man's ruling passion' (pp. 262–3), Jude returns to Christminster – a place of spiritual and physical death – on Remembrance Day – in Father Time's words, 'the Judgment Day' – to die. And if Jude castigates Sue for falling under the sway of religious superstitions, he too appears to have succumbed once again to New Testament doctrines. Indeed, critics have suggested that Jude's end is a repetition of Christ's passion:[18] like Christ, Jude has returned to Christminster/Jerusalem, coming, in Sue's words, 'from Caiaphas to Pilate' (p. 261). He has come to the place of the Martyrdom and the Crucifixion, as witnessed in the premonitory hanging deaths of his three children. In addition, Jude is analogised to Saint Paul; as he addresses the crowd on Remembrance Day, Hardy compares him to Paul before the Lycaonians. And, like Sue, Jude repeatedly quotes from Paul's writings to explain their tragic impasse: '"We are acting by the letter; and "the letter killeth"' (p. 308).

Sue, for her part, cannot succeed as the moon goddess Diana in Victorian England. As much as she has immersed herself in Classical pagan culture, she has nonetheless been born into a Christian world and has been permanently marked by it. This is a culture that cannot accept as legitimate the notion of a woman who has thoroughly assimilated pagan culture. Nor can it accept the pagan concepts of male and female equality and complementarity, of the harmonious coexistence of chastity and fertility in a woman, of female 'one-in-herselfness'. In its fundamental misunderstanding of Sue's paganism, it labels her as a monstrous being. But Sue's monstrosity is presented as a perverse sexlessness – a deliberate and cruel withholding from the male.

The hold that Christian culture has over Sue is, as critics have remarked, apparent from the first. The statues of Apollo and Venus that she buys early in the novel quickly become those of St Peter and Mary Magdelen. At the same time Sue quotes from Swinburne's *Hymn to Proserpine*, a poem that acknowledges the triumph of the 'pale Galilean' and relegates Proserpina permanently to the underworld. Like Diana, Proserpina cannot, according to Swinburne, exist as a duality, living half in sunlight, half in darkness; she must remain forever underground. Such is Sue's fate as well. Sue's attitude toward Christian culture is most forcefully expressed, however, in her account of her rereading and rewriting of the New Testament: '"I altered my old one [New Testament] by cutting up all the Epistles and Gospels into separate *brochures*, and rearranging them in chronological order as written, beginning the book with Thessalonians, following on with the Epistles, and putting the Gospels much further on. Then I had the volume rebound"' (pp. 121–2). In so rewriting the New Testament, Sue is pursuing two contradictory critical impulses. First of all, she raises the question of the chronological ordering of the New Testament books. The dating of the Gospels and the Epistles can be established primarily by referring to events recorded and dated in the texts themselves. Such scrutiny of the biblical text inevitably leads, however, to the chief issue in nineteenth-century biblical criticism: the verification of eyewitnesses, the reliability and authenticity of their accounts, and thus the question of whether the Bible is ultimately history or myth, a fable with multiple authors or divine revelation. Sue, then, is in fact deconstructing the Bible to suggest that it is not a divine text, a continuous narrative that embodies a myth of absolute origins but, on the contrary, a discontinuous narrative suggesting gaps and absences rather than presence.

After having deconstructed the Bible, however, Sue then sets about reconstructing it, and in her new version she places the writings of St Paul first. St Paul is, of course, as Hardy's contemporary Nietzsche knew so well, the chief promulgator of Christian patriarchal law; he is the apostle who first set down in writing – fixed and codified – the teachings of Christ, formulating in particular Christian attitudes toward women: in his epistles he pronounces on such questions as the evils of sexuality, the dangers of marriage in turning the faithful away from God, the necessity of procreation only as a duty to God, the importance of the silence of women in the church. With St Paul, we have indeed moved far away from the concepts of womanhood embodied in the moon goddess Diana. It is his doctrines that triumph at the end as, after the death of her children in Christminster, Sue completely gives herself over to them. Pauline law punishes her for her pagan attempts at one-in-herself-ness; quoting from I Corinthians she tells Jude: "'We are made a spectacle unto the world, and to angels, and to men'" (p. 267). And Pauline law encourages her to adopt a stance of total self-abnegation; relying again on I Corinthians, Sue maintains that "'every successful man is more or less a selfish man. The devoted fail. ... 'Charity seeketh not her own' ...'" (pp. 286–7).

Through the tragic fates of Jude and Sue, Hardy in his novel portrays the irreconcilable conflict between pagan and Christian cultures – Hellenism and Hebraism – in Victorian England. In addition, however, *Jude the Obscure*, like George Eliot's novels, testifies to the failure of book learning in general to help men and women make their way through the debased conditions of life in the modern age, Hesiod's 'age of iron'. For Jude dies a pitiful death with both his Classical and Christian texts heaped carelessly around him, useless and indifferent to his pain. The survivors at the end of the novel are Arabella and the physician Vilbert who are both contemptuous of book culture and live by their natural instincts of trickery and deceit. The uselessness of books in helping individuals deal with the complexities of modern life, in particular its emotional aspects, had already been intimated by Sue in childhood in her 'tragic' recital of Poe's 'The Raven' recalled for us by Aunt Drusilla. For, if the poem records a young man's vain quest to recapture his dead mistress, Lenore, it also records a similarly vain search for intellectual knowledge: the student is seen pondering 'weak and weary, / Over many a quaint and curious volume of forgotten lore'; the raven 'of saintly days of yore' who comes to visit him and 'perche[s] upon a bust of Pallas' represents the quest for intellectual knowledge; and, finally, Lenore becomes the ideal goal of the quest, a goal that the raven assures the student he will never be able to attain through books. Poe's poem provides, then, an apt commentary on both Jude's and Sue's situations; the student functions as a specular image for both of them. Faced with the meaninglessness of book culture to help them sort through the complexities of their situation, both Jude and Sue regress back into the past and become dominated by a compulsion to repeat. Sue returns to Phillotson and remarries him, thus affirming the triumph of the father and his Christian laws. Jude returns to Arabella and, in remarrying her, embraces death.

In *Jude the Obscure*, then, Hardy's narrator constructs an ironic narrative that totally subverts the earlier cultural myths of the Romantics. Through his ironic rereading of Shelley's poems, Hardy's narrator denies any possibility of a harmonious complementarity of sun and moon, male and female. In the conflict between pagan and Christian that rages both within each protagonist and between them, he denies Mme de Staël's earlier Romantic vision of a synthesis of these divergent cultural traditions. Finally, in its structure, the narrative of *Jude the Obscure* may be seen as an ironic version of the Romantic quest paradigm as described by M. H. Abrams.[19] Jude and Sue do indeed return home to Christminster, though not to complete the figure of the spiral as did Shelley's Laon and Cythna, for example. They have indeed left home on a quest; they have experienced alienation, fragmentation, and isolation; but their return brings them no illumination, no final understanding of self, only increased despair and pain, continued false actions, repeated compulsive behaviour, and, in Jude's case, death. The defeat of Hardy's characters is so total that the narrating function must be assumed by a third-person narrator who, from a vantage point of complete anonymity and detachment, quite unlike the more involved stance of Eliot's narrator, dispassionately and systematically deconstructs those Romantic cultural myths that his protagonists still hoped to live by. In fact, with *Jude the Obscure*, the possibilities of thought and action open to earlier Romantic protagonists seem to have reached a dead end. As a consequence, Hardy abandoned fiction writing to seek in poetic discourse other forms of language and thought that would better help him to explore the culture of his age.

From Carla L. Peterson, *The Determined Reader: Gender and Culture in the Novel From Napoleon to Victoria* (New Brunswick, NJ, 1986), pp. 207–26.

NOTES

[This essay is taken from Carla L. Peterson's wide-ranging critical study, *The Determined Reader: Gender and Culture in the Novel from Napoleon to Victoria*. This book takes as its point of departure the figure of the reader-protagonist, the fictional hero (male or female) whose reading experience is central to their representation. She suggests that, in such narratives, reading functions as a kind of private ritual in which interpretation of reading of a cultural text also 'encompasses a reading of self, of others, of reality' (p. 1). Readers are 'determined', as her title has it, by their gender and class, which give particular inflections to their relationships to their experiences of texts. Noting the frequency with which reader-protagonists are isolated, she comments that 'For the reader-protagonists the ritual process begins with an acute sense of loss of identity arising from orphanhood and entry into a stepfamily ... [They] feel that they have lost their name, their real family, their history. They secretly turn to books, and reading becomes their ritual experience' (p. 31). The female reader-protagonist in a book by a male author, she suggests, embodies the male artist's anxiety as a feminised, marginal figure in a patriarchal culture.

In this chapter, the particularly feminist component of her analysis derives from her insistent recognition that Jude is not the novel's only reader-protagonist, and that part of the similarity between the novel's central couple lies in their intellectual complementarity. Exemplifying here what, in her introduction, she calls her 'method of radical comparativism' (p. 4), she seeks to explore the relatedness and the difference of the male and female experience portrayed, as well as the intersection of distinctions of class and gender.

All quotations in this essay are from the Norton Critical Edition of *Jude the Obscure*, ed. Norman Page (New York, 1978). Ed.]

1. Matthew Arnold, 'Culture and Anarchy', in *The Complete Prose Works* of *Matthew Arnold*, ed. R. H. Super (Ann Arbor, MI, 1965), vol. 5, pp. 163, 165, 167. See also Frank M. Turner's discussion of the significance of Arnold's essay in 'Victorian Culture' in *The Greek Heritage in Victorian Britain* (New Haven, CT, 1981), pp. 17–36. For an earlier discussion of Hebraism and Hellenism in *Jude the Obscure*, see Ward Hellstrom, 'Hardy's Scholar-Gipsy', in *The English Novel in the Nineteenth Century*, ed. George Goodin (Urbana, IL, 1972), pp. 196–213.

2. Frank M. Turner, *The Greek Heritage in Victorian Britain* (New Haven, CT, 1981), p. 21.

3. 'To Sir Edmund Gosse', 10 November 1895, Norton Critical Edition of *Jude the Obscure*, ed. Norman Page (New York, 1978), p. 349.

4. See Michael Millgate's recent biography of Hardy, *Thomas Hardy: A Biography* (New York, 1982).

5. See also Perry Meisel's comments on history in *Jude the Obscure* in *Thomas Hardy: The Return of the Repressed* (New Haven, CT, 1972), p. 140.

6. See René Girard, *Deceit, Desire and the Novel: Self and Other in Literary Structure*, trans. Yvonne Freccero (Baltimore, MD, 1965), pp. 7–10. See also J. Hillis Miller, *Thomas Hardy: Distance and Desire* (Cambridge, MA, 1970), p. 125.

7. Horace, 'Carmen Saeculare', in *The Odes and Epodes*, trans. C. F. Bennett (London, 1934), p. 355.

8. Friedrich Nietzsche, *The Birth of Tragedy*, trans. Walter Kaufmann (New York, 1967), p. 35.

9. Esther Harding, *Woman's Mysteries, Ancient and Modern* (New York, 1971), pp. 102–4.

10. Elizabeth Hardwick, 'Sue and Arabella', in *The Genius of Thomas Hardy*, ed. Margaret Drabble (New York, 1976), p. 71.

11. D. H. Lawrence, 'Study of Thomas Hardy', in *Phoenix: The Posthumous Papers of D. H. Lawrence*, ed. E. D. McDonald (New York, 1936), pp. 497–510. A much needed corrective to Lawrence's patriarchal vision has been provided by more recent critical studies. See, for example, Mary Jacobus, 'Sue the Obscure', *Essays in Criticism*, 25 (1975), 304–28, and Penny Boumelha, *Thomas Hardy and Women: Sexual Ideology and Narrative Form* (Brighton, 1982), pp. 135–56 especially. [Reprinted in this volume – see pp. 53–74. Ed.]

12. Hesiod, 'Works and Days', in *Hesiod and Theognis*, trans. Dorothea Wender (Harmondsworth, 1973), ll. 185–8.

13. See also Jerome Buckley's brief discussion of Jude and Sue as doubles in *Season of Youth: The Bildungsroman from Dickens to Golding* (Cambridge, MA, 1974), p. 176.

14. Percy Bysshe Shelley, *Laon and Cythna* in *The Complete Poetical Works of Percy Bysshe Shelley*, ed. Neville Rogers, vol. 2 (Oxford, 1975), canto 2. st. 24. All references in the text are to this edition.

15. For a fuller discussion of Shelley's poem, see, for example, two recent excellent books, Nathaniel Brown's *Sexuality and Feminism in Shelley* (Cambridge, MA, 1979), and Michael Scrivner's *Radical Shelley* (Princeton, NJ, 1982).

16. For a different interpretation of the meaning of *Epipsychidion* in *Jude the Obscure*, see Michael E. Hassett, 'Compromised Romanticism in *Jude the Obscure*', *Nineteenth-Century Fiction*, 25 (1971), 432–43.

17. Percy Bysshe Shelley, *Epipsychidion* in *Shelley's Poetry and Prose*, ed. Donald H. Reiman and Sharon B. Powers (New York, 1977), ll. 25–32. All line references in the text are to this edition. Shelley's poem has of course been widely commented upon. For a recent study, see Earl Schulze, 'The Dantean Quest of *Epipsychidion*', *Studies in Romanticism*, 21 (Summer 1982), 191–216.

18. F. B. Pinion, *Thomas Hardy: Art and Thought* (Totowa, NJ, 1977), pp. 110–13.

19. See M. H. Abrams, *Natural Supernaturalism: Tradition and Revolution in Romantic Literature* (London, 1971).

5

Hardy's Fist

JOHN GOODE

> What has Providence done to Mr Hardy that he should rise up in his arable land of Wessex and shake his fist at his creator?
>
> (Edmund Gosse)

> That is the voice of the educated proletariat speaking more distinctly than it has ever spoken before in the English Literature
>
> (H. G. Wells)[1]

ONE CANNOT CHOOSE ONE'S READERS

Of course no text, however hard it tries, stands free within its frame. But *Jude the Obscure* rejoices in its entanglement:

> Growing up brought responsibilities, he found. Events did not rhyme quite as he had thought. Nature's logic was too horrid for him to care for. That mercy towards one set of creatures was cruelty to another sickened his sense of harmony. As you got older, and felt yourself to be at the centre of your time, and not at a point in its circumference, as you had felt when you were little, you were seized with a sort of shuddering, he perceived. All around you there seemed to be something glaring, garish, rattling, and the noises and glares hit upon the little cell called your life, and shook it and warped it.
>
> (I. 2)

Lying down behind the pigsty, sacked for having been kind to the birds he is paid to scare, this hitherto safely ironised innocent, failing to find a coherent discourse (discourses seek to rhyme, to harmonise) is granted instead that authoritative second person as though the ' of speech remains unclosed. For 'he perceived' is tagged on too late to keep the third and fourth sentences in the frame of free indirect style, and the perception is not only as sophisticated as the implied author, but deliberately inverts the traditional development of knowledge, which is that you learn to be part of a larger whole. Growing up is an ordeal of centring and you, the reader, are dragged in to be made part of that ordeal. It happens again in Part I, chapter 4: 'but nobody did come because nobody does'. We are supposed to be watching the development of a poor young boy, but he keeps taking charge of our end of the syntax and our tense. The particular is not generalised, it is universalised. The very language pulls you in to the picture: Jude is not one of many (typical) – he is one of us.

Again and again the novel breaks out of its frame. Another, more representative, example follows the death of the children:

> 'I am a pitiable creature,' she said, 'good neither for earth nor heaven any more! What ought to be done?'
> She stared at Jude and tightly held his hand.
> 'Nothing can be done,' he replied. 'Things are as they are and will be brought to their destined issue.'
> She paused. 'Yes! Who said that?' she asked heavily.
> 'It comes in the chorus of the *Agamemnon*. It has been on my mind continually since this happened.'
> 'My poor Jude – how you've missed everything! – you more than I, for I did get you! to think you should know that by your unassisted reading, and yet be in poverty and despair.'
>
> (VI. 2)

It's all in the worst possible taste. The children have been found hanging on the back of the door, and not only does Jude produce an apt quotation which shows his knowledge more than it illuminates the situation, but Sue suddenly looks out of her understandable hysteria and both awards him an accolade and tells the reader how to assess his quotation. The novel frequently annoys the reader in this way, preventing him from 'identifying' with the situation (by which I really mean keeping it out there as a self-contained game, for this is so 'unbelievable', isn't it?) and, what is worse, doing the critic out of a job, since analysis and comparison are, as Eliot says, the critic's tools, and Sue and Jude frequently do both.

Worse still, the novel bedecks itself with precedents either by quotation, or allusion or direct comparison: '"it makes me feel as if

a tragic doom overhung our family, as it did the house of Atreus."
"Or the house of Jeroboam," said the quondam theologian' (V. 4).
The novel not only ruins the prospects of interpretation by explicit
discussion but also offers its own system of literary allegiances,
which makes it difficult for the critic to determine influences or
place it in a tradition (though this has not deterred many from doing
it). And it breaches decorum in other ways such as when, again at
the centre of a highly charged scene that any respectable writer
would let us enjoy for all it was worth, Jude warns Phillotson that it
is dangerous to sit on stone without a covering and offers him some
sacking, presumably so that his rival does not get piles. Obviously it
reminds us that Jude is more intimate with material contingency
than the schoolteacher, but it still seems an oddly affectionate and
'irrelevant' gesture. Hardy keeps preventing us from reading this
novel as 'story' – as illusion, as fable, as vision. *The Woodlanders*
and *Tess of the d'Urbervilles* subvert the reader they call into being.
Jude the Obscure does not even acknowledge the reader as a self-
defined and separate subject. It is simply not fit for consumption.[2]

Or to put it positively, it is a text that can only be called into
being as an event. It certainly *was* an event as the reviews and letters
about it to Hardy show. The *Life*[3] mainly stresses the hostile response, and the 1912 Preface says that this cured him of novel-
writing. But this flagrantly misrepresents what happened. If the
Bishop of Wakefield publicly burnt the novel and Mrs Oliphant
took it as evidence of Hardy's membership of an anti-marriage
league, a whole group of reviewers – Gosse, Ellis, Wells, Hannigan,
Le Gallienne – wrote about it with a passionate commitment which
effectively embraced the text more as a cause than as the object of a
professional judgement. Nor can Hardy have had any other intention (despite the disingenuous protests of aesthetic disinterestedness)
than to make an intervention in highly controversial issues of the
day, most notably that of marriage. As soon as Jude is married, he
makes an explicit comment about the nature of marriage which is
directly linked not only with the host of novels which dealt with
'the new woman' but also with the prolonged debate of 1891–3
about marriage which dominated the journals and to which Hardy
himself contributed.[4] If he could justifiably claim that the novel is
not merely about marriage but also about education, that theme is
presented within the parameters of theology, which links it with the
current polemic about religion (see the correspondence with
Clodd).[5] And bearing in mind that the big sensation in fiction of the

previous decade was precisely a novel, Mrs Humphrey Ward's
Robert Elsmere, which dealt with the contact between education and
theology particularly in the way an Oxford intellectual's theological
doubts can be made positive by his recognition that working-class
people are likely to be blasphemous and revolutionary without some
religious values, the Bishop of Wakefield was surely right to burn
Hardy's novel. Beside anything it said about sex, it also portrayed
the absolute failure of Christianity to provide any ethical or ontological guidance.

This is doing scant justice to the topicality of the novel,[6] but I
only want to indicate that it is conceived as an intervention, and
that it is in those terms that we still read it. Education and the
family, in Althusser's phrase, form the ideological couple of late
capitalism,[7] and that is the concern of this novel (that is, not one
and the other but the coupling of them): it is the double call of the
self into the world that determines and constructs it. The effect of
the disframing is precisely that it negotiates the eventfulness of the
text's reference as an eventfulness of its action or the act of reading
it. We are agitated by its vulgarity. This is guaranteed by two formal
devices, a structural strategy and an intertextuality.

We are used by now to Hardy's triadic structure, whether as sequence, as in *The Mayor of Casterbridge* and *The Woodlanders* or as
the overlaying and refocusing of levels of discourse as in *Tess of the
d'Urbervilles*. *Jude the Obscure* develops this in an extreme way,
constructing a triadic 'series of seemings' which I take to mean not
the charting of a mental history, since the novel is much too bound
up with the contingent and the necessary for that, but a sequence of
illusory modes which comment on one another. Specifically, it is
structured according to a determinative role of place which presents
us with a precise graph of the socialisation of the characters. 'At',
the word which links the title of each part, implies a double negation of the subject since although it defines a location it does not
suggest, in fact in most cases positively denies accommodation –
thus at various stages the characters are placed but have no place.
Moreover, there is a shift in the significance of place progressively
from the purely given (Marygreen) to the chosen by gesture
(Christminster), the chosen by compromise, blocked gesture
(Melchester and even more Shaston), the determined solely by economic necessity (Aldbrickham and elsewhere). The arbitrariness is
vital: they both have to go to these places and these places have no
meaning for them. Thus finally the arbitrarily asserted return is the

locative equivalent of the nevertheless which we have encountered as the key action of the late fiction, but significantly *as* return and not as a gestural metonymy.

This gives us a triadic structure in two ways. First it constitutes an onion, since Marygreen and Christminster again both universalise their predicaments in metaphysical terms. Christminster and Aldbrickham are both about the condition of the working class, and at the centre, Melchester and Shaston, preoccupied as they are with training and marriage respectively, personalise, so that there is a vortex of particularisation. But in terms of a linear structure it also means that the first and last sections act as a symbolic frame for the realistic narrative (which is one reason why the novel seems to have no frame, since frames should not really be in the picture). That use of the second person which I indicated as important earlier is the keynote of Marygreen, which centres on the field and which in spite of sharp social observation, works out to a highly generalised level.[8] 'But nobody did come because nobody does' indicates a shift from the condition of Jude to the condition of man: the field is the ontology of the unnecessary life. As soon as he moves to Christminster, Jude embarks on a history marked by the specific institutions of his time and the specific relationship to them he has as working man (and Sue as woman). It is not the field and God's gardener, but the city, the stonemason's yard and the Master of Biblioll, the marriage bed and the husband. At the end, however, the novel is transformed again. Just as the metonymy of the gesture ('thither J. F.') lifts the novel out of its field and into the urban life of the nineteenth century, so the metonymy of the return is to 'the centre of my dream' – to 'the *reflected* sunshine of its crumbling walls' (my italics). It is a return to a symbolic mode but not a symbolism generated by the metaphoric eye of the narrator (making the actual field the field of life), but a theatrical gesture generated out of the protagonists' despair of dealing with life 'realistically'. Jude's speech, Father Time's euthanasic infanticide, Sue's conversion and histrionic remarriage make the text a performance. The novel restates itself – as 'myth', as social problem novel, and as (avant-garde) theatre.

The intertextuality functions also both to alienate the text (in a Brechtian sense) and to radicalise its effect. This is an area I have to dispute with critics with whom I am broadly in sympathy but who, I think, take 'the letter killeth' as too global and one-dimensional an instruction about what to do with the literature incorporated.[9] First, we should recall that Hardy's relationship to writing is dialectical – it is both an institution which has to be negotiated and an agency of self-improvement. The letter killeth is after all a perception only available to the literate who know their Bible.[10] Moreover, killing isn't only a bad thing. Some things need to be killed, and one thing the literature that is invoked in this text can kill is the unquestioning acceptance of authority emanating from Biblioll and the marriage laws. Moreover, the actual context in 2 Corinthians indicates that by letter is meant the law, the scripture, as voiced, to invoke Derrida once more. To suggest that the display of learning merely signifies the dead illusion that Jude is betrayed by is to read the allusiveness undialectically (although I accept that if you follow many of the quotations through they cast an ironic light on the text, as Ingham in her excellent Introduction indicates).

The key to this is the episode of the grammars. Jude is to think that the possession of the grammars will give him instant access to the ancient languages and therefore to a distinguished career as a bishop (though to regard him as hypocritical because he fancies having money is a middle-class judgement). He is disabused, of course, but two things follow from it. In the first place, Hardy let us know that partly Jude is only under an illusion because he has no access to modern linguistics, Grimm's Law. This theme pervades the whole learning process. It is not just that Christminster is difficult to enter, it is also that it is a place of ignorance, like the British elite in general, not only impervious but second-rate. Thus there is a way of learning which Jude is denied. But secondly, he takes on the pedestrian grammars and works his way through them, which is what brings him to Christminster, and if not to the University to Sue, and the echo of the undergraduate and the enlightened liberation from the darkness of theology and marriage. The written may be identical with the walls (see II. 2 as Wotton points out[11]) but it is also the obscured signpost, J. F.

The texts of Jude form their own antagonistic canon, which is deliberately a contradiction in terms, because what opposes itself to rubric and cardinal is an apocrypha, and in more ways than one the textual allegiances of this novel are apocryphal.

In the first place, there is a highly polemical secularisation of the sacred text itself. Not only are there frequent references to the actual Apocrypha (including, for example, the Gospel of Nicodemus, which actually presents Pilate in a sympathetic light) but also Sue calls attention to the absurd way the Song of Songs is canonised, and the book most frequently quoted from is the Book of

Job, which Leslie Stephen had described as the agnostic's book of the Bible and which had been the subject of a great deal of non-Christian commentary such as that of Renan and Mark Rutherford.[12] Even the New Testament citations which occur more frequently as we should expect when Sue begins to retreat into the Church, tend to privilege the epistles to the Corinthians, which are actually not very Pauline in their liberal attitude to dogma.[13] So the Bible is evoked not as a sanctified authority but as a document of human experience that privileges love, sex and the resistance to oppression.

There is also a secular use of a poetic succession. The poets most often cited are Shelley, who was sent down from Oxford for atheism, Browning, who became disillusioned with higher education and who was radicalised by his reading of Shelley, and Swinburne, who was a notorious rebel at Oxford and whose most immediate mentor was Browning. And Hardy too, of course, was immediately inspired by Swinburne, and exchanged letters with him comparing the reception of *Jude the Obscure* with that of *Poems and Ballads*. All of them at some point oppose Christianity and marriage. And they can in this respect be linked with the other recurrent presence, Gibbon, whose fifteenth chapter is cited several times and who is, of course, one of the inspirations of the poem quoted about Julian the Apostate.

But this leads to the dialectical effect of these citations. On the one hand there is a radical agnostic tradition which underwrites the intellectual emancipation of the novel. On the other hand, of course, all these writers, including Gibbon, had the privilege to go to the University, even if, through their integrity, they rejected its values.

Gibbon's account of the rise of Christianity in his fifteen and sixteenth chapters makes continual use of the words 'obscure' and 'obscurity' to describe both Judaism and early Christianity. For him a fundamentally rational polytheistic civilisation hardly noticed the rise of this grubby little religion from Palestine. In the sixteenth chapter he relates how the grandsons of St Jude, supposedly the brother of Christ, were arrested in Rome because they were thought to be pretenders to the mantle of King David. To prove their innocence, they showed their hands, 'hardened with daily labour'. 'The obscurity,' Gibbon contemptuously remarks, 'of the house of David might protect them from the suspicions of a tyrant.' Hardy's novel enters a tradition of a radical discourse knowing it to be socially apart. The reaction to Gibbonnian rationalism implicit in its evocation is parallel to Marx's response to Feuerbach. Ideologically Feuerbach explained the deformative effect of religion but failed to understand its material foundation. The 'theoretic unconventionality' which the intertext invokes is not denied, on the contrary it is very important, but its limits are seen.[14]

In terms of his own immediate cultural situation, Hardy knows that he can call on what we can accurately term an avant-garde (the case of Shelley, for example, is partly mediated through Dowden's biography, which provoked the reactionary essay of Arnold in 1886).[15] Theoretically, avant-gardes are not elites, since there is nothing to prevent anybody who cares to master the intellectual parameters of such groups from entering them. But, of course, only certain privileged groups are ever in a position to choose. *Jude the Obscure* exists exactly at this interface. In a letter, ironically to Mrs Henniker, one of Hardy's society ladies, he pointed out that his novel was written for those into whose soul the iron had entered, and would not be appreciated by frequenters of drawing-rooms. But, he added, one cannot choose one's readers.[16] A little earlier, the eminently bourgeois feminist Millicent Fawcett, admiring *Tess of the d'Urbervilles*, asked him to write a novel warning working people of the disastrous consequences of hasty marriage. Hardy declined, but it is tempting to think that his last novel is a considered ironic response to that banal request.[17] For all that it was written with a certain support assured, there is a level on which Hardy is writing for the future.

Of course, that future is observed in Wells's review. But the educated proletariat, sharp as the phrase is, is a contradiction in terms. For in this world, to be educated (led out) is to cease to be proletarian. It is a way out of the field to which there is no return. *Jude the Obscure* rallies the avant-garde in the name of the excluded, and it remains an event because that means it poses the question of knowledge and its ideology, knowledge as education and carnality, the wall and the garden of bourgeois order. For to open them out is to admit the obscure, and that is the decline and fall of an empire.

Ingham argues that the outcry against the novel was the recognition of a revolutionary novel.[18] I agree with the spirit and not the letter of this, for if the novel distances itself from the official public it does so under cover of the avant-garde. The question is whether the avant-garde relates to the proletariat, those whose soul the iron has entered and in terms of the historical formation of the novel, its existence as a totality, surely not. Significantly the word Ingham reaches for is 'subversive'. The *revolutionary* novel is still to be made, out of the recalling of the reader into a double reading. Having dragged in the reader, it devises a sequence of concrete universals. The field is the result of labours but becomes the symbol of the human condition; Christminster is both the wall against the self-taught and the ideological formation of the nineteenth century; marriage is about the new woman but is actually about the family. We need two readings, one representational, which is the field and leads to the coming universal wish not to live, and the other representative of the voices unsilenced within it. We can thus transform the totality that the novel represents to the totalisation of which it is a representative, or, to put it another way, to understand the agency of its structuration.

MY SCHEME OR DREAM

'At' doubly decentres – it is an exclusion, since none of the places demand your presence, and an imprisonment since only by being domiciled at that place can you get work. This is to become a novel, literally about finding a lodging: knowing your place means knowing you have no place. Yours is an unnecessary life because its necessities are not reciprocated. The cell called your life is at once an incarceration, the thick wall, as Pater puts in, of personality,[19] and always, at the same time, part of a whole. It turns the organic inside out – instead of the part being itself and being part of a greater self, the part is cut off from the whole and for all that is not free to be itself.

Marygreen thus inverts the obvious fictional structures to which it makes reference. Classically enough it begins with a departure, but this is not the setting out of the protagonist, but his abandonment – he is left behind, alone but not on the road. Sent to the well, which is as ancient as the village itself, he finds only 'a long circular perspective ending in a shining disk of unquivering water' which offers him no mirror, but merely assimilates the tear of his desolation into its depths. His thoughts are *interrupted* by his aunt. Three possibilities of relationship are at once denied. The only link with a present, with the teacher who is leaving, is reduced to the stored, unplayed piano. The link with the past and the quivering water is denied by the reversal and absorption of the well process (that is, instead of drawing water from it, he drops a tear into in which is never to be heard of again, which makes no mark). And finally his aunt disrupts even his relationship to his own thought, so that when he does operate the well it is overshadowed by the negations of fear and stress.

I term the section mythic only because of its quality of generalised explanation, 'how it came to pass'. It clearly parodies the opening of *Tom Sawyer*, where the importunity of the aunt provokes the division of labour. Jude has no such resources – this will not be a comic novel about the origins of capitalism or about the retarding interval of childhood. What he finds instead of a negotiable world is the apparently transcendent presence of the field:

> The brown surface of the field went right up towards the sky all round, where it was lost by degrees in the mist that shut out the actual verge and accentuated the solitude. The only marks on the uniformity of the scene were a rick of last year's produce standing in the midst of the arable, the rooks that rose at his approach, and the path athwart the fallow by which he had come, trodden now by he hardly knew whom, though once by many of his own dead family.
> 'How ugly it is here!' he murmured.
> The fresh harrow-lines seemed to stretch like the channellings in a piece of new corduroy, lending a meanly utilitarian air to the expanse, taking away its graduations, and depriving it of all history beyond that of the few recent months, though to every clod and stone there really attached associations enough and to spare – echoes of songs from ancient harvest-days, of spoken words, and of sturdy deeds. Every inch of ground had been the site first or last of energy, gaiety, horseplay, bickerings, weariness.
>
> (I. 2)

There are two manifest forms of obscurity here. First the obscurity of social marginalisation which is how it is dominantly used throughout the text (obscure means poor, as Ingham says).[20] Also, however, there is an obscurity of mind. The field of vision (though, of course, it is also a field in which he works and a battlefield of Darwinian nature), doubly darkens Jude's view: first by stretching up to the horizon and obliterating its verge; equally, as the second paragraph makes clear, the brown utilitarian surface obscures its history which has to be supposed by a self-advertising, omniscient narrator ('though to every clod and stone ... '). Thus the self is abandoned to this apparently unbounded real without a history, though in fact, as the text keeps telling us, there is nothing exceptional about it since he is one among the many which be cannot see. This gives him nothing, for the many are obliterated. Only the well survives as an ancient relic and the church is 'erected on a new piece of ground by a certain obliterator of historic records'. Not, either, that the historic records hold much comfort, since insofar as the invisible past is authorially voiced it is largely a history of deceit and oppression.

None the less it has its marks, and thus a third kind of obscurity: a rick of last year's *standing*, a path *athwart* the fallow, and the rooks, '*inky* spots on the nut brown soil'. They are marks of a kind of opposition, residual, transversal, despoiling. The obscurity of Gibbon's little sect is about to overwhelm the world and it will be Julian's philosophy that will be described as obscure.[21] Now look at Jude's response – 'how ugly it is here!' It is a strange way for a young boy to respond to his oppression. The objection is aesthetic, and the only gesture he makes imaginative: 'his heart grew sympathetic with the birds' thwarted desires … A magic thread of fellow feeling united his life with theirs.' 'Thwarted' recalls the path athwart and the thwarted aspirations of the unseen buried. The magic thread, which clearly echoes the Paterian web, comes from the perception that their life 'much resembled' his own. Later, he will see Christminster as phantasmogoria, 'either directly seen or miraged', and he will look at his learning as at a magic lantern. I do not mean that this novel has a teleology, though at the point of his death Jude will operate a theatrical representation, having tried to survive through the creation of images, first in stone and then in cake. Rather it constitutes a mode of relationship for the reader of what would otherwise be a self who disappeared into the field. Jude too, by his voice (note), which is opposed to the noise he is paid to make, is a mark, unedited by the world he inhabits since he has no value, no family, no community, only the prospect of 'the fall of the curtain' on his unnecessary life. Hardy has called you into the being of what Virginia Woolf will later call the obscure life. The obscure life is the subject without a predicate, the margin that calls into question the page from which it is excluded.

The field carries only marks, to which we shall return; but the opening momentum is the necessity of moving out of the field, which can obviously only happen in disorganic ways (since organically, the field would have to open itself to the subject athwart it, which would be absurd). Verges are boundaries, here lost in mist. They propose both limits and edges that the Marygreen section defines, thus achieving its ontological status. The dialectic of limits and edges is narratively embodied in the marriage to Arabella and the grammars respectively, though neither of these are simply assigned to one concept (since edges are always limits and vice versa). But their confrontation is dramatised in the walk during which Jude stares at his future and is struck with a prick.

The limits are stated by the two women in Jude's life as a quadrilateral which could enclose a field. They are presented as four syntactically axiomatic statements:

1 'Pigs must be killed. Poor folks must live' (Arabella)
2 'She or he "who lets the world, or his own portion of it choose his plan of life for him, has no need of any other faculty than the ape-like one of imitation"' (Sue, quoting J. S. Mill)
3 'Feelings are feelings' (Arabella)
4 'We should mortify the flesh, the terrible flesh' (Sue – this is not strictly axiomatic, but it is her inductive logic consequent on 'because we are too menny')

These are all true and borne out by the narrative, but obviously they contradict one another. There is a primary opposition between Arabella and Sue. Statements 1 and 2 embody the polarities of evolution, since on the one hand evolution is the struggle for survival and on the other the recognition of the development of species and choice becomes part of the definition of being human. Statements 3 and 4 embody the polarity of emotion, since the only way to protect the feelings is to mortify the flesh and the only means of mortification is the privileging of feeling over other demands. Thus these pairs might seem to deal antinomously with the objective and subjective respectively. Moreover, they respectively represent working-class and middle-class verges, since Arabella's are realistic (natural and sexual selection as the binary form of ''tis nature and what do please God') and Sue's aspirational, postulating the world as the field of the self – self-fulfilment, self-discipline. For, of course, the working class is the predicate of the middle-class subject, which is why if we do not sentimentalise, working-class culture can too often look like a programme of acceptance and evasion. Equally however 1 and 3 and 2 and 4 are as incompatible with one another as 1 and 2 and 3 and 4. In this opposition within the character, Arabella would have to be taken as representing 'nature' (Darwinian and romantic respectively) and Sue 'culture' as the illusion of free will and equality and the superior choice of spirituality respectively.

There is nothing *really* natural about Arabella, but she uses this term frequently (for example about her grief for little Jude) and tries in several ways to imitate natural processes like pregnancy and hair growing. Of course the Other of Arabella is only another mode of assertion into the symbolic order, since what she offers is a trap to make a marriage. Arabella's sexuality is never separated from conventionality: the barmaid becomes the landlady. Lawrence's later reading of Arabella as some kind of natural energy only shows that he was as vulnerable to barmaids as the rest of us. But her dimple making and hair enhancing are not *qualifications* of her sexuality – they are part of it. Even the Other trajectory (literal) of the pig's prick is bound up with the economic system it serves. After all it is not mere realism that locates the enticement and breakdown in the dismemberment and demolition respectively of the pig. Not only is Jude's sexuality at variance with his theological ambition, it is the sign of his proper place within the economy of pig killing – that is, lower-class marriage. 'Feelings are feelings', Arabella's furthest excursion from the symbolic order, is a return. It has nothing to do with the loving kindness of Jude's sympathies in the field. When she expresses her grief over the death of the children she admits that she feels much more for Father Time 'as is natural'. Sue and Jude have already shown us something very different from this natural which serves the social. The natural is the symbolic order. The Other is only what the structure licenses – carnivals are not revolutions, but ways by which revolutions are avoided.

Nor is there anything intrinsically civilised about Sue, who recognises that she is pre-medieval, but nevertheless is forced to retreat into urban ideologies, theoretic unconventionality or ritualism (the Anglo-Catholic arena she disappears into was a very urban movement). Thus, she schematically voices the extremes of civilisation – liberty (via Mill who rejects 'Nature') and repression.

Along these axes Arabella moves from a zero by which the natural law is made to serve the existing order of things to an affirmation by which human desire is brought within the compass of nature to justify not a disruption of the order (since although she is about to reseduce Jude it is so that she can reobtain a husband) but its manipulation (which is a subversion, it is true, but one which finally strengthens what it subverts). Sue on the contrary moves from an affirmation which is as chronologically modern as Arabella's zero (since the text from which she quotes was published very shortly before the story takes place)[22] to a negation (which is precisely medieval, or medievalist). Her zero is the ontology of the railway station (where you choose your journey and where you experience, as Sue does, the overwhelming sense of the vast train stopping just for you) as the negation is that of the cathedral in which personal aspiration is abolished. Both women move between the symbolic order and the Other but on opposing levels (nature and culture) and in opposing directions (plus and minus). Although these statements are articulated for Jude by his women (and that has a bearing on the sexual politics of the novel), they can be traced to his original ordeal at Marygreen. Thus the Arabella axis is absolutely defined (though only the zero statement is made) within the field, since what Jude has to learn is that what was good for God's gardeners was not good for God's birds *but* the only mode of inclusion offered is the magic thread of feeling. The field obliterates human continuity but can only do so because that continuity underlies it and leaves the marks without which Jude would have no place in them at all: or, to put in more starkly, if the inky blots of the birds were not there Jude would not be employed, though he is employed to enforce their absence. Jude's work is thus his own cancellation as it will be at Christminster where he repairs the walls that keep him out. After he has decided that he does not want to be a man, 'then like the natural boy, he forgot his despondence and sprang up' (I. 2). The natural keeps you going in order to rule you out – the only way he can prevent being a man is by not being a natural boy (an omen that is clearly fulfilled).

The Sue axis is hardly present since Jude's contact with civilisation is minimal. Nevertheless the section opens and closes with the choice of a departure – Phillotson's scheme or dream – and Jude's own signpost. 'He who chooses his *plan* of life for himself,' Mill's text goes on, 'develops all his faculties.'[23] All the planning and scheming and dreaming belongs with Sue's affirmation, but also, at the end of the paragraph from which this quotation comes, Mill compares human nature to a tree 'which requires to grow and develop itself on all sides, according to the tendency of the inward forces which make it a living thing'. I don't know how consciously Mill is appropriating that organistic image of human society as a tree which is central to Burke and Carlyle (and later to Yeats) but it is clear that he does exactly the opposite with it, for instead of it becoming a metaphor of subordination, it becomes a metaphor of self-development (inward forces). Sue is as axiomatic as Arabella because she gives voice to the inward forces which remain as a part of the field as the utilitarian surface. Thus it shares a common base with 'feelings are feelings' since although both are affirmations they are as determinate as the negations. To be me at all I have to develop myself irrespective of the social order which demands that I come into being. Sue's negation, that we should mortify the flesh, obviously recalls the way in which sexuality literally puts a stop to Jude's dream when Arabella throws a 'piece of flesh' at his self-dedication to being the *beloved son* of Christminster, in other words at the point at which he sees himself entering the symbolic order. (Given his orphanage, Jude's address to the Alma Mater adds another resonance to the merely trivial ambition of which he is wrongly accused.)

Thus the field is defined by the inclusive oppositions of survival, love, freedom and self-discipline. They are modes of being all of which are modes of determination. There aren't any ways out through them. They are the invisible verges.

Unless we understand the inexorability of this landscape we cannot understand the extraordinary inclusiveness of Jude's own journey. Let me recapitulate the sequence. Jude's sense of justice loses him his place. Having reported this to his aunt, he lies down behind the pigsty (which is, as we know, a very significant place to be behind) and meditates on the flaw in the terrestrial scheme of things. This leads him to reject the prospect of growth, but 'the natural boy' springs up and forgets (it is anti-Wordsworthian since in Wordsworth the child is father to the man and wishes his days to be bound each to each). Jude, on the contrary, *steals* out of the hamlet and returns to his field not to work but to follow the path athwart. At the edge of the ploughing, another ironic echo, this time of the end of *Paradise Lost*, marks off the field from the world, but the world is only a bleak open down, *crossed* by a solitary road at right angles to the neglected Icknield Way (the monumental significance will be obvious). It is a flat, low-lying country 'under the very verge' of his upland world, so his ascent merely gives access to a drop, and the only way to move is via a cross. Until, that is, he finds a *ladder* which can literally lift him to a point of vision from which he can see Christminster or its mirage. He obliterates his despondence, he climbs out of his field and sees, whether truthfully or not is indeterminate, what is at least light. The whole process is disruption, misery and the way out (to echo Morris's title).[24]

Christminster is the last monument. As with the Barrow, the amphitheatre and Stonehenge it persists as the record of endeavour and oppression. Jude successively becomes aware of each of these dimensions. At night, he hears the broken voices of the inmates who, under the umbrella of his naïvety, or (to exercise the principle of the grammars again) the reduction anthologisation which is history, speak in a succession which glosses over their actual incompatibility. There is an obvious irony in juxtaposing, say, Gibbon with Newman, or Arnold with Peel, and it reflects Jude's indiscriminate awe, *or* the fate which awaits polemic in time. By day, in the meantime, he recognises the walls' barbarian oppression (thus echoing the term Arnold used for the aristocracy and summing up the irony of Christminster which, designed for the poor, is the citadel of the ruling class), and feels a bond not with the voices of the past, but 'as an artizan and comrade' (this latter word is crucial in the novel, and is obviously chosen by Hardy throughout with deliberate care) who made and remake the walls, as we now recognise, into pages that can be read. The monuments are petrified residuums of the Barn, or rather the Barn blended with Church and Castle from which it is distinguished in the precarious utopianism of *Far From the Madding Crowd*. But unlike the other monuments, Christminster is still active, and reminds us that the novel as a whole relates as a grotesque mirror of *Far From the Madding Crowd*, and its activity is to do with work including the intellectual work (Jude's invocation of the ghosts is imagined to have been heard by a student working late), but work here does not bring people together – it is precisely a separating process. 'Artizans and comrades' recalls the cancelled tension of the novel which follows *Far From the Madding Crowd*, in which the heroine's brother, also a stonemason, maintains a recalcitrantly radical position in the face of her entryism.

Of course, Christminster is merely a place of fetishists and ghost seers, and this leads radical critics to see Jude's aspiration as mere illusion. Ingham, for example, correctly notes that it is neither coherent nor disinterested.[25] It is merely the mirage of social integration which is confirmed by the parodic names which echo its petrifaction. But if Jude is merely to confront an illusion, what is the point of the universalising of the opening section? It is as though a wide-angled narrative, which drags the reader in as unseparated subject, is suddenly narrowed down to a patronising tale of lost illusions. The negative answer is already clear from the analysis of the movement out of the field. Jude is not offered a place which he chooses to leave. As we have seen he is both abandoned and constrained. His 'illusion' is not an illusion in respect of the identity which awaits him. It is the primary condition of his obscurity that there is no true self for him to find. Christminster is at least a place where there are no farmers. Phillotson refers to 'my scheme or dream', which aptly encapsulates the double bind of the obscure life. For how can you be human without choice, and yet how can this choice be anything other than a dream? Jude picks up Phillotson's word when he realises he has trapped himself into marriage which is the field, 'a social ritual which made necessary a cancelling of well-formed schemes involving years of thought and labour' (I. 9).

We know that the well-formed scheme involves illusions that will be quickly disabused. Doesn't the first breakthrough in classical learning teach him a poem which induces 'a polytheistic fancy' inconsistent with the 'ecclesiastical romance in stone' but which voices precisely the need that will initially deprive him of it? His only resource is system, just as with the grammars it has been doggedness. When he has abandoned the pagan classics, his resolution to go to the city of light and lore is approached with a logic as abstract as his ethical decision to abandon the sheer love of reading: 'What was required by the citizen? Food, clothing, and shelter. An income from preparing the first would be too meagre; for making the second he felt a distaste ... They built in a city: therefore he would learn to build' (I. 5). To work out a programme of action in such terms is a sign of your unnecessary life. There is no reason why *you* should follow this course. Jude seeks in Christminster not merely enlightenment but 'a place' – 'it has been the yearning of his heart for something to anchor on' (I. 3). The yearning has to embody itself therefore through a sense of order. Jude is not trying to escape from his place, because he has no place. He has no choice but to make a choice to improve himself and that is no choice at all. That is why the dream is a scheme or the scheme a dream. The only 'place' for Jude is displacement.

Jude is to find that the order which Christminster is, is not orderly in terms of his own consciousness but only in terms which exclude him. That is a condition of his specific social construction. But the specific social construction is not realised as such until that construction has become normative – the product of the ethical decision, the logical assessment of possibilities. That is why I stress the universalising rhetoric of the first section. It is not a question of Jude's typicality but of the universalised terms of his situation – Jude's field is the field of life, which does not make the novel more representative but more importunate. He may absurdly see

Christminster as the New Jerusalem but the way of seeing it is contrasted by way of Gibbon with St John the Divine who sees it with the eye of a diamond merchant. This partly just relativises our judgement (that is, if Jude aspires towards an illusion, it is at least more morally just than that of the author of Revelation). But also it is related to the fact that the contradiction in Jude's encounter with Christminster is not singular but double. There is the contradiction within the superstructure that Christminster represents, between learning and culture which the Horatian Ode foreshadows and the contradiction between superstructure and base, that is the historical deformation of Christminster as an institution – 'You are one of the very men Christminster was intended for when the colleges were founded' (III. 4). Christminster is a place full of fetishists where you are elbowed off the pavement by millionaires' sons. This is not two contradictions, but one. On the one hand there is the pagan proletarian, on the other the established bourgeois. It is a question of knowing your place, remaining in your own sphere, which is terribly sensible advice but a hard slap after ten years of labour. And what else is the sphere of the labourer?

Christminster is the city of Light and the Tree of Knowledge grows there. But the celestial city is the giver of order and the tree of knowledge a forbidden fruit. Education is about the training of traditional intellectuals and universities are the modes of organising them into socially acceptable, if not useful, cadres (for in bourgeois society one way of handling the intellectual is to shut him away in an institution – see Walter Pater's *Emerald Uthwart* if you think I am importing a 1960s accent). This raises a problem of how to read Christminster which, unlike anything earlier in Hardy, must be read parodically. You cannot think of Christminster as you must of Casterbridge as an entirely independent name (for Casterbridge has nothing to do with Dorchester, that is clear). But Jude hears the voices of real people all but one of whom are associated not with Christminster but with Oxford. So we cannot but think of the history of Oxford, and the history of Oxford is complex and revealing. Given the structure of his learning, what Jude goes to find is the Tractarian movement. What he finds there, insofar as he gets anywhere near, is the second-hand residue of the undergraduate's scepticism which resembles the climate of criticism of the scriptures which surfaced in the publication in 1860 of *Essays and Reviews* and which had led to Pusey's unsuccessful persecution of Jowett, and to some extent the heterodox Hellenism presided over by Pater.

The master of Biblioll's terribly sensible advice is a good instance both of the way in which the text works parodically and of the complex relationship between criticism and containment in the debates of the sixties. Biblioll clearly reminds us of Balliol whose Master, Jowett, who died in 1893, was the subject of articles by Swinburne and Stephen (and therefore topical both to the time of the story and the time of the production of the text). As a contributor to *Essays and Reviews* and as a general liberal presence he was a valued ally of the kind of enlightened opinion to which Hardy's novel owes its admittedly ambiguous allegiance. In a letter of 1867, Jowett defined 'the object of reading for the schools' as 'to elevate and strengthen the character for life'. The three ways of attaining this have a clear bearing on Jude. First and second respectively are hard work and 'a real regard for truth and independence of opinion'. On the other hand, alas, we also need 'a consciousness that we are put here in different positions of life to carry out the will of God, although this is rather to be felt than expressed in words'.[26] A wall of silence thus intervenes between what is rational for the ruling class and sensible for the worker. In his radical essay 'on the Interpretation of Scripture', Jowett makes it clear that no amount of truth is sufficient to alter institutions:

> An ideal is, by its very nature, far removed from actual life. It is enshrined not in the material things of the external, but in the heart and conscience. Mankind are dissatisfied at this separation. They fancy that they can make the inward kingdom and outward one also. But this is not possible. The frame of civilisation, that is to say, institutions and laws, the usages of business, the customs of society, these are for the most part mechanical, capable only in a certain degree of the higher spiritual life. Christian motives have never existed in such strength, as to make it safe or possible to entrust them with preservation of the social order … For in religion as in philosophy there are two opposite poles; of truth and action, of doctrine and practice, of idea and fact.[27]

The way in which it appropriates a rational materialism (laws and institutions are not absolute) for a deeply conservative end (they are mechanical and therefore not accountable to the intelligence) is beautiful and its detailed appropriateness to Jude's ordeal is obvious (we note how many practices are dispersed to the 'frame' so that very little is left on which 'mankind' can have any effect). Thus the Tractarian aspiration towards an organic totality (an anchor) is displaced by a dialectically educating and excluding liberalism.

Moreover, Jude is deprived of the reconciliation of culture and learning that emerges in the dominant, reorganising figures of the interim between the story and the text (the seventies and eighties) who were busy recuperating the learning roaming unfettered and dangerously through the ruins of theology. I think not only of Ruskin, who became Slade Professor in 1870, and Arnold, who had been professor of poetry from 1857 to 1867 but also the English Hegelians, above all Bradley and Green, who used a highly radical philosophical system to provide new strategies of containment. Bradley demolished any basis for conduct other than 'my station and its duties', and is another presence in the terribly sensible advice. Green worked apparently more progressively by the dialectical elaboration and practical application of the transindividual consciousness.[28] Jude is never allowed into the city of light; but through the mediation of Sue, that is through the woman, he is allowed to eat of the forbidden fruit. He cannot, however, make this a fortunate Fall because, as we have seen, the world is not all before him where to choose. On the contrary, the world beyond the field, that is beyond his station and its duties, is an open plain below the verges marked only by a cross and a forgotten Roman way. Moreover, he only begins to benefit from the actual current of ideas when he is displaced from Christminster to Melchester.

Robert Elsmere, on which Hardy made extensive notes, clearly demonstrates the straight ideological version of this and is deeply relevant to the novel. It was the great success of the 1880s if you take success to be a matter both of sales and respectability. For a novel to be a bestseller (my copy of 1889 claims to be the twenty-fourth edition) and to have received favourable reviews from Gladstone and Pater it has to be quite special. Furthermore it has a remarkable pedigree, being written by Matthew Arnold's niece, and dedicated to the memory of T. H. Green. The hero, who is a paragon of learning but suffers from a strange physical condition, comes down from Oxford to inherit his father's rural living. This is on the estate of a Gibbonesque scholar who after a long series of complex confrontations finally induces a religious crisis by way of the Higher Criticism which leaves him unable to go on seeing Christ as a God or working as a rector. (Elsmere has no trouble with Darwinism though he does decide to keep quiet about it to his wife; the Higher Criticism alienates him completely from her – it is very stirring stuff.) Through the influence of a character who is a thinly disguised version of T. H. Green, he takes up instead a secular pastorship in working-class London. Both as rector and pastor, he works largely by telling stories to the lower orders (thus resembling ironically enough Hardy's Ethelberta). But what is important for us is that he re-embraces Jesus (not as God but as the ultimate image of human purity) in reaction to a series of blasphemous cartoons circulated by radical artisans depicting Mary Magdalen speaking obscenities to the crucified Christ. You see where this scepticism leads to!

The Tractarians and the Oxford Hegelians offer some kind of break with Utilitarianism. They offer the Tree of Knowledge as the City of Light. *Robert Elsmere* shows how careful such an ideology has to be, since it cannot be offered to the working class without becoming subversive of society as a whole and the family in particular. The undergraduate helps Sue, and thus Jude, to a pagan joyousness which grows out of pagan learning and the decanonisation of scripture. Green, on the other hand, sees the Greeks as merely selfish and regards Institutions as 'facts beyond' to which consciousness should submit.[29] The agents of emancipation are the walls that contain, the verges which are invisible in the mists. The 'new idea' of going to an obscure hamlet which takes him to Melchester is both Tractarian and Hegelian and depends on Jude not listening to Sue (Jude praying).

Education is an anchor, a leading out which holds him in place. The second dislocation which locates is sex. Like knowledge, it is both self-escape and repair. If it opposes the career of learning through Arabella, it also through Sue opposes the dislearning of theology. Jude recognises that twice his path athwart has been thwarted by women. In the case of Arabella, this is 'the natural' reclaiming him to the symbolic order and it is not ironic merely that he is helped out of that by Spinoza, for the escape from Arabella is a version of his endeavour.[30] Sue is more complex since both Jude and Phillotson seek to bring her within the symbolic order. On one level she continues the radical theme of education and exposes its containment. She is free of the Jerusalem but can accommodate intellectually by reproduction. She does not seek the City of Light – she has it already. In the Training-School episode she clarifies the social control latent in the emancipatory agency of education, literally, as later she exposes marriage, by jumping out of the window.

Sue gets caught between image and utterance. It is the requirement of clothes and image that she leaps out of. The clothes episode recalls the climax of Sarah Grand's *The Heavenly Twin* (1893), the apparently feminist bestseller of the nineties, in which the female twin Angelica, who has maintained in drag an intimate but sexless relationship with a wonderful tenor, nearly drowns in the river and has to be rescued and stripped by him. As it is all in the dark her naked body is not actually revealed, but it does lead to a recognition which ends the relationship. Luckily he dies of pneumonia and she returns to the husband who, being twenty years her senior, she calls 'Daddy' and achieves equality with him by writing his speeches. Such chaste and liberal fantasies must have struck Hardy with an irony picked up in the image of Phillotson fondly contemplating Sue's handwriting.

In marriage, Sue becomes a voice. It is her imprisonment and his torture. Just as the education motive is inevitable but part of the field – a way out which is a walling in, so here not only is marriage the inevitable, but so too is the end of marriage. Feelings are feelings and this binds Sue and Jude into their fate, though briefly they have something different.

The key figure here is Father Time. In another novel extensively extracted by Hardy and having many links with *Jude the Obscure*, Pater's *Marius the Epicurean*, the hero in a journal he keeps at the end shows that no philosophy can work. A return to the golden age (to the simplicity Jude and Sue feel they have found at Stoke Barehills) would not eradicate 'that root of evil, certainly of sorrow, of outraged human sense in things, which one must carefully distinguish from all preventable accidents ... were all the rest of man's life framed entirely to his liking, he would straightway begin to sadden himself over the fate, say of the flowers'.[31] Jude's son clearly shares the same response. Marius's final vision is shaped by looking at the lives of the poor and the way in which what is valuable for them is the love they feel for one another (especially children) and how likely that love is to be destroyed by death. Watching a boy who has brought his labouring father lunch he foreshadows both the young Jude and the consciousness of his logical successor: 'He is regarding wistfully his own place in the world there before him. His mind, as he watches, is grown up for a moment; and he foresees, as it were, in that moment, all the long tale of days, of early awakenings, of his own coming drudgery at work like this.'[32]

Marius's only solution to the 'inexplicable shortcoming' on the part of nature is a 'candid discontent' in the face of the very highest achievement, but a 'minor peace' in the acceptance of a Christian martyrdom that privileges 'humanity standing free of self pity', and it is not really suicide (though Marius does not believe in

Christianity), since its function is to preserve another character who will voice 'the plea which humanity would ever possess against any wholly mechanical and disheartening theory of itself'. For Marius the children who dominate the latter part of the novel relieve the iron outline of the horizon about him 'with soft light beyond'. Of course, the children provide no soft light for Jude: their hanging bodies speak only for the outline, clarify the verges which had been lost in a mist. The logic of both novels is towards the Schopenhauerian opposition to the will to live. This is not incompatible with the evocation of Christ, which is apparently incongruous in a novel which so firmly rejects theology. Each of the re-organising ideologies it encounters – Hegelianism, Arnoldism, Aestheticism – come back to Christ as model (even Marius). Even Schopenhauer himself, who might seem to negate Christianity by proclaiming the unforgivable sin as the supreme virtue, sees his own work as a New Testament in that it 'declares that the Law is insufficient, and indeed absolves man from obedience to it, and that the soul of the New Testament is undoubtedly the spirit of asceticism'.[33] This is abandoning the letter (he cites Romans 7) and mortifying the flesh; moreover, asceticism is 'precisely the denial of the will to live'. Sue and Father Time between them take the novel from the Old Testament of 'merely moral virtue' to the new gospel of the will not to live.

Nevertheless they are only voices, and both are heard not as the novel but as voices within it whose performative context includes ironic distance (not to say grotesqueness, since the suicide note is a grotesque pun). Even the doctor's explanation is the report of an opinion and immediately placed as a historical phenomenon. In other words the last section of the field is decentred. It has been closed up by the events of the middle which have led to that something external which, despite its lack of specific identity, is very specific in its triadic negation of learning, labour and love. It is not falsified but it is not a place of rest. It does not say amen to the novel. Hardy seems to want to stress this by the way in which the word tragedy is employed in the final section in a deliberately journalistic manner to refer to the death of the children, and not to the total situation of Jude and Sue. It confers no literary status on the totality of events. Even as he reports the doctor's 'explanation' Jude collapses into grief: 'He's an advanced man the doctor, but he can give no constatation to ... '

The field is unanswerable. Its positives – choice and feelings – are the functions of its zeros – self-denial and survival. If we underestimate the pessimism of the novel's intelligence we shall not be able to embrace the optimism of its will. The only way out of the field structured at the beginning is the reflected illusions which are finally endorsed at the end. This impasse derives from specific conditions in the base but those conditions are not made typical, and not given a historical term but universalised. Nothing works to change them. The educated proletariat becomes the species man – the iniquity of the system is 'something external'. But the voice of the obscure articulates this and thus it calls out the replies it does not seek. Jude is condemned to repair and imitation, but 'how ugly it is here' is a sign athwart his furrow.

From John Goode, *Thomas Hardy: The Offensive Truth* (Oxford, 1988), pp. 138–60.

NOTES

[This essay is taken from John Goode's extensive critical study, *Thomas Hardy: The Offensive Truth* (Oxford, 1988). Goode was throughout his career a Marxist critic, but his work was also increasingly influenced by poststructuralist theory, with its argument that language does not merely reflect a pre-existing reality but actively constructs the ways in which people experience, understand and interpret the world. The two critical modes are brought together throughout this book which, as its title suggests, considers the various ways in which Hardy's writing is 'offensive' in its challenges to and subversions of various forms of orthodoxy. In this chapter on *Jude the Obscure*, he is concerned with the radicalism of the novel's refusal to respect the boundaries of good taste, as they were understood at the time. He also, importantly, analyses the novel's habit of 'annoy[ing] the reader' and 'doing the critic out of a job' by flaunting its own textuality through quotation, allusion and satirical reference to authoritative texts. Drawing on the theory of the 'alienation effect' proposed by the Marxist playwright and theorist Bertolt Brecht, he argues that the novel's textual self-consciousness productively impedes the conventional practices of reading – such as identification with the characters, or interpretation of the author's intention – which might be brought to bear on it, forcing the reader into active thought. In an important sense, the novel's stress upon its own textuality *is* its radicalism, in this reading.

No standard edition is used for quotations in this essay. Roman numerals are used to indicate Part or Book numbers, Arabic for chapter numbers. Ed.]

1. R. G. Cox (ed.), *Thomas Hardy: The Critical Heritage* (London, 1970), pp. 269, 283.

2. See T. Eagleton, *Criticism and Ideology: A Study in Marxist Literary Theory* (London, 1976), p. 131. I argue, however, that the strategy is less 'provisional' and more fully co-ordinated with the divided cultural situation it encounters.

3. F. E. Hardy, *The Life of Thomas Hardy, 1840–1928* (London, 1965), p. 104. This highly coded text, emulating the 'life and letters' format of official Victorian biographies, is universally regarded as Hardy's equivalent of an autobiography.

4. 'The Tree of Knowledge', *The New Review*, 10 (1894), 681.

5. *The Collected Letters of Thomas Hardy*, ed. Richard Little Purdy and Michael Millgate (Oxford, 1978–88), vol. II (1893–1901), p. 92.

6. See Penny Boumelha, *Thomas Hardy and Women* (Sussex and New York, 1982), pp. 63–97, and Patricia Ingham (ed.), Introduction and Notes to *Jude the Obscure* (Oxford, 1985). [Ingham's essay is reprinted in this volume – see pp. 20–31. Ed.]

7. Louis Althusser, 'Ideology and Ideological State Apparatuses (Note Towards an Investigation)' (1969), in *Lenin and Philosophy, and Other Essays*, trans. from the French by Ben Brewster (London, 1971), p. 146ff.

8. Not that we should underestimate that observation. The novel is not a series of seemings in the sense that it deals merely with a world of consciousness. On the contrary it is difficult to find equally accurate and internal presentations of working-class life to compare with, let us say, the pig-killing episode, and indeed the whole 'world' of the novel.

9. T. Eagleton, 'Introduction' to *Jude the Obscure* (New Wessex edn, London, 1974), pp. 9–20; Patricia Ingham (ed.), 'Introduction' to *Jude the Obscure* (Oxford, 1985), pp. xi–xxii. Ingham's edition is extremely valuable, as are her two articles on 'The Evolution of *Jude the Obscure*', *Review of English Studies*, 27 (1976), 27–37, 159–69, which develop her theory about the allusions further.

10. 2 Corinthians, 3: 3–6. The imagery has a clear bearing on the novel.

11. G. Wotton, *Thomas Hardy: Towards a Materialist Criticism* (Dublin and Totowa, NJ, 1985), p. 104.

12. L. Stephen, *An Agnostic's Apology* (London, 1931), p. 58. The essay from which this comes, 'Dreams and Realities', was first published in 1874, but the first edition of the collection appeared in 1893. The book as a whole is deeply relevant to *Jude the Obscure*. The word 'agnostic', which is one of the indicators of the date of the story, is made by Stephen to be the bearer of a legitimated obscurity: 'we can say, though obscurely, that some answer exists, *and would be satisfactory*, if only we could find it' (p. 2; my italics).

13. See M. Arnold, *Literature and Dogma*. See *The Complete Prose Works of Matthew Arnold*, ed. R. Super (Ann Arbor, MI, 1960–77), vol. VI, p. 175.

14. E. Gibbon, *The History of the Decline and Fall of the Roman Empire* (London, 1897), vol. II, p. 91.

15. E. Dowden, *Life of Percy Bysshe Shelley* (London, 1886); M. Arnold, *Essays in Criticism*, Second Series, *The Complete Prose Works of Matthew Arnold*, ed. R. Super (Ann Arbor, MI, 1960–77), vol. XI, p. 327. It is worth contrasting this with *Shelley's Socialism: Two Lectures*, by Eleanor Marx and Edward Aveling, to the Socialist League, 1888. Hardy's own ideas about Shelley are more likely to have been based on J. A. Symonds, *Shelley* (London, 1881), see especially pp. 182–3: 'The anomaly which made his practical career a failure, lay just here. The right he followed was too often the antithesis of ordinary morality.'

16. *The Collected Letters of Thomas Hardy*, ed. Richard Little Purdy and Michael Millgate (Oxford, 1978–88), vol. II (1893–1901), p. 94.

17. Ibid., vol. I, p. 264.

18. Patricia Ingham (ed.), 'Introduction' to *Jude the Obscure* (Oxford, 1985), p. xxii.

19. W. Pater, *The Renaissance: Studies in Art and Poetry*, ed. Donald Hill (Berkeley, CA, 1980), p. 187. The notorious 'Conclusion' from which this phrase is taken was restored to the text in 1893 after being omitted in the second edition of 1877.

20. Patricia Ingham (ed.), Introduction to *Jude the Obscure* (Oxford, 1985), p. xiv.

21. E. Gibbon, *The History of the Decline and Fall of the Roman Empire* (London, 1897), vol. II, p. 437.

22. J. S. Mill, 'On Liberty', in *Collected Works of John Stuart Mill*, ed. J. A. Robson (1977), vol. XVIII, p. 262.

23. Ibid., p. 263.

24. William Morris, 'Misery and the Way Out', May Morris, 'William Morris, Artist, Writer and Socialist' (1936) in William Morris, *Collected Works* (New York, 1966), vol. II, pp. 150–64.

25. Patricia Ingham (ed.), Introduction to *Jude the Obscure* (Oxford, 1985), p. xii–xiii.

26. Evelyn Abbott and Lewis Campbell, *Life and Letters of Benjamin Jowett* (London, 1897).

27. F. Temple et al., *Essays and Reviews* (London, 1861), p. 356.

28. F. H. Bradley, *Ethical Studies*, 2nd edn (London, 1962), p. 163. It is worth noting, with respect to my point about the topicality of Hardy's

novel, that Bradley referred to this work in a note to a text that might seem directly related to *Jude, Appearance and Reality* (Oxford, 1893); T. H. Green, *Prolegomena to Ethics*, 4th edn (Oxford, 1899), p. 60–1; cf. also pp. 296–7. A properly historical analysis of *Jude the Obscure* would have to take much fuller account of Green, who is relevant on a number of levels. His book on Hume is a radical critique of empiricism, his ethics provides a direct link between phenomenology and community, and his political influence reconstructs the principles of liberalism.

29. T. H. Green, 'Lectures on the Principles of Political Obligation', in F. Nettleship (ed.), *Works of Thomas Hill Green* (London and New York, 1911), vol. II, p. 428 (first published 1886).

30. This is another instance of the complex effect of the allusions. To do good cheerfully is a very weak translation of 'agere et laetere'. Had Jude really been able to read Spinoza he would have had a clearer idea of the relation of necessity and desire, as had two earlier translators, Eliot and Rutherford, neither of whom renders Spinoza like this. Hardy read a relatively perceptive article on Spinoza in *Chambers' Encyclopaedia*.

31. W. Pater, *Marius the Epicurean* (1892) (London and New York, 1896), vol. II, pp. 197–8 (ch. 25).

32. Ibid., p. 193. Hardy made extensive notes on this text and, like *Robert Elsmere*, and *An Agnostic's Apology*, it is consistently relevant to his novel. On the other hand, see Michael Ryan, 'One Name of Many Shapes: *The Well-Beloved*', in Dale Kramer (ed.), *Critical Approaches to the Fiction of Thomas Hardy* (London, 1979), pp. 172–92, for a view that *The Well Beloved* is a parody of Pater's novel.

33. A. Schopenhauer, *Essays and Aphorisms*, selected and translated by R. J. Hollingdale (1970), p. 62. John Stokes reminds me that Schopenhauer did not advocate suicide, which substitutes an apparent redemption from misery for a true one (ibid., p. 78). But he did absolve it from condemnation, and in any case it is not entirely clear that Hardy understood the distinction. See Thomas Hardy, *Literary Notebooks* (1909).

6

Ill Wit and Sick Tragedy: *Jude the Obscure*

CHRISTINE BROOKE-ROSE

'BOOKS AND OTHER IMPEDIMENTA' (I.i)

That Hardy, deprived of university education, became obsessed with the acquisition of knowledge and methodical note-taking for incorporation of 'items' into his novels, is particularly stressed in Gittings' biography,[1] as well as his general conviction that everything could be learnt, even the writing of poetry, by consulting the right books. It is this last aspect which is so savagely treated in *Jude*. That he also became a well-educated man 'in a way that Dickens, Trollope and James were not', as argued by Rehder,[2] is no doubt true but irrelevant to my purpose. What interests me here is the peculiar intensity and the intense peculiarity of Hardy's use of knowledge in *Jude*, not only as narrative theme but as narration itself.

As narrative theme, it has been amply (and of course contradictorily) treated, and I shall merely summarise my reading. There is the clear equivalence of intellectual knowledge and carnal knowledge, each proving evasive and illusory, each killed by the 'letter' of the epigraph. Knowledge is desire and Christminster is clearly female: 'like a young lover alluding to his mistress' (I.iii); or female fused with God the Father: 'my Alma Mater, and I'll be her beloved son, in whom she shall be well pleased' (I.vi); the recurrent image of the wall that keeps him out (e.g. II.ii) is paralleled by Sue's behaviour, both inviting and refusing, and by: 'Now that the high window-sill stood between them, so that he could not get at her, she seemed not to mind' (IV.i); and when he has lost both, it is Sue who becomes a ghostly presence in Christminster, replacing that of poets and divines of earlier days (III.viii). As Rehder puts it: 'The tragedy in Hardy's novels is often the end of a dream. The awakening is a prelude to destruction, as if knowledge were forbidden [...] knowledge comes with the force of a blow.'[3]

The two types of knowledge are also antagonistic, and Jude is perfectly aware, both during and after the early relationships, that two women have prevented his studies (I.ix, II.iv, IV.iii). At the same time the reader is made aware that Jude falls, with varying degrees of blindness, into every trap (a facile Freudian reading would say that he doesn't *really* want to study), and that his problematic love for Sue replaces, at least in the narration, his single-minded project of 'reading most of the night after working all day' (II.ii).

There are also complex polarities in types of knowledge, first and very early (I.v) between knowledge as classics and knowledge as theology, a tug incarnated by Sue herself as 'pagan' versus Jude as Christian, with the parallel reversal which is the basis of the novel's structure. But both these unite against other knowledge, as when Jude 'reads', as craftsman, 'the numberless architectural pages round him' (II.ii), and has 'a true illumination, that here in the stone yard was a centre of effort as worthy as that dignified by the name of scholarly study' – though the narrating author steps in: 'But he lost it under the stress of his old idea' (II.ii). And after the crash of his dream he discovers for a moment, though as mere spectator still, 'the real Christminster life', the town life, which 'was a book of humanity' (II.vi). A deal of 'reading', but of what might be called 'ordinary' knowledge. It is thus rather odd to find him opposing Divinity as 'ordinary' knowledge to classics, and a moment later also reducing the classics to 'the ordinary classical grind'.

> It was a new idea ... A man could preach and do good without taking double-firsts in the schools of Christminster or having anything but ordinary knowledge ... It would be necessary that he should continue for a time to work at his trade while reading up Divinity, which he had neglected at Christminster for the ordinary classical grind.
>
> (III.i)

What is 'ordinary' knowledge? In Tinker Taylor's words: 'I always saw there was more to be learnt outside a book than in' (II.vii). But knowledge, whatever it is of, is always a taking IN what is OUT, in order to pass it OUT again, in teaching, in bringing up, in communicating, in living: like money or other acquisitions, it circulates, but you can't take it with you.

And yet, though Jude has read and experienced much, he does not die with greater self-knowledge, or even with the deep knowledge of the other that he thought he had. It is news (event) rather than knowledge as such that 'comes with the force of a blow' (Rehder), and his bookish quotation from Job as he dies seems abysmally pathetic and irrelevant, as does that from *Agamemnon* after the children's death, and Sue's reaction to the latter is amazingly condescending in the circumstances:

> My poor Jude – how you've missed everything! you more than I, for I did get you! [he got her too, so she must mean he didn't to the same full extent] To think that you should know that by unassisted reading, and yet be in poverty and despair!
>
> (VI.ii)

In no novel that I have ever read do words of knowledge seem to occur quite so frequently. The plot manipulations depend on it (knowledge as secrecy and revelation), as do all the thematic elements: knowledge as books ('books and other impedimenta' says the narrating author, of Phillotson's baggage in the first chapter, and we need knowledge that the Latin plural means baggage, to see the full irony); knowledge as common sense, as craftsmanship, as superstition, as misleading items from ignorant others; knowledge like money, as access to knowledge ('to get ready by accumulating money and knowledge', II.ii); knowledge as self-awareness, as knowledge of the other, perpetually contradicted, or as fear of the other's knowledge, or as self-assurance (Phillotson in VI.v, 'they don't know Sue as I do' or Sue in VI.iii, 'I am convinced I am right'); or as public knowledge of private facts: for their troubles, too, are largely due to the paradox that their illicit union gets 'known', so that they have to keep moving to where they are 'unknown', while inversely, the theme of their legalistic marriage depends also on the knowledge (or non-knowledge) of consummation: 'if the truth about us had been known' says Sue on getting a divorce under 'false pretences'. It seems that only the vulgar Arabella reads life correctly, from her viewpoint of survival, and she is gifted with quite an animal knowledge: she can tell, not from 'knowing' Sue but simply from looking at her, that her marriage had not, and has now, been consummated (V.ii), and naturally imparts this knowledge to Phillotson.

'BUT NOBODY DID COME BECAUSE NOBODY DOES' (I.iv)

What about knowledge in the narration itself?

When the boy Jude has at last obtained his Latin and Greek Grammars and learnt, as his first great shock, that a grammar is not a simple prescription or rule or 'secret cipher, which, once known, would enable him by merely applying it, to change at will all words of his own speech into those of the foreign tongue', the narrating author (after giving us extraneous information about Grimm's Law to show that he knew better), ends the chapter:

> Somebody might have come along that way who would have asked him his trouble, and might have cheered him by saying that his notions were further advanced than those of his grammarian. But nobody did come, because nobody does, and under the crushing recognition of his gigantic error Jude continued to wish himself out of the world.
>
> (I.iv)

Nobody does, except the narrating author, who tells us (wrongly as it happens, Grimm's 'Law' not being a law in the sense needed here), but withholds knowledge from him. And all his life, Jude will seek 'a secret cipher' to life, and end up wishing and getting himself out of the world.

Knowledge circulates incessantly in any narrative, which depends on it, and the proper questions are how much, what kind, and whether external or internal to the fiction; and, within the fiction, whether external or internal to a character.

In the nineteenth-century Realist novel, especially in its Naturalist version (Zola), a vast amount of knowledge about the world circulated in various ways, and since the ideology of Realism (to show, to teach, a rich, pre-existent but capturable world) was inhabited by the basic contradiction of all pedagogy (a plethora of information vs the need for readability),[4] all sorts of disguises had developed.

Hardy had presumably mastered all these, though he is often accused of clumsiness, notably with point of view. Taking it rather as mastery, two modern critics, Penny Boumelha and David Lodge, each treat Hardy as highly innovative.[5]

Boumelha discusses the 'formal experimentation' with genre, voice and structures of perceptions that were explored by the 'New Woman' novels of the eighties and nineties, but which had already marked Hardy's earlier career, and were now 'given a significant contemporaneity by the practices of these lesser-known writers'.[6] These structures attempted a dissolution of the boundaries between author and character, as opposed to the 'objective', 'scientific', authoritative 'narrator' of the Naturalistic novel. *The Woodlanders*, she says, is Hardy's 'most experimental' novel, with a 'continuing multiplicity of generic elements almost to end', so that in

> the crucial figure of Grace Melbury, for whom no coherent personality ... is constructed ... the full play of ambiguities and tensions is enacted in the shifts and vacancies of her role as narrative centre. It is not by coincidence that Grace is also the focus of Hardy's most radical attempt so far to confront the issues of sexuality and marriage in his fiction.[7]

Here two ways of writing emerge, the attempt to give a 'scientific authoritative encompassant that will shape the narrative of Tess Durbeyfield, and the deflected and overtly partial mode of narration that will grant to Sue Bridehead an inaccessibility pushing beyond the emptiness of enigma'.[8] *Jude*, she says later,

> is a novel that threatens to crack open the powerful ideology of realism as a literary mode, and throws into question the whole enterprise of narrative. 'The letter killeth' – and not only Jude ... Sue is progressively reduced from a challenging articulacy to a tense and painful silence that returns her to the fold of marriage – a conclusion which ironically duplicates the death of Jude. Writing comes increasingly to resemble an instrument of death.[9]

I am not sure that generic mixture as such (by which she means re-using traditional elements from other genres, popular ballads, theatricality, and so on) is 'experimental', but the word has become pretty meaningless. As for the 'cracking open' of Realism's ideology, it is treated (as the quotations from Boumelha show) much more thematically, so that 'writing' (and 'experiment'?) as instrument of death seems rather a sleight of hand. Her 'overtly partial' mode of narration simply means that the narrative adopts mostly Jude's point of view in what is today called 'internal focalisation', but this is hardly innovative and this does not efface the distance between narrating author and character, nor does the notion of 'partial' mode prove their fusion, as Boumelha appears to think. However, without basically disagreeing with Boumelha in other respects, I want to show that it is paradoxically through misuse of traditional elements that a novel so concerned with knowledge should turn out to be, in the modern sense, so unknowable.

Inversely, David Lodge has stressed Hardy's modernity by showing how cinematic his treatment of perspective is: aerial shots of diminutive figures on a huge landscape (= vulnerability of human creatures and the indifference of nature) or the illuminated figure inside observed by the unobserved observer outside (= imperfect understanding and defective communication). Or the 'hypothetical or unspecified observer', a sort of 'second narrator' who 'might have seen' which (though strictly speaking impossible in the cinema which would have to show such a figure) Lodge argues is like a different camera-angle that needs no such explanatory supposition (but then of course any 'narrator' can switch viewpoints, for instance in dialogue, without need for a 'hypothetical' observer). Lodge adds that what is so original in Hardy is commonplace in film, which must narrate in images only, so that transposition of a Hardy novel into film is difficult.[10]

Here too, I doubt whether Hardy's treatment of perspective is all that new. Balzac was doing it in the first half of the century, as were Hawthorne, Melville, Scott, and Dickens. Indeed it could be argued that the cinema inherited all the by-then clichés of the novel except the 'narrative voice', and took another quarter-century to free itself.

Balzac's fascination with visual treatment has been well analysed by Jean Paris and by Le Huenon and Perron,[11] notably for the descriptive aporia it often entails. The knowledge imposed is both postulated and concealed. 'Every reader of Balzac is familiar with those introductory descriptions set into play by an image, a picture, a vision that is immediately indexed as lack of knowledge.'[12] This refers specially to Balzac's many 'hypothetical observers' (already in Stendhal), and similarly Jean Paris shows that Balzac's use of this device produces indetermination. Poe uses it also for the ambiguity of the fantastic, for instance in *The Fall of the House of Usher* (1845): 'Perhaps the eye of a scrutinizing observer might have discovered a barely perceptible fissure ...'

'But what is the nature of knowledge?' the authors ask, and reply by quoting Balzac on the *Comédie humaine*, on knowledge moving from effects to causes, and then to principles. 'The customs are the spectacle, the causes are the wings and the machinery. Principles, that's the author.[13] They comment: 'This, taken literally, postulates a sharp dissociation between the realm of representation and the realm of knowledge'.[14]

Above all, it postulates the place of representation as the place of accident, chance, and the subject of knowing as 'principle'. The 'author' will, for instance, interpret an obscure inscription on a house (his technical knowledge), while the idle passer-by (the hypothetical observer) stays at the level of appearance. Where Jameson[15] sees in this ordered visual topos the constitution of the bourgeois subject and narrative strategies that block development, Le Huenon and Perron suggest on the contrary another space of knowledge:

> These interminable comings and goings are final moments in the constitution of a new space, a new knowledge where the subject cannot find a place; they are the end terms of transformation processes that take archaic spaces of knowledge originally inscribed in the text, redistribute them, and re-present them according to an incoherent and incomprehensible logic.[16]

One might almost be reading about Hardy. Doesn't Sue rearrange the books of the New Testament in the order in which they were written, which shocks Jude, but makes it 'twice as interesting'? (III.iv). Except that, for Hardy, there were (ultimately) no 'principles'. And therein will lie the contradiction.

'THE SAME WOMANLY CHARACTER' (III.vi)

Hardy, to be sure, achieves his indetermination in other ways. When Balzac uses the hypothetical observer it is to create a mystery, an as-yet-unknown, a 'veiled indexation of knowledge'. In Hardy it has already become an empty tic, which can even abolish the hypothetical observer:

> An hour later his thin form ... could have been seen walking along the five-mile road to Marygreen. On his face showed the determined purpose that alone sustained him but to which his weakness afforded a sorry foundation.
>
> (VI.viii)

The external focalisation necessary to a hypothetical observer is contradicted by information only the author can know, whereupon the hypothetical observer, already weak, textually vanishes. Similarly the device of the 'pretended unknown', already a cliché in Balzac, is used for pointless exclusion of the reader who nevertheless knows from immediate context:

[previous paragraph about Sue]
On an afternoon at this time a young girl entered the stonemason's yard ... 'That's a nice girl ... Who is she ... I don't know ... Why yes' [identification by the craftsman] Meanwhile the young woman had knocked at the office.

(II.iv)

Meanwhile a middle-aged man was dreaming a dream of great beauty concerning the writer of the above letter [whom we know to be Sue]. He was Richard Phillotson [whom we already know, and know to be interested in Sue], who [description and analeptic information ...] These were historic notes, written in a bold womanly hand at his dictation some months before ... the same womanly character as the historic notes ... frank letters signed 'Sue B' ... written during short absences with no other thought than their speedy destruction ... forgotten doubtless by the writer ... In one of them ... the young woman said ...

(III.vi)

The viewpoint of the craftsman is taken in the first passage, though there is no particular narrative point or realist interest in this. The viewpoint of the second passage becomes aporetic. Who speaks? Both the narrating author and Phillotson know who wrote the letter, as does the reader. Only the first can know the 'thought', and Phillotson could be said to guess ('doubtless') the forgetting. There is an uncertain hovering between the 'pretended unknown', Narration and Represented Thought (RT). 'The 'pretended unknown', frequent still in *Jude*, has become a pointless trick of pseudo-exclusion of the reader for its own sake, pseudo-suspense.

Elsewhere however, readers are, on the contrary, as in melodrama, let *in on* the terrible traps that are preparing for Jude, and this with ultra-simplistic shifts of focalisation derived from popular forms, almost of the 'little-does-he-know' type, usually signalled by 'Meanwhile Arabella', 'Meanwhile Sue' and so on; like cutting in the cinema, where it is a fundamentally popular technique but also, as Lodge does not say, authoritarian as to camera angle for limitation or revelation. Today the trick has become mechanical and meaningless in soap opera. And what the readers are and are not told can seem visibly arbitrary. In *Jude* for instance (to remain with trivial items), we are let in on Arabella's false dimples (and so watch Jude discover them), but not on her false hair, which has been elided (we discover it with him). Similarly the frequent voyeuristic or overhearing scenes sometimes tell us something new (Sue walking close to Phillotson, II.v) and sometimes not; Jude overhearing Arabella's friends on their 'advice' to her (I.x) – and even then he only surmises, so that some readers may feel exasperated at his stupidity, as throughout his courtship.

Thus, on the level of plot, readers are ostentatiously manipulated, as Jude is (Hardy said Jude was a 'puppet') and made to enter a crudely ironic structure rather like that of a Punch-and-Judy show where the children cry 'look out!', and not an identifying one that makes them share the experience.

With other elements of knowledge, however, such as self-awareness (wisdom), or knowledge of the other (insight), we are on the contrary drawn into an identifying structure, but in a peculiar way, through a similar dialectic of the hidden and the revealed but on a different scale, a dialectic as cock-teasing as Jude's 'ever-evasive Sue'. And this is achieved through:

(1)   a skilful use of dialogue to conceal what it suggests (and this is rather modern)
(2)   a heavy-handed use of narration
(3)   a blurred use of Represented Speech and Thought (see note 20).

'YOU DON'T KNOW HOW BAD I AM, FROM YOUR POINT OF VIEW' (III.i)

By definition the most mimetic parts of a narrative are in Direct Speech ('Language can only imitate language', says Genette[17]). Hardy is a master of dramatic form, and *Jude* has perhaps more dialogue than any of his other novels. Dialogue has a revealing/concealing structure since we reveal ourselves through utterance, but only to the limits of what can be articulated. It thus draws us IN and keeps us OUT, guessing. It is not by chance that Sue and Jude are interesting chiefly in dialogue and when they are talking about the *problems* of their relationship (and of the book): 'You must take me as I am', says Sue, twice, the first time meaning one thing (non-consummation, V.i), the second time another (she is about to leave him, VI.iii): there too she says 'Ah – you don't know my badness!' and he exclaims vehemently 'I do! Every atom and dreg of it! You make me hate Christianity, or mysticism, or whatever it may be called, if it's that which has caused this deterioration in you.' A big IF. And much earlier she had said 'Only you don't know how bad I am, from your point of view', meaning her paganism, but also perhaps 'The Ishmaelite' (III.i, III.ii), and later she repeats 'I said you didn't know how bad I was', meaning (apparently) what 'people say', that 'I must be cold-natured – sexless' (III.iv).

Not all the dialogue is so 'writerly' (the readers fill in).[18] More often it is punctuated by author-comment: 'with the perverseness that was part of her' (III.i), 'with a gentle seriousness that did not reveal her mind' (III.vi), 'in the delicate voice of an epicure of the emotions' (III.vii), or her 'tragic contralto' (IV.i). And even here all these perceptions might be Jude's, in RT, since we are in dialogue and he is present as perceiver. The late realist novel does not distinguish clearly between narration in internal focalisation and RT, but comments after dialogue usually still come from the narrating author. Either way the perceptions are outside Sue, even though she is speaking. The blurring of author-comment and Jude's perceptions is important to understand Jude. But the viewpoint of Sue, and above all the nature of their relationship, its quality, its texture (what attracts two such different people apart from loneliness, especially on Sue's side), this is treated much more bizarrely, from regular distancing to total occultation, whereas we are given all the scenes with Arabella straight – a much simpler affair.

'A CHRONICLER OF MOODS AND DEEDS'

At their first meeting, Jude and Sue at once go off to see Phillotson, and any conversation they might have had on the way is elided. When they arrive, Jude's interest shifts at once to Phillotson, then the walk back is distanced by narrative summary in internal focalisation on Jude (II.iv). This is followed by a practical discussion about why she has to leave and Jude's fatal suggestion that she should go to Phillotson as pupil-teacher. And this sort of occultation will mark the whole development: desperate dialogue, desperate messages, internal focalisation on Jude, author-comment on both, or ellipsis of Sue, although Hardy is by no means averse to the classical-viewpoint change for other characters.

We do, of course, have separate access to Sue, but only in dialogue or letters with Phillotson, or in dialogue with Arabella or with Mrs Edlin, and hardly at all in internal focalisation.

The most remarkable occultation is that of their happiness. The kiss which 'was a turning point in Jude's career', for instance, is elided, then hinted at by a hypothetical observer (who however has authorial knowledge) as he returns from the station: 'in his face was a look of exultation not unmixed with recklessness', then told in summary analepsis: 'An incident had occurred' (IV.iii). And when Sue at last comes to live with Jude they merely have another intense conversation about their situation, then a scene about Arabella, then we switch to Phillotson and Gillingham. The next section starts:

> How Gillingham's doubts were disposed of will most quickly appear by passing over the series of dreary months and incidents that followed the events of the last chapter.
>
> (V.i)

The same happens after the consummation, finally achieved through Jude playing on her jealousy and followed after the normal Victorian ellipsis by a sad absent-mindedness on Sue's part and immediate departure, out of guilt, to see Arabella, and a switch to the arrival of Jude's son. Then:

> The purpose of a chronicler of moods and deeds does not require him to express his personal views upon the grave controversy above given. That the twain were happy – between their times of sadness – was indubitable. And when the unexpected apparition of Jude's child in the house had shown itself to be no such disturbing event as it had looked ...
>
> (V.v)

The sleight of hand is obvious: the reader's desire is not for the chronicler's personal views but for the moods and deeds. And after the incident which makes them decide to leave Aldbrickham the narration resumes:

> Whither they had gone nobody knew, chiefly because nobody cared to know. And anyone sufficiently curious to trace the steps of such an obscure pair might have discovered ...
>
> (V.iii)

Nobody knows, chiefly because the author, momentarily hiding behind 'nobody', does not care to tell us, though as usual the hypothetical observer does tell us at once, but in summary. And suddenly we're at the Kennetbridge Fair, in dramatic form again, but between

Sue and Arabella, and Sue has two children of her own. As Patricia Ingham says in her excellent introduction to the Oxford edition: 'The joy is looked forward to and back, but it is never actually there',[19] at least, when evoked, it is always as 'veiled indexation of knowledge', as vanishing-point in the narrative technique, the narrating author heavily marking or not marking his ellipses and sudden shifts.

The reason is the *author's* knowledge: what matters to Hardy is desire (male), while marriage is death: hence the allowance we have to make, not for Sue's (and Hardy's?) horror of sex (a Victorian commonplace no odder than the post-Freudian treatment of sex-refusal as abnormal), but for her horror of *legalised* marriage, three times endorsed separately in author-comment and clearly a euphemism for the death of desire through familiarity, or knowledge possessed and therefore undesired, since desire is by definition for something absent. The equally obvious fact that it is sometimes not so, that some rare people have the ludic art of love – another form of 'knowledge' – does not interest Hardy, or indeed most novelists, since narrative is based on desire, yet for this of all relationships, where so much depends on that mysterious quality called companionship (which is what Sue wanted), the imaginative effort should have been made. It is a serious lack, for it pushes the reader further OUT, and alienates him from both Jude and Sue.

'A VOICE WHISPERED THAT, THOUGH HE DESIRED TO KNOW HER …' (II.iv)

Author-comment pulls us OUT, as does narration in external focalisation. Narration in internal focalisation gives the viewpoint of the character but as told by the narrating author, in summary for instance, or in what Genette calls 'narrativised discourse', which summarises a character's words (spoken or thought) without giving them.[20] Represented Speech and Thought (here almost entirely Thought, RT) draws us much further IN, since it gives the character's idiom, but still in narrative sentences. It has now become an extremely blurred narrative cliché of average realist fiction, where it is often used to pass narrative information that could not be going through the character's mind in that form. And this we already get in Hardy.[21]

The distinction is very clear when the knowledge is author-knowledge extraneous to the fiction: information about Roman Britain is passed through Jude's mind in RT (I.viii), but the history of

Shaston comes from the author in IV.i (transferred from III.vi where it presumably formed part of Phillotson's interests). But when the knowledge is the content of a consciousness the distinction is much less clear. This blurring seems to me to begin with Hardy and is, together with simple occultation, largely responsible for the indetermination, the (later fashionable) 'ambiguities and tensions', the 'shifts and vacancies' (Boumelha) or the 'incomprehensibility that constitutes the novel's effect' (Goode).[22] No doubt this is what Boumelha means by 'fusion' of 'narrator' and character. Hardy constantly shifts from narrative sentences to RT, and it is often impossible to discern 'who speaks':

> To be sure she was almost an ideality to him still. Perhaps to know her would be to cure himself of this unexpected and unauthorized passion. A voice whispered that, though he desired to know her, he did not desire to be cured.
>
> (II.iv)

We start in RT ('to be sure', 'Perhaps', 'would be'). But does one think to oneself 'a voice whispers'? Does not that voice also 'represent' author-comment? Here it is unimportant but there are strange moments of aporia with Sue:

> Sue paused patiently beside him, and stole critical looks into his face as, regarding the Virgins, Holy Families, and Saints, it grew reverent and abstracted. When she had thoroughly estimated him at this she would move on and wait for him before a Lely or Reynolds. It was evident that her cousin deeply interested her, as one might be interested in a man puzzling out his way along a labyrinth from which one had oneself escaped.
>
> (II.ii)

Evident to whom? Who says 'her cousin'? Until then we could be either in narration (internal focalisation) or (less likely) in RT (the 'would' as future, but more convincingly as iterative), then suddenly we veer, not just to narration but to an implied hypothetical observer, followed by author-comment. Or:

> to keep him from his jealous thoughts, which she read clearly, as she always did
>
> (IV.i)

> But Sue either saw it not at all, or, seeing it, would not allow herself to feel it
>
> (IV.ii)

Grammatically both could be RT. but who says 'as she always did'? Since Sue is rarely treated in RT we must assume that it is narrational, but then it is either untrue, or Sue must be interpreted (elsewhere) as consciously cruel. And in the second example the narrating author is explicitly not telling.

One of the rare instances of RT with Sue immediately veers to author-comment:

> Meanwhile Sue ... had gone along to the station [NS], with tears in her eyes for having run back and let him kiss her [NS/RT]. Jude ought not to have pretended that he was not her lover, and made her give way to an impulse to act unconventionally, if not wrongly [RT]. She was inclined to call it the latter [NS/RT]; for Sue's logic was extraordinarily compounded, and seemed [... NS]
>
> (IV.iii)

These various unclarities naturally happen all the time with Jude, who is treated regularly in RT, which critics do not always distinguish from narration (or even from their own comments). In fact it will be easier to show the blurring by quoting one good critic producing just that confusion. Patricia Ingham writes:

> Rather disconcertingly for the reader, the narrator, whose sympathy with Jude has been acute so far, now berates him for 'mundane ambition masquerading in a surplice' and rebukes him for that social unrest, that desire for upward mobility, which from the 1870s had been an explicit reason for Oxford in particular holding back the spread of adult education to the working class in order to protect 'the over-crowded professions'. The narrator's volte-face sets the future pattern. He may condemn Jude sometimes but elsewhere, for instance in Jude's speech to the crowd at Christminster, he will support his attempt to 'reshape' his course and rise into another class ...[23]

The 'narrator' does not 'berate' Jude for mundane ambition, June berates himself, since the passage is in RT (III.i, opening, 'It was a new idea ...' partly quoted p. 123). Nor *a fortiori*, does he rebuke him for 'that social unrest' and all that follows, since all that follows is the critic's language (outside the text), whereas the text says, more vaguely, 'a social unrest which had no foundation in the nobler instincts; which was purely an artificial product of civilization'. Nor for that matter does the 'narrator' 'support' Jude during his speech at Christminster since it is given by Jude in Direct Speech (DS), with no author-comment but plenty of disapproval from Sue as well as irony of event: she keeps saying they ought to find a room first, and

Jude's ignoring her leads to their difficulty in finding a room and the boy's disastrous reactions.

Ingham also says first that 'the narrator makes clear from the start the delusory nature of the boy's [Jude's] quest, *and*, later, that 'Jude and the narrator are seized with the desirability of the learning that the university offers', and then again (after dealing with the irony of the quotations): 'What Jude only learns of life's cruelty the narrator knows from the start: he is already aware of the ironic irrelevance of the literary text.'

This seems to be having it all ways, and like the previous example, comes from a misreading of narrative techniques, which are much clearer than this reading implies. The 'delusory nature of the boy's quest' refers to his seeing or perhaps not seeing Christminster from Marygreen as a boy, but this is told in internal focalisation and dialogue without author-comment, and to say 'the narrator makes clear from the start' is to mistake narration in internal focalisation for author-comment. Nor is the 'narrator' at any point seized with the 'desirability', and so on; only Jude, and the ghastly irrelevance of the bits of classical knowledge and theological authors he tries to study on his own is not commented, it can only be *at once* clear to the reader (as opposed to later) from a shared cultural code (knowledge again, but outside the text), which varies in time and space and from reader to reader, irony being culturally determined. Ingham's last statement fuses what she calls the 'narrator' with the author, which shows (once again) how misleading the term 'narrator' can be.

It is probable that in Hardy the narrating author only speaks clearly as such when he is giving us information unknown to the characters, and this he does a great deal (he didn't know, didn't notice, had an illumination ... but forgot it, etc.), sometimes heavily and oddly, as when he tells us that Jude (then a boy), 'was the sort of man who was born to ache a good deal before the fall of the curtain upon his unnecessary life should signify that all was well with him again' (I.ii); sometimes wrongly, as when he says that 'Sue did not for a moment, either now or later, suspect what troubles had resulted to him [Phillotson] from letting her go' (IV.vi – later? she obviously learns it eventually); or dogmatically: 'He did not at that time see that mediaevalism was as dead as a fern leaf in a lump of coal' (II.ii – which is the author's view). All the internal focalis-ation on Jude, however, hovers between narration and RT. And much of the 'ambiguity' lies here. But 'ambiguity' can also lie in careless critical reading.

'OR IS IT THE ARTIFICIAL SYSTEM OF THINGS?' (IV.iii)

John Goode quotes Jude asking what Goode takes 'to be the funda-mental ideological question posed by the novel' and found unforgiv-able by the critics who cannot take Sue:

> What I can't understand in you is your extraordinary blindness now to your old logic. Is it peculiar to you, or is it common to woman? Is a woman a thinking unit at all, or a fraction always wanting its integer?
>
> (VI.iii)

If this question (Goode continues) is asked in the novel, it is surely naïve to ask it of the novel.

> What is important is that this question should be asked; it poses for Sue only one of two possibilities – that the nature of her blindness to her own logic must be explained either by her 'peculiarity' or by her belonging to womanhood. Either way, she is committed to being an image, and it is this that pervades the novel. Nobody ever confronts Jude with the choice between being a man or being peculiar. The es-sential thing is that Sue must be available to understanding. We might want to deduce that Hardy feels the same way as Jude at this point, but I think to do so would go against the consistency of the novel and against Hardy's whole career as a writer [his theme being woman as the object of male understanding].[24]

The point is excellent, but I am not so sure of his last arguments for the author not sharing Jude's feelings. Jude had of course already expressed a similar view before, in ambiguous RT then in DS to himself, when he reflects on two women blocking his aspira-tions: 'Is it that the women are to blame; or is it the artificial system of things, under which the normal sex-impulses are turned into devilish domestic gins ...'? (IV.iii). But a few paragraphs later it is unambiguously the author who says 'for Sue's logic was extraordin-arily compounded'. And after all it is the author who makes Sue change her logic. The 'artificial system of things' is of course made by men but neither Jude nor the author seems aware of that. Elsewhere Jude exclaims that he is not against her, 'taking her hand, and surprised at her introducing personal feeling into mere argu-ment' (III.iv). This is narration not RT, and a gender-image, for Jude himself takes her arguments personally all the time. There is, moreover, Jude's own blindness to his 'old logic' (his reverence for the classics and Divinity, or his own past belief in legalistic marriage, which allowed him to sleep with Arabella and then be horrified to learn of her bigamous remarriage: 'why the devil didn't you tell me last night?' (III.ix); or his total unawareness that his speechifying was as much the cause of the tragedy as were Sue's careless answers to the boy, whereas it is Sue's awareness of these (her long habit of apparently neurotic self-reproach) that destroys her:

> 'Why did you do it, Sue?'
> 'I can't tell, it was that I wanted to be truthful. And yet I wasn't truthful, for with a false delicacy I told him too obscurely. Why was I half wiser than my fellow-women? and not entirely wiser! Why didn't I tell him pleasant untruths, instead of half realities! It was my want of self-control so that I could neither conceal things nor reveal them!'
> (VI.ii)

As always. And like the author. But if her self-imposed penance seems excessive, at least she is given to know that it is for this 'half' wisdom, and whatever the readers feel about her description they must surely know during the scene with the boy (and think 'look out!') that the boy is being wholly misled. Jude however talks here of 'our peculiar case', and his only apparent self-reproach is that he 'seduced' her, and 'spoilt one of the highest and purest loves that ever existed between man and woman' (VI.iii). This shows a very peculiar logic and a very limited self-awareness, for it is no more than the simplistic Victorian dualism of purity vs sex, and his own remarriage and self-imposed penance of death seem far blinder than hers. Thus Sue, whose complex inner feelings are occulted throughout, turns out, in dialogue, to be far more self-aware and less blinded than he is, while the gender-images of Jude, despite constant internal focalisation, are left for some readers to see and some not to see. Sue must be pin-pointed for Jude as image of guilt and blindness.

'GOOD-BYE, MY MISTAKEN WIFE. GOOD-BYE!' (VI.iv)

The multi-meaning of 'mistaken' is painful: *she* has been mistaken all along: *he* has been mistaken in marrying her: *he* has mistaken her for someone else (an ideal); *he* has mis-taken her. The debit is on his side. And all because of 'the artificial system of things'.

Lance Butler[25] has argued that Hardy is one of the rare writers who does not have a 'world-view', whereas for most literary texts we do a 'doublethink' and 'make allowances' for cosmological orders that are 'frankly ludicrous' (for example, Dante, Dickens's innocent children, George Eliot's providential endings). He takes the endings of six major Hardy novels and shows a clear progression from various compromises (there is a providential structure) to *Jude* where Hardy finally achieves 'an ending that isn't false'. Since the novels are minutely planned and orchestrated, the paradox is that the order imposed 'implies that there is no final order ..., that in this rich patterned universe, there is no ultimate meaning. Whatever happens in Hardy's major fiction, however much he manipulates and controls it, he finally finds out how to prevent it from falling into a contrived moral or supernatural order'.[26]

But we are not told how, apart from the endings, which are summarised. This leaves us with one highly reductive content (the absence of plan), which could also be said of many books including Voltaire's *Essais sur les moeurs* (and Jude twice accuses Sue of being Voltairean); and it seems to me in the 'how', in the meaning-production differentials of language, that the difficulties arise. Butler says that Hardy has received too much formal attention, so that his supposed 'faults' have excluded him from the company of the great. I have had the opposite impression that traditional attention had been thematic, and formal attention superficial, often falling back on the famous descriptions, and that Hardy is now being revalued in many exciting ways, while Boumelha's formal study turns the 'faults' into high experiment and Lodge's turns them into anticipations of film. I have tried to go further and point up, within the 'experiment', basic contradictions that in no way belittle Hardy (as deconstruction is not demolition) but seem deeper than that of careful (literary) structure revealing absence of (cosmological) structure.

For the attempt to blur the gap between the narrating author's discourse and the character's discourse is already traceable in *Daniel Deronda* twenty years earlier, together with an attempt, more radical than anything in Hardy, to disrupt the determinism of sequence and plot, and these will not fully flourish until Virginia Woolf (see Gillian Beer[27]). Hardy is part of that struggle, but his endings, like those of George Eliot, still 'exceed the book's terms' or 'strive structurally for a unity its perceptions will not fully permit'

(Beer on Eliot), if for inverse reasons: a clinging to providential structure in Eliot, a rejection of providential structure in Hardy. And I see little difference between 'making allowances' for Dickens's innocent children and doing so for (among other things) a concept of tragedy that depends so heavily on organised stupidity, that is, on limitation (a secular version of a theological stance, the orthodox Augustinian one), while the characters blame institutions and faintly hope for a change (a Pelagian stance, whose secular version was liberal socialism). I agree with Lance Butler about the 'doublethink' we bring to literature (though that is part of the pleasure, unless we read only for our own period 'truth'), but I do not agree that Hardy is as exempt from these allowances as he claims, or that he 'speaks to us today, as Shakespeare does and Beckett does, because he faces the ultimate penury of the world.'[28]

For Shakespeare wrote plays, and Beckett wrote either plays or novels in what Bakhtin calls 'free direct discourse',[29] that is, one voice, but wholly dialogical, indeterminable. Hardy's indeterminacy seems addressed to different readers (which is why I have been using the plural rather than THE reader of theory):[30] readers whose relation with the text may be submissive and coerced, readers whose relation with it may be subversive or conflicting or resisting. This may well explain his universal appeal despite the 'allowances' we have to make, which can thus be regarded as internal to the period fiction, like the 'allowances' we make for, say, the divine right of kings in Shakespeare.

Formally however, I suggest that Hardy's *poetic* indeterminacy, the feeling of a meaningless chasm behind the very precision, comes from his handling of direct speech, while the *pointless* indeterminacy and compensating pinpointing come from his handling of traditional narrative devices, which he has if anything weakened rather than enriched, and which have largely vanished except as fatigued stereotypes. They may of course return, if the present philosophy of 'ultimate penury' is succeeded by another period of firm beliefs, as Voltaire (and the concomitant eighteenth-century games with narrative authority) was succeeded by Victorian faith and its crises. But then, like the faith and authoritarian certainties, they would surely return in a refreshed and more energetic form.

Sentimentality, says Butler, 'is not simply an error of taste but the inevitable product of a world-view in which man comes into the world trailing clouds of glory'.[31] I wholly agree, but would add: the blurred and empty use of old ironic devices is not simply an error of taste but the inevitable result of a world-view in which, however 'not false' one's endings, someone controls things, but indifferently and unfairly. A double-think world-view. Hardy stands between the two centuries, a great traditional figure.

For the treatment of knowledge, in narrational terms, wraps up all the fundamental ideological questions, telling us, like the cinema, too much when we would rather not know and, like the cinema, blurring the very origin of knowledge when we want to know 'who speaks' (or why that camera angle). This, so stated, can be interpreted as highly modern, but it can also be said to mean that, in the practice of reading, the narration still mimes God.

For example, if Jude's quotations are 'ironic' because incomplete, he may or may not know this, and the readers depend on outside knowledge, a cultural code. On the other hand, Jude doesn't know that the epigraphs frame his story. Or *does* he? He quotes that of the book to Sue: 'Sue, Sue, we are acting by the letter, and "the letter killeth"' (VI.viii). Is Jude, after all, a dialogical character carrying on a 'secret polemic' with his author or any other defining entity? In whom he loses faith.

But no. The quotation is 'ordinary' knowledge, available to authors and characters and readers alike, and he quotes it only about their legalistic marriage, not about the deathly and lifely power of language to say the opposite of what it says. We are still too much in traditional, ironic, monological modes, however indeterminate, the author manipulating the very indeterminacy before our eyes: now you see it, now you don't. There is Christminster, there it maybe isn't. There is knowledge, there it isn't. There is desire, there it isn't. There is the voice that utters, there it isn't, it was only Jude, the obscure.

From Christine Brooke-Rose, *Stories, Theories and Things* (Cambridge, 1991), pp. 103–22.

NOTES

[A distinguished novelist, critic and academic, Brooke-Rose maintains a sceptical closeness to literary theory. In her introduction to this book, she distinguishes two current notions of theory: as a technique for reading, represented by the study of literary devices and conventions, and as an approach to questions of meaning, represented by philosophy. Her own interest, as a critic, lies primarily with the first. She comments at some length on the value of narratology, the systematic study of narrative forms and structures, before considering the claims of deconstruction, psychoanalysis, feminism and semiotics to critical pre-eminence. However, no one theoretical perspective in the end seems to her to be adequate to the representation and exploration of individual creativity.

In this essay, Brooke-Rose draws particularly on linguistic theory for the analysis of narrative technique. She adopts Ann Banfield's term, from *Unspeakable Sentences: Narration and Representation in the Language of Fiction* (London, 1982), of Represented Speech and Thought (here, RST) for what is often called free indirect discourse. RST represents a character's thoughts, or remembered or imagined speech, in the third person (as in supposedly objective narration) but keeps the deictics of direct speech such as exclamations or questions. By bringing such technical analysis to bear on the novel's writing, Brooke-Rose distinguishes different kinds of indeterminacy in *Jude* and their relation to forms of knowledge accessible to character and reader.

No standard edition is used for quotations in this essay. Roman numerals are used to indicate part or book numbers, Arabic for chapter numbers. Ed.]

1. Robert Gittings, *Young Thomas Hardy* (London, 1975).

2. R. M. Rehder, 'The Form of Hardy's Novels', in Lance St John Butler (ed.), *Thomas Hardy After Fifty Years* (London, 1977), pp. 13–27.

3. Ibid., p. 24.

4. See Philippe Harmon, 'Un discours contraint', *Poetique*, 16 (1973), 411–45; reprinted in *Littérature et réalité* (Paris, 1982), pp. 119–81, and Christine Brooke-Rose, *A Rhetoric of the Unreal: Studies in Narrative and Structure, Especially of the Fantastic* (Cambridge, 1981).

5. Penny Boumelha, *Thomas Hardy and Women: Sexual Ideology and Narrative Form* (Sussex and New York, 1982). David Lodge, 'Thomas Hardy as a Cinematic Novelist', in Lance St John Butler (ed.), *Thomas Hardy After Fifty Years* (London, 1977), pp. 78–89.

6. Penny Boumelha, *Thomas Hardy and Women* (Sussex and New York, 1982), p. 93.

7. Ibid., p. 113.

8. Ibid., p. 114.

9. Ibid., p. 146. [Reprinted in this volume – see p. 53–74. Ed.]

10. David Lodge, 'Thomas Hardy as a Cinematic Novelist', in Lance St John Butler (ed.), *Thomas Hardy After Fifty Years* (London, 1977), pp. 78–89.

11. Jean Paris, *Balzac* (Paris, 1986). Roland Le Huenen and Paul Perron, 'Reflections on Balzacian Models of Representation', *Poetics Today*, 5:4 (1984), 711–28.

12. Roland Le Huenon and Paul Perron, 'Reflections on Balzacian Models of Representation', *Poetics Today*, 5:4 (1984), 716.

13. Honoré de Balzac, *Lettres á Mme Hanska*, vol. 1 (Paris, 1967), p. 270.

14. Roland Le Huenen and Paul Perron, 'Reflections on Balzacian Models of Representation', *Poetics Today*, 5:4 (1984), 722.

15. Fredric Jameson, 'Balzac et le problème du sujet', in R. Le Huenen and P. Perron (eds), *Le roman de Balzac* (Montreal, 1980), p. 69.

16. Roland Le Huenen and Paul Perron, 'Reflections on Balzacian Models of Representation', *Poetics Today*, 5:4 (1984), 728.

17. Gérard Genette, 'Discours du récit', in *Figures III* (Paris, 1972); trans. Jane E. Lewin, *Narrative Discourse* (Ithaca, IL, 1980).

18. See Roland Barthes, *S/Z* (Paris, 1970); trans. R. Howard (New York, 1974).

19. Patricia Ingham (ed.), Introduction to *Jude the Obscure* (Oxford, 1985), p. xx. [Reprinted in this volume – see p. 20–31. Ed.]

20. Gérard Genette, 'Discours du récit', in *Figures III* (Paris, 1972) analyses these types of discourse as ways of varying Distance (under Mood), the most distant being 'narrativised discourse', the least 'direct discourse' (the character's words). In *Nouveau discours du récit* (Paris, 1983), p. 38, Genette summarises Brian McHale, 'Free Indirect Discourse: A Survey of Recent Accounts', *Poetics and Theory of Literature*, 3:2 (1978), 249–87, who proposes 7 degrees of distance to his 5.

21. I am adopting Ann Banfield's term (*Unspeakable Sentences – Narration and Representation in the Language of Fiction* [London, 1982]), of Represented Speech and Thought (here RST) for 'free indirect discourse'. For a full discussion see Christine Brooke-Rose, *Stories, Theories and Things* (Cambridge, 1991), ch. 5, pp. 63–80.

    In brief: RST represents a character's thoughts, or remembered or imagined speech, by shifting the 'I' of Direct Speech (DS) to the 3rd person, and any future tense to the conditional (I shall go/He would go), and keeping the deictics of Direct Speech such as exclamations, questions, etc. However, when there are no deictics and future tense, a sentence in RST can be formally indistinguishable from a narrative sentence, so that only the active presence (walking, watching, etc.) of the character thinking remains as a criterion. E.g., from Banfield: 'He [Frank Churchill] stopped and rose again and seemed quite embarrassed. *He was more in love with her than Emma had supposed*' (my italics) (Jane Austen, *Emma*), where the last sentence can be read as narrative (therefore true), but on second reading only as RST (Emma's thought, wrong as it turns out). Banfield gives a linguistic argument for the sentence to be RST independently of second reading. This subtle device, wholly an invention of the novel, is still subtly used in Joyce and Virginia Woolf, but rapidly becomes a blurred narrative cliché of much realistic fiction, misused to pass narrative items that could not be going through the character's mind in that form.

22. See Penny Boumelha, *Thomas Hardy and Women* (Sussex and New York, 1982), p.113, and John Goode, 'Sue Bridehead and the New Woman', in Mary Jacobus (ed.), *Women Writing and Writing About Women* (London and New York, 1979), p. 108.

23. Patricia Ingham (ed.), Introduction to *Jude the Obscure* (Oxford, 1985), p. xiii–xiv.

24. John Goode, 'Sue Bridehead and the New Woman', in Mary Jacobus (ed.), *Women Writing and Writing About Women* (London and New York, 1979), p. 103.

25. Lance St John Butler, 'How It Is For Thomas Hardy', in Lance St John Butler (ed.), *Thomas Hardy After Fifty Years* (London, 1977), pp. 116–25.

26. Ibid., p. 125.

27. Gillian Beer, 'Beyond Determinism – George Eliot and Virginia Woolf', in Mary Jacobus (ed.), *Women Writing and Writing About Women* (London and New York, 1979), pp. 80–99.

28. Lance St John Butler, 'How It Is for Thomas Hardy', in Lance St John Butler (ed.), *Thomas Hardy After Fifty Years* (London, 1977), p. 119.

29. Mikhail Bakhtin, *Marxism and the Philosophy of Language*, published under the name V. N. Voloshinov (1929); trans. L. L. Matejka and I. R. Tibunik, under that name (New York, 1973).

30. See Mary Louise Pratt, 'Ideology and Speech Act Theory', *Poetics Today*, 7:1 (1986), 59–72.

31. Lance St John Butler, 'How It Is For Thomas Hardy', in Lance St John Butler (ed.), *Thomas Hardy After Fifty Years* (London, 1977), p. 118.

7

Male Relations in Thomas Hardy's *Jude the Obscure*

RICHARD DELLAMORA

I AMBITIOUS AND EROTIC AIMS

In a classic study of the female novel, Nancy K. Miller has drawn attention to Sigmund Freud's assumption that, for women, ambitious wishes are subsumed in erotic ones.[1] In his essay, 'The Relation of the Poet to Daydreaming' (1908), Freud argues that novelistic fictions represent the fulfilment of their authors' 'unsatisfied wishes': 'The impelling wishes vary according to the sex, character and circumstances of the creator; they may easily be divided, however, into two principal groups. Either they are ambitious wishes, serving to exalt the person creating them, or they are erotic. In young women, erotic wishes dominate the phantasies *almost exclusively*, for their ambition is *generally comprised* in their erotic longings; in young men egoistic and ambitious wishes assert themselves plainly enough alongside their erotic desires.' Freud asserts that the protagonists of the popular novel move confidently forward to the realisation of their dreams; 'this ... invulnerability very clearly betrays – His Majesty the Ego, the hero of *all daydreams* and *all novels*'.[2]

While Miller's main interest is in whether Freud reserves 'a *place*'[3] for the ambitious wishes of young women, I am interested in the connection between the 'ambitious wishes' and the 'erotic desires' of young men. When Freud speaks of these desires as occurring 'alongside' (*neben*) ambitious wishes, he might consider the conjunction in his own life of his engagement with Martha Bernays in June 1882 with his discovery, in the same month, of the 'key' to psychoanalytic theory.[4] Regarded in another light, however, Freud's erotic desires appear 'alongside' his professional involvement in his mentor Josef Breuer's study of hysteria in a much more intimate way. Freud, in his own words, 'first became aware of the power of the unconscious' when, at the end of her treatment, Anna O., a patient of Dr Breuer, suddenly experienced the pains of a 'hysterical childbirth'.[5] In the view of Wayne Koestenbaum, Freud fantasised his collaboration with Breuer as a sexual union in which Freud became mother of the text of psychoanalytic theory while simultaneously supplanting Breuer as father because Breuer refused to acknowledge the processes of transference and countertransference that accounted for Anna O.'s delusion.

This account suggests that the relation between erotic and ambitious wishes in young men may be far from 'plain enough'. And while Victorian novelists who consider the possible confusions tend to focus, as does Freud in the 1908 essay, on the choice of a suitable partner in marriage, the example of Freud and Breuer suggests another set of relations in which the mingling of wishes is liable to be especially occluded, namely the connection between mentor and protégé. In recent years Eve Kosofsky Sedgwick has emphasised that, in order to 'get on', men in late Victorian England needed mentors and friends in all-male institutions like the public schools, the older universities, or the professions. Such relations existed in a double bind in which 'the most intimate male bonding' was prescribed at the same time that 'the remarkably cognate' homosexuality was proscribed.[6] Whether institutionalised in public schools in friendships between older and younger boys or in relationships between teacher and student, pedagogic eros helped motivate educational reform and was a major aspect of the ethos of school during the century.[7] Such friendships could likewise be idealised by men like Thomas Hardy who lacked similar advantages.

A venerable literary tradition authorised intimacy between tutor and pupil. And although the emotional power of these relationships in literature was usually baffled in the sentimental language of schoolboy friendship and swathed in a Platonising rhetoric, Greek paederastic tradition made writers aware of the sexual undertones.[8] These relations were also capable of taking perverse shape as represented in masked form in Victorian writing in which women whip men, a kind of pornography that Steven Marcus has associated with fantasies of public school life and that he describes as 'a kind of last-ditch compromise with and defence against homosexuality'.[9] In A. C. Swinburne's extensive writing about boy-spanking, both participants are male. Edmund Gosse reports that Swinburne

> said that the taste for this punishment had come to him at Eton, and he wrote in 1863, 'Once, before giving me a swishing that I had the marks of for more than a month, [the tutor] let me saturate my face with eau-de-cologne ... He meant to stimulate and excite the senses by that preliminary pleasure so as to inflict the more acute pain afterwards on their awakened and intensified susceptibility. ... He was a stunning tutor; his one other pet subject was *metre*, and I fairly believe that my ear for verses made me rather a favourite. I can boast that of all the swishings I ever had up to seventeen and over, I never had one for a false quantity; I made it up in arithmetic.'[10]

For young Swinburne, physical chastisement makes a sort of corporeal rhythm whose melody is male–male desire.

This synaesthetic investment in tutor and rod depends, however, on the sense of security afforded by an aristocratic background as well as on an indulged sense of perverse play inimical to the characters, narrator, and author of *Jude the Obscure*.[11] In Victorian fiction, the teacher–student relation between males is more likely to be governed by tropes of a sadism that exhausts itself in cruelty and debasement. One thinks, for instance, of the advertisement in Charles Dickens's *Nicholas Nickleby* for 'Mr Wackford Squeers's Academy, Dotheboys Hall', which includes in its syllabus 'single stick (if required)'.[12] Dickens's allegation in the Preface that his account is based on 'trials at law ... involving such offensive and foul details of neglect, cruelty, and disease, as no writer of fiction would have the boldness to imagine'[13] implies possible sexual abuse as does the very name of the school ('Do-the-boys') and the cognomen of its proprietor ('s-queer'). Moreover, although Squeers's is a middle-class boarding school, sadomasochism is the note of Dickens's representation of Bradley Headstone, the former 'pauper lad'[14] turned school teacher of working-class children in *Our Mutual Friend*.[15] Significantly, Headstone too is musical in a fashion: he 'plays the great church organ'[16] badly.

Mr Phillotson's marital rape of Sue late in *Jude the Obscure* makes him a sadist too. As well, by the logic of Shelleyan twinning that merges the ego boundaries of Jude and Sue (pp. 239, 295, 301), Phillotson's violence against Sue is visited, metaphorically but vividly, upon Jude's racked body.[17] My main point in the present context is, however, the unsuitability *for reasons of class* of Phillotson as a vehicle of Jude's ambitions. Even in cruelty, the humble teacher is especially associated with vulnerability – as in an article in the *Spectator* in 1845 which reports that a charity school teacher, 'Mr Michael Donovan, a schoolmaster in St Aloysius Catholic School at Somers Town, has been committed for trial from Clerkenwell Police-office, on a charge of cruelly beating James Cavanagh, a little boy nine years of age.' While condemning the use of flogging in schools, the article points out the hypocrisy of focusing prosecution upon teachers of 'the smaller and more helpless class'.[18]

II   SAME-SEX FRIENDSHIPS

At the start of *Jude the Obscure* its male protagonist is much in need of a mentor. An orphan in the charge of his spinster great-aunt, he knows chastisement early – at the end of chapter 2 he is soundly spanked by Farmer Troutham, for whom 'he's a-scaring of birds' (p. 17). Like other sensitive young men in Hardy, Jude as he grows older tries to improve himself by way of the distinctly Oxonian medium of culture – though despite the attraction to Oxford Jude's ambitions are translated into the modest goals of becoming a teacher or clergyman. In order to raise himself above the decayed village culture in which he finds himself, Jude Fawley needs connections across lines of class to his betters. His approaches, however, are coolly turned back. For instance, when he writes for advice to the Master of Biblioll College, he receives the following word:

> 'Sir, —— I have read your letter with interest; and, judging from your description of yourself as a working-man, I venture to think that you will have a much better chance of success in life by remaining in your own sphere and sticking to your trade than by adopting any other course. That, therefore, is what I advise you to do. Yours faithfully,
> 'T. Tetuphenay.
> (p. 125)

Later, after Sue Bridehead leaves Melchester to teach under Phillotson at Shaston, Jude, once more alone and aware of the strength of his 'passion' for Sue, seeks solace by searching out the author of a new hymn, 'a strangely emotional composition', entitled 'The Foot of the Cross' (p. 202). Jude hopes for understanding, for guidance, and for friendship: '"He of all men would understand my difficulties," said the impulsive Jude. If there were any person in the world to choose as a confidant, this composer would be the one, for he must have suffered, and throbbed, and yearned' (p. 203). After reaching 'the quaint old borough' (p. 203) in which the composer lives, Jude makes an initially favourable impression: 'Being respectably dressed, good-looking, and frank in manner, Jude obtained a favourable reception' (p. 204). The musician, however, opens the conversation by talking about money, then gives Jude a circular and confides that he is about to go into 'the wine business' (p. 204). When he learns that Jude is an unlikely customer, his attitude changes: 'When the musician found that Jude was a poor man his manner changed from what it had been while Jude's appearance and address deceived him as to his position and pursuits' (p. 204). The musician approaches the meeting as one of potential practical benefit; as Hardy precisely notes, Jude's approach is based on unexamined impulse. He too seeks benefit, namely help in his struggle for education; but he also seeks emotional communion with a sharer of 'yearning'. Jude represents this aim to himself by way of absorption in the composer's music, a form of art closely associated with sexual passion in the nineteenth century – as it is in Swinburne's memory of his 'stunning' tutor. Jude, however, is excluded from the possibility of intimacy with the musician because he has no *quid pro quo* to offer. Even the musician's 'business' comments ironically on the erotic aspect of the situation. In some Oxford writing, what Walter Pater refers to in an essay of 1876 as 'the bitterness of wine, "of things too sweet"', signifies a sexually self-conscious desire for other men.[19] On this occasion, however, passion is to be exchanged only for a cash equivalent.

If Hardy is sardonic about the limits and exclusions of friendship across lines of class, he is mordant about Jude's working-class connections. Jude's acquaintances among upwardly mobile members of the working class regard his sexual nonconformity as a slur on their respectability – though the form that difference takes for Jude, namely common-law marriage with Sue, was scarcely unconventional among workers.[20] Jeffrey Weeks has stressed that conservative values of family among skilled workers should be read as evidence both of 'a growing sense of class identity' at the end of the century and of 'a claim to full citizenship'.[21] In this context Jude's relationship with Sue may be construed as a lapse of class discipline – hence his exclusion from the Artizans' Mutual Improvement Society at

Aldbrickham. To fellow artisans Jude's marriage is a symptom of the social disorganisation that they associate with members of the lower working class. The 'young men' fail to grasp the fact that Jude's situation depends rather on his and Sue's efforts to live by a higher, disinterested standard that, insofar as it does have a class location, emanates from bohemian revolt among the professional classes. Such a distinction is incomprehensible to the members of the Society, who associate culture with 'Improvement', not with domestic patterns that mimic those of workers lower in the social scale.

Jude's involvement with the Society marks the high point of the 'success' that is open to him if he remains, as Tetuphenay has advised, within his own class. As a member of the Society, Jude speaks in the voice that a contemporary reviewer heard Hardy himself speak in the novel: 'the voice of the educated proletarian, speaking more distinctly than it has ever spoken before in English Literature'.[22] Hardy writes:

> Fawley had still a pretty zeal in the cause of education, and, as was natural with his experiences, he was active in furthering 'equality of opportunity' by any humble means open to him. He had joined an Artizans' Mutual Improvement Society established in the town about the time of his arrival there; its members being young men of all creeds and denominations, including Churchmen, Congregationalists, Baptists, Unitarians, Positivists, and others – Agnostics had scarcely been heard of at this time – their one common wish to enlarge their minds forming a sufficiently close bond of union. The subscription was small, and the room homely; and Jude's activity, uncustomary acquirements, and above all, singular intuition on what to read and how to set about it – begotten of his years of struggle against malignant stars – had led to his being placed on the committee.
>
> (pp. 314–15)

In this context the 'malignant stars' are all too evidently the exclusions that are the opposite face of the coin of class privilege. In resistance, however, Jude for a moment comes into his own as a working-class intellectual able to integrate his 'experiences' with his reading in ways that help others and gain respect for himself. But this moment of *éclaircissement* is immediately eclipsed. In the succeeding paragraph comes the news that the committee forces him to resign because of the common-law status of his marriage.

If fellow artisans see Jude as falling below them because of an erotic idealism more appropriate to Pre-Raphaelites than to workers, his friends among casual labourers see his educational attainments as an act of class betrayal. Although Raymond Williams has remarked on Hardy's ability to communicate a sense of solidarity between working people, Jude's relations with members of the lower working class are destructive.[23] The appearances of Tinker Taylor, 'a decayed church-ironmonger' (p. 127), and his mates are bitter moments for Jude. Early in the novel, egged on by fellow workers and by two Oxford undergraduates, he disgraces himself by reciting the Nicene Creed in Latin for a crowd in a pub. When he returns to Christminster as a defeated man late in the novel, one of his former fellow masons, Jack Stagg, mocks him as 'Tutor of St. Slums' (p. 335), and Tinker Taylor reminds Jude of 'the night of the challenge in the public-house' (p. 336). Further on, when Arabella stages a party in order to keep Jude drunk for a few days, 'in a saturnine humour' (p. 393) he suggests inviting Stagg and another mason, Uncle Joe. Taylor, passing by, also joins the festivities. At the end of the novel Arabella leaves Jude on his deathbed to watch the boat races with 'Stagg and one or two other of Jude's fellow stone-workers' (p. 419).

Tinker Taylor's jeering reference to Jude's knowledge of Latin is apt. From early childhood Jude is obsessed with learning the classical languages, a prime badge of membership among the professional classes forming in the mid-nineteenth century. Early on, he secures orders for the itinerant 'Physician' Vilbert in exchange for schoolbooks, schoolbooks that Vilbert forgets to bring. Earliest and most important is Mr Phillotson, Jude's 'much-admired friend' (p. 34), who at the beginning of the novel leaves the school at Marygreen in order to seek admission to the university at Christminster, Hardy's fictional term for Oxford. The Latin grammar that Phillotson sends Jude is one of the few tokens of friendship that Jude receives.

The boy's struggles with the textbook provide an especially poignant instance both of his thirst for improvement and of the obstacles that stand in his way:

> Ever since his first ecstasy or vision of Christminster and its possibilities, Jude had meditated much and curiously on the probable sort of process that was involved in turning the expressions of one language into those of another. He concluded that a grammar of the required tongue would contain, primarily, a rule, prescription, or clue of the nature of a secret cipher, which, once known, would enable him, by merely applying it, to change at will all words of his own speech into those of the foreign one. ... He assumed that the words of the

required language were always to be found somewhere latent in the words of the given language by those who had the art to uncover them, such art being furnished by the books aforesaid.

(p. 35)

When Jude eagerly opens the schoolbook, he has an unpleasant surprise: 'He learnt for the first time that there was no law of transmutation, as in his innocence he had supposed (there was, in some degree, but the grammarian did not recognize it), but that every word in both Latin and Greek was to be individually committed to memory at the cost of years of plodding' (p. 35).

In the passage, Latin is a metonymy for the perquisites that accompany an elite education. The 'transmutation' that Jude seeks is transmutation from one class to another. His frustration indicates just how unlikely he is – by either 'cipher' or 'plodding' – to learn the 'art' of the 'foreign' language of the upper middle classes – much less to find *his* language translated without change of meaning into theirs. The passage reveals how far he is from realising that his cultural ambitions are mixed with ambitions of class, status, and money. Even if traversed, his chosen paths of advancement will at best still not raise him beyond the limits of a laborious lower-middle-class existence. Indeed, one could argue that even if he were to succeed in these ways, his function, like that of Phillotson's, would be one of preparing young males for service on the lower rungs of business, industry, and public service. Accordingly, to achieve culture would mean to repeat in himself and others the construction of a newly fashioned corporate subject.

Unable either to merge with his class or to enter the paths of entitling friendship, Jude is peculiarly isolated. Sue's similar isolation is, if anything, yet more pronounced. In contrast to *Tess of the d'Urbervilles*, in which Tess bonds strongly with her female fellow workers at Talbothays Dairy, Sue is left high and dry. Hardy goes out of his way to deprive her of the sustaining relationships with other women that were one of the most positive aspects of Victorian middle-class life.[24] She is first observed working in a religious arts shop run by the spinster daughter of a deceased 'clergyman in reduced circumstances' (p. 101); Miss Fontover runs a sisterhood for profit. Michael Millgate notes that Sue has no friends at Melchester Training School for teachers even though Hardy was familiar with such relations as a result of his sisters' experiences in a similar school and even though after 'visiting two London training colleges for women in 1891' he 'had been moved by the thought of such friendships'.[25] Later the 'neighbouring artizans' wives' (p. 308) of Aldbrickham drive Sue and her family out of town.

The careful hedging of Sue from intimacy with other women has a valence within the male homosocial economy of the book since Hardy was aware that her wish to retain control of her own body was liable to be construed in contemporary sexology as a sign of sexual inversion.[26] His concern accounts for an imbalance in the sympathy with feminism that one finds in the book. On the one hand, the focus on issues of sexual choice and control over reproduction are consonant with concerns among contemporary feminists such as Elizabeth Wolstoneholme Elmy.[27] Hardy's refusal to endorse motherhood as a defining female virtue and the absence of female friendship, however, are distinctly at odds with late Victorian feminism. This absence, especially in light of ways in which Hardy associates Sue with difference,[28] serves to dampen erotic connotations in male relations in the novel, especially in that of Jude and Phillotson. Obliquely, however, Hardy signals this element by his account of Sue's life, 'like two men almost', with a young graduate of Christminster. Sue shares a sitting room with the young man in London for fifteen months yet resolutely rebuffs his advances: 'he wanted me to be his mistress, in fact, but I wasn't in love with him' (p. 155). Her desire for security in a platonic relationship based on shared intellectual interests is modelled not on a 'curious unconsciousness of gender' (p. 156) as Jude surmises but on the manipulation of conventional ignorance, including her own, concerning the erotic investments involved in male friendships. While Jude's scepticism (not to mention Hardy's) refers in the first instance to the prospect of an intimacy between men and women that is not sexual, it also refers to the norm of male–male bonding on which Sue bases her compact with the young man.

III   ENTER PHILLOTSON

In the first manuscript version of the novel Jude's erotic and ambitious aims were to focus on the figure of a young woman, Sue, who at this earlier stage was to be the adopted child of the head of a Christminster college. Her live artisan father and the relationship with the undergraduate were later changes. In the manuscript, Hardy describes young Jude's vision of Christminster as follows:

He set himself to wonder on/wondering/the exact point in the glow where his cousin might be; she who never communicated with his branch of the family/anyone at Fawn (Mary) Green now/who was as if dead to them here. In the glow he seemed to see her soul standing at ease like one of the forms in Nebuchadnezzar's furnace.

He had heard that breezes travelled at the rate of ten miles an hour and the fact now came into his mind. He parted his lips as he faced the north-east, & drew in the wind as if it were a sweet liquor.

'You,' he said, addressing the breeze caressingly, 'were in Christminster city between one & two hours ago: floating along the streets, pulling round the weather-cocks, touching Sue's face, being breathed in by her; & now you be here, breathed in by me; you, the very same.'[29]

Only afterwards did Hardy add Phillotson and make him the focus of Jude's ambitious wishes.

Patricia Ingham thinks that the element of desire involved in Jude's preoccupation with Christminster is 'oddly inappropriate in connection with a middle-aged schoolmaster'.[30] Hardy writes: 'The city acquired a tangibility, a permanence, a hold on ... [Jude's] life, mainly from the one nucleus of fact that the man for whose knowledge and purposes he had so much reverence was actually living there' (p. 27). Phillotson, however, is a more plausible motive of Jude's ambition than Sue, since the route to education and Oxford usually lay through male connections; and Ingham forgets that at the opening of the novel Phillotson is a young man. In a slightly roundabout way, Hardy adverts to the shy romance of the scene: Jude 'was not among the regular day scholars, who came unromantically close to the schoolmaster's life, but one who had attended the night school only during the present teacher's term of office' (p. 14). The locution leaves open the possibility of sentiment on both sides of the relationship – although it is significant that Phillotson does not know how to play the piano that he leaves behind for a time in Old Miss Fawley's fuel house. Afterwards he confesses that he has forgotten that he had confided his dream to the boy: 'You know what a university is, and a university degree? It is the necessary hallmark of a man who wants to do anything in teaching. My scheme, or dream, is to be a university graduate, and then to be ordained' (p. 14).[31]

At the opening of part 2, three years after Jude's unsuccessful marriage to Arabella, he finally leaves for Oxford/Christminster. He does so, however, on an impulse that though directed toward a woman nonetheless includes Phillotson at the edge:

The ultimate impulse to come had had a curious origin – one more nearly related to the emotional side of him than to the intellectual, as is often the case with young men. One day while in lodgings at Alfredston he had gone to Marygreen to see his old aunt, and had observed between the brass candlesticks on her mantelpiece the photograph of a pretty girlish face, in a broad hat with radiating folds under the brim like the rays of a halo. He had asked who she was. His grand-aunt had gruffly replied that she was his cousin Sue Bridehead, of the inimical branch of the family; and on further questioning the old woman had replied that the girl lived in Christminster though she did not know where, or what she was doing.

His aunt would not give him the photograph. But it haunted him; and ultimately formed a quickening ingredient in his latent intent of following his friend the schoolmaster thither.

(p. 84)

The passage is replete with erotic cross-directions. The invocation of Sue as an Angel in the House, with her haloed image flanked by candlesticks, her 'girlish' attractiveness, her cognomen, are contradicted by Jude's evident fascination. At the same time, the aunt's reminder of domestic misfortune warns against sexual involvement and sounds the motif of the marriage theme, what Hardy in the Preface to the first edition refers to as the 'disaster that may press in the wake of the strongest passion known to humanity' (p. v). Similarly, Jude's 'latent intent of following his friend the schoolmaster' is both invoked and sidelined as an exclusively 'intellectual' interest. In contrast to the rejected passage cited earlier, this one is normalising in character: deleting the references to inspirer and hearer characteristic of Greek paederastic tradition, to the 'sweet liquor' of the breeze 'pulling round the weather-cocks', and to the male 'forms in Nebuchadnezzar's furnace'.

Curiously, once Jude does find Sue, he immediately introduces her to his former patron. After the cousins meet the man, reduced by years of work as a village schoolteacher, Jude persuades Sue to let him offer her to Phillotson as an assistant. Although this offer is rationalised as arising from Jude's reluctance to let Sue, who has just lost her employment, leave the vicinity, he places her in the role of protégé to Phillotson that he has occupied in fantasy since childhood. It is odd that Jude should be oblivious of the possibility of a marriage proposal emanating from such a working relationship,[32] even odder that he should cede to an unattractive older man the proximity of a woman with whom Jude is already falling in love. Jude thereby initiates a triangle familiar in male homosocial culture and strongly marked by homophobia though one might also consider the relations in terms of mentor and protégé. Sue becomes mentor to Jude while becoming protégé to Phillotson in a pattern: Jude : Sue :: Sue : Phillotson. Thereby Sue substitutes for Jude in his idealised relation to Phillotson. Given 'the extraordinary sympathy, or similarity, between the pair' (p. 239) that Phillotson notes, Sue may function similarly in Phillotson's imaginary although, as mentioned above, what Hardy emphasises is Phillotson's amnesia about his former pupil.

Likewise, Sue's former relation with the graduate of Christminster/Oxford may be triangulated with Jude though again the pattern of mentor–protégé is equally or even more revealing: in this case, Jude : Sue :: Sue : the young graduate of Christminster. Sue's connection equips her to become Jude's entry to advanced thinking of the 1860s;[33] the doubling, however, indicates obliquely the sort of friendship upon which Jude's hopes depend. In this respect, Sue's life with a university man, in part because of its erotic ambiguity, is a more suitable model for Jude than his projection of friendship with Phillotson.

Mary Jacobus is correct in arguing that the 'sense of life which in Hardy's earlier novels sprang from rural activity or landscape derives in *Jude* from conversation. Sue's attempts to articulate her changing consciousness ... make her a vital counterpart to Jude'.[34] Hardy makes evident his commitment to an ideal of affective and intellectual equality between men and women. Nonetheless, Sue's role as mentor signifies in part Jude's lack of connection with a university man. Yet even if an appropriate male mentor were to appear, the relation would remain sexually anxious since intellectual friendship between a young man of rural background and an upper-class male was fraught, in the middle-class imagination, with anxieties about the effeminising effect of such a dependency, in particular the negative effect on 'an enterprising mind, an inquisitive spirit, a liberal ambition' (p. 255).[35]

IV   EXPERIENCE

In the late 1850s and early 1860s, Hardy became the friend of Horace Moule, a brilliant young man eight years Hardy's senior and son of a distinguished clergyman, the Rev. Henry Moule, the vicar of Fordington St George. In the words of Hardy's biographer,

'Moule's impact upon Hardy was immense. He was handsome, charming, cultivated, scholarly, thoroughly at home in the glamorous worlds of the ancient universities and of literary London. Although only eight years Hardy's senior, he was already an accomplished musician, a publishing poet and critic, and an independent thinker. He not only helped Hardy with his Greek but introduced him to new books and ideas.'[36] Moule inducted Hardy, who yearned for a university degree and harboured a wish to become a clergyman, into contemporary liberal thought, including the polemic against Evangelical Christianity of *Essays and Reviews* (1860) that Sue draws on in the course of the novel.[37]

The attention was flattering in the extreme – since Moule enjoyed advantages of personal charm, education, class, money, and status relative to Hardy, son of a West Country builder. Millgate observes that Moule and his brother 'exacerbated' Hardy's 'sense of inferiority and incited his ambition for self-improvement'.[38] Moule, however, was a checkered figure, unable to complete his university degree at either Oxford or Cambridge, troubled by alcoholism and possibly opium addiction, and the subject of gossip concerning sexual misadventures. At the time of his death in 1873 he held the post of assistant Poor Law inspector for East Anglia.

During the 1860s Moule wrote educational manuals and tutored students for examinations. Millgate comments upon Moule's 'ambiguous sexuality which seems to have constituted the obverse, so to speak, of his gifts as a teacher and his devotion to the boys and young men who were his pupils'.[39] When Hardy began publishing novels at a quick clip in the early 1870s, the balance of the relationship shifted. Moule responded with both enthusiasm and condescension, pointing out 'slips of taste' in *A Pair of Blue Eyes* in a letter of May 1873. Millgate believes that on the evening of Hardy's last conversation with Moule at Queens' College, Cambridge, in the following month, the older man made an explicit approach to Hardy – an approach to which he responded with anger.[40] Three months afterwards to the day, Moule committed suicide at Cambridge. Hardy was devastated, and from this time onward in his fiction 'never portrayed a man who was not, in some way, maimed by fate'.[41]

While the circumstances of the final meeting will never be known, Moule's appeal likely made utterly clear to Hardy the fact that this particular relation included a sexual motive, a discovery yet more disturbing in that Hardy was socially subordinate. One hears his outrage still echoing in *Jude the Obscure*. The worst betrayal in male friendship was sexual.

Hardy's poetry, however, indicates a more self-aware response to the incident. He memorialises his connection with Moule in a poem entitled 'Experience', which is addressed to 'My friend', a phrase 'which Hardy always reserved, in other poems, for Moule'.[42] In the poem Hardy characterises the relation with the same imagery of afflatus, drawn from paederastic tradition, that in the manuscript passage quoted earlier he associates with Jude's attraction to Sue:

> But there was a new afflation –
> An aura zephyring round
> That care infected not:
> It came as a salutation,
> And, in my sweet astound,
> I scarcely witted what
> Might pend,
> I scarcely witted what.[43]

Another poem, which is based on an incident that occurred during Hardy's final visit to Moule's room, addresses the issue of how aware Hardy had been of sexual undertones in the friendship.[44] In the poem, the speaker touches the drippings from a candlestick that have taken the form of a shroud. According to folk tradition, the act indicates that he will soon die. Although critics usually read the poem, 'Standing by the Mantlepiece', subtitled 'H.M.M. 1873', as a dramatic monologue addressed to a woman who has rejected the speaker, Millgate suggests that it makes more sense to read the poem as addressed by Moule to Hardy. If so, then the speaker's reproach is directed toward Hardy himself:

> Let me make clear, before one of us dies,
> My mind to yours, just now embittered so.
> Since you agreed, unurged and full-advised,
> And let warmth grow without discouragement,
> Why do you bear you now as if surprised,
> When what has come was clearly consequent?[45]

The question, touching precisely on the point of sexual complicity in male friendship, implicitly acknowledges Hardy's shared responsibility for the failure of sympathy that had occurred.

V   CONCLUSION

In her more recent writing, Sedgwick has argued that 'there exists ...
a plethora of *ignorances*, and we may begin to ask questions about the
labour, erotics, and economics of their human production and distribution'.[46] In *Jude the Obscure* Hardy pluralises sexual ignorance. For
Jude desire for a woman is itself a form of unknowing. Because of the
occlusion of desire in male relations and the pervasive inequality of
men and women, Jude and Sue both tend to bifurcate the many pleasures of friendship from those of 'the strongest passion known to
humanity' (p. v). For them sexual desire for a member of the opposite
sex is 'gross' (p. 275). Jude's wife, Arabella, first attracts his attention
by hitting him in the face with a pig's 'pizzle',[47] which Hardy in the
novel euphemistically calls 'the characteristic part of a barrow-pig'
(p. 43). The incident implies her function as a substitute for an
achieved masculinity, confused in the minds of both young people
with the *membrum virile*. She is also a figure of castration since, in
order to become a man, Jude needs to possess Arabella or someone
like her; but with Arabella the act reduces him to a mechanical function and hence blocks the achievement of selfhood. Hardy further suggests Arabella's disabling power by alluding to the picture of Samson
and Delilah that hangs on the wall of the inn where the couple stop
during their first Sunday outing. To say that Arabella castrates Jude is,
however, misleading. The castrating woman is a figure of a male
fantasmatic. Rather, Jude is unmanned, at the very moment of sexual
initiation, by an unconscious ideology that identifies manliness with a
body part – and that part in relation to the vagina. In this respect,
Arabella too is an ideological construct, a female orifice designed to
receive the phallus. What Jude near death refers to as 'my weakness
for womankind' (p. 366) is more nearly the gnostic view that he takes
of himself as an intellectual and emotional 'spirit' in conflict with a
debased 'flesh' (p. 202). But again this erotophobic attitude, though
characterised psychologically, is institutional in character.

The most evidently destructive ignorance in the novel is ignorance
about birth control, which Arabella uses to trick Jude into marrying
her at the start of the novel. Later, in the three-year period following
the fair at Stoke-Barehills, Sue gives birth to two babies and is expect-
ing a third. Jacobus attributes these continual pregnancies, which sap
Sue's resilience, to 'the absence of contraception'.[48] But as Penny
Boumelha has pointed out, the 'female pills' that Hardy mentions
early on are abortifacients.[49] They provide evidence of the effort

made by country folk to control the rate of reproduction. With her independent views, one might expect Sue to take measures to protect herself from unwanted pregnancies – though one should also bear in mind that while a Victorian feminist like Annie Besant in the 1870s promoted sexual activity and the use of the vaginal sponge, 'the majority of the women's movement were in strong opposition' to artificial contraception.[50] Given these contradictions within feminist sexual politics, my surmise is that Sue and Jude may practise coitus interruptus, a practice liable to failure that would also have adverse psychological effects. At any rate, whether or not the couple are imagined as using this or any other method of contraception, the emotional, physical, and economic strains brought on by the repeated onset of pregnancy for Sue underscore ways in which bodily processes undermine her well-being. Her inability to control the most intimate bodily functions provides ample impetus for the body hatred that she exhibits late in the novel. Moreover, her cruel predicament makes male desire yet more problematic since it becomes synonymous for her with the experience of powerlessness. One may assume further guilt, as well, on the part of Jude, whose intimacy with Sue poses Malthusian consequences.

Little Father Time's role in the tragic denouement of the novel brings the circle round again to the experience of desire between men. In what Florence Hardy referred to as 'the tragedy' of Moule's life, 'Moule had had, or had been persuaded he had, a bastard child by a low girl in his father's parish at Fordington'. Purportedly, the child was raised in Australia and later hanged.[51] (Father Time, also the result of a dubious pregnancy, is raised in Australia, and later hangs himself along with Jude and Sue's two children.) Given the fact that Father Time shows symptoms of congenital syphilis,[52] an infection associated with sexual delinquencies both between men and across genders, the boy's place in the novel suggests the decadent effects of phallic touch whether between males or between men and women.

The unhappy end of Sue and Jude follows from a society incapable of tolerating difference. Conscious desire tends to be forced into the mould of marriage, a relationship that determines all others. To their own cost but predictably so, Sue and Jude introject this intolerance. Given the biographical association of Father Time with Horace Moule's illegitimate son, the boy's diseased condition further suggests Hardy's subliminal inability to deal with the wandering desires of a man like Moule. At this point, the novel (and

Hardy) seem to reach endgame since Hardy regards the conserving defence against difference in marriage as a solution destructive of both men and women. As well, conventional marriage provides a means whereby the poor are influenced to control and damage one another while at the same time remaining vulnerable to the injustices of class. Father Time is, however, even more a figure of the consequences of social intolerance than he is of the effects of desire (p. 348). Hardy perceives that a life of 'Greek joyousness' (p. 307) cannot be sustained in face of what he takes to be the laws of nature and society. But he also sees that increased knowledge of 'the nature of things' might contribute to making it easier for individuals to live with themselves and others. Then too desire and the body might become less problematic.

In 1911 Hardy presented the holograph manuscript of the novel to the Fitzwilliam Museum at Cambridge. The manuscript contains an unusual passage, extremely critical of Victorian conventions, which appears in no published version of the novel. The quotation provides another instance of the censored and at times self-censored speech of men in nineteenth-century England who realised the need to attend to questions of masculine desire. Hardy included the passage in the hope that one day there would be those who would speak and listen. In the manuscript Jude speaks the words to a female friend, the Widow Edlin:

> When men of a later age look back upon the barbarism, cruelty & superstition of the times in which we have the unhappiness to live, it will appear more clearly to them than it does to us that the irksomeness of life is less owing to its natural conditions, though they are bad enough, than to those artificial conditions arranged for our well being, which have no root in the nature of things![53]

From *Papers on Language and Literature*, 27 (1991), 453–72.

NOTES

[Richard Dellamora's critical project has been more extensively set out in his earlier book *Masculine Desire: The Sexual Politics of Victorian Aestheticism* (Chapel Hill, NC, 1990). There, taking the work of Michel Foucault on discourse and on sexuality as his starting-points, he is concerned to examine desire between men in Victorian culture. It is important to notice that, by this, he does not mean to discuss only overtly, actively sexual relationships between men. Instead, he sets out to look at the constructions of the restraints upon male–male desire in a whole range of relationships and institutions, including friendship, education, and the professions.

Similarly, in this essay, Dellamora revealingly brings to light a series of what might be called melancholy, desirous relationships between Jude and other men, and his attraction towards what was at the time of the novel's composition the particularly male enclave of Oxford. The point is not to argue that Jude is 'really' homosexual, whatever that might mean, but rather to throw a new analytical light on the novel's representation of both its heterosexual couples and its same-sex relationships. In this, it offers a genuinely original interpretative framework for the novel.

All quotations in the text are from the Macmillan Edition of *Jude the Obscure* (Toronto, 1969). Ed.]

1. Nancy K. Miller, *Subject to Change: Reading Feminist Writing* (New York, 1988).

2. Ibid., p. 32; emphasis added.

3. Ibid., p. 32.

4. Wayne Koestenbaum, *Double Talk: The Erotics of Male Literary Collaboration* (New York, 1989), pp. 22, 27.

5. Ibid., pp. 26, 17.

6. Eve Kosofsky Sedgwick, 'The Beast in the Closet: James and the Writing of Homosexual Panic', in *Speaking of Gender*, ed. Elaine Showalter (New York, 1989), p. 152.

7. Louis Crompton, *Byron and Greek Love: Homophobia in Nineteenth-Century England* (Berkeley, CA, 1985), pp. 74ff., and John Chandos, *Boys Together: English Public Schools 1800–1864* (New Haven, CT, 1984), ch. 14.

8. Louis Crompton, *Byron and Greek Love: Homophobia in Nineteenth-Century England* (Berkeley, CA, 1985), pp. 267–8; Gert Hekma, 'Sodomites, Platonic Lovers, Wrong Lovers: The Backgrounds of the Modern Homosexual', *Journal of Homosexuality*, 16: 1/2 (1988), 435–40.

9. Steven Marcus, *The Other Victorians: A Study of Sexuality and Pornography in Mid-Nineteenth-Century England* (New York, 1977), p. 260.

10. A. C. Swinburne, *The Swinburne Letters.*, ed. Cecil Y. Lang (New Haven, CT, 1960–62), vol. 6, p. 244.

11. As Swinburne's disturbed response to early reviews of *Poems and Ballads, First Series* (1866) indicates, security is a relative phenomenon; nonetheless, I believe it to be crucial to the insouciance of his recollection of his 'stunning tutor'.

12. Charles Dickens, *Nicholas Nickleby*, ed. Paul Schlicke (New York, 1990), p. 26.

13. Ibid., p. xl.

14. Charles Dickens, *Our Mutual Friend*, ed. Stephen Gill (Harmondsworth, 1976), p. 267.

15. See Eve Kosofsky Sedgwick, *Between Men: English Literature and Male Homosocial Desire* (New York, 1985), ch. 9; Terrence Whaley, 'The Dickensian Image of the School Teacher', in *From Socrates to Software: The Teacher as Text and the Text as Teacher*, Eighty-ninth Yearbook of the National Society for the Study of Education. Part 1, ed. Philip W. Jackson and Sophie Haroutunian-Gordon (Chicago, 1989), pp. 36–59.

16. Charles Dickens, *Our Mutual Friend*, ed. Stephen Gill (Harmondsworth, Middlesex), p. 266.

17. For the Shelleyan resonances see Michael E. Hassett, 'Compromised Romanticism in *Jude the Obscure*', *Nineteenth-Century Literature*, 25 (1971), 432–43.

18. 'Flogging in Small Schools', *Spectator* (1 February, 1845), p. 109. I am grateful to Anita Wilson for providing me with a copy.

19. Walter Pater, *Greek Studies* (1910; reprinted New York, 1967), p. 42.

20. Jeffrey Weeks, *Sex, Politics and Society: The Regulation of Sexuality since 1800* (New York, 1981), pp. 60–1. Although common-law marriages could be both scandalous and violent, Judith Walkowitz's discussions indicate the customary and durable character of such relationships. See 'Jack the Ripper and the Myth of Male Violence', *Feminist Studies*, 8 (1982), 542–74, and other writings.

21. Jeffrey Weeks, *Sex, Politics and Society: The Regulation of Sexuality since 1800* (New York, 1981), p. 74.

22. Mary Jacobus, 'Sue the Obscure', *Essays in Criticism*, 25 (1975), 327, note 5.

23. Raymond Williams, *The English Novel from Dickens to Lawrence* (New York, 1970), p. 116.

24. For the extensive literature dealing with this phenomenon, see among others Nancy F. Cott, 'Passionlessness: An Interpretation of Victorian Sexual Ideology, 1790–1850', *Signs*, 4 (1978), 219–36; Lillian Faderman, *Surpassing the Love of Men: Romantic Friendship and Love Between Women From the Renaissance to the Present* (New York, 1981); Carroll Smith-Rosenberg, 'The Female World of Love and Ritual: Relations Between Women in Nineteenth-Century America', *Signs* (1975), 1–29; and Martha Vicinius, *Independent Women: Work and Community For Single Women 1850–1920* (Chicago, 1985).

25. Michael Millgate, *Thomas Hardy: A Biography* (New York, 1982), p. 352.

26. I discuss the situation in Richard Dellamora, *Masculine Desire: The Sexual Politics of Victorian Aestheticism* (Chapel Hill, NC, 1990), ch. 10.

27. See Sheila Jeffreys, *The Spinster and Her Enemies: Feminism and Sexuality 1880–1930* (London, 1985), ch. 2.

28. I refer to her crossdressing, to Hardy's use of an epigraph from Sappho at the head of part 3, to her sympathy with Swinburne, etc.

29. Quoted in Patricia Ingham, 'The Evolution of *Jude the Obscure*', *Review of English Studies*, 27 (1976), 166.

30. Ibid., 166.

31. Eve Kosofsky Sedgwick in 'The Beast in the Closet: James and the Writing of Homosexual Panic', in *Speaking of Gender*, ed. Elaine Showalter (New York, 1989), has drawn attention to the significance for male self-knowledge of the confidences that a protagonist forgets that he has made to a sympathetic listener.

32. At the time of her engagement Sue tells Jude:

    'I have promised – I have promised – that I will marry him when I come out of the Training-School two years hence, and have got my Certificate; his plan being that he shall then take a large double school in a great town – he the boys' and I the girls' – as married school-teachers often do, and make a good income between us.'

    'O, Sue! … But of course it is right – you couldn't have done better!' (p. 140).

33. Robert Gittings, *Young Thomas Hardy* (Harmondsworth, 1978), pp. 139–41.

34. Mary Jacobus, 'Sue the Obscure', *Essays in Criticism*, 25 (1975), 307.

35. The words of Caleb Williams, from William Godwin's novel, *Caleb Williams*, ed. David McCracken (New York, 1970). I am indebted for the general point to Robert J. Corber, 'Representing the "Unspeakable": William Godwin and the Politics of Homophobia', *Journal of the History of Sexuality*, 1 (1990), 85–101.

36. Michael Millgate, *Thomas Hardy: A Biography* (New York, 1982), pp. 67–8.

37. Robert Gittings, *Young Thomas Hardy* (Harmondsworth, 1978), pp. 134–41 believes that the incident recalls the influence upon Hardy's religious beliefs of a young, unidentified woman, probably a schoolteacher of extremely modest background, to whom he was close in the mid-1860s.

38. Michael Millgate, *Thomas Hardy: A Biography* (New York, 1982), p. 68.

39. Ibid., p. 70.

40. Ibid., pp. 150–1, 155–6.

41. Ibid., p. 264.

42. Thomas Hardy, *The Complete Poems*, ed. James Gibson (London, 1979), p. 65.

43. Ibid., pp. 615–16.

44. Michael Millgate, *Thomas Hardy: A Biography* (New York, 1982), pp. 153–4.

45. Thomas Hardy, *The Complete Poems*, ed. James Gibson (London, 1979), p. 887.

46. Eve Kosofsky Sedgwick, 'Privilege of Unknowing', *Genders*, 1 (1988), 104.

47. Florence Emily Hardy, *The Later Years of Thomas Hardy: 1892–1928* (London, 1930), p. 41.

48. Mary Jacobus, 'Sue the Obscure', *Essays in Criticism*, 25 (1975), 318.

49. Penny Boumelha, *Thomas Hardy and Women: Sexual Ideology and Narrative Form* (Madison, WI, 1982), p. 152. [Reprinted in this volume – see p. 53–74. Ed.]

50. Sheila Jeffreys, *The Spinster and Her Enemies: Feminism and Sexuality 1880–1930* (London, 1985), p. 44.

51. Robert Gittings, *Young Thomas Hardy* (Harmondsworth, 1978), pp. 257, 262.

52. Elaine Showalter, 'Syphilis, Sexuality, and the Fiction of the Fin de Siècle', in *Sex, Politics, and Science in the Nineteenth-Century Novel*, ed. Ruth Bernard Yeazell, Selected Papers from the English Institute, 1983–84, 10 (Baltimore, MD, 1986), p. 108.

53. Quoted in Patricia Ingham, 'The Evolution of *Jude the Obscure*', *Review of English Studies*, 27 (1976), 37.

8

Jude the Obscure and the Taboo of Virginity

MARIA A. DiBATTISTA

In support of Gibbon's warning that 'insulted Nature sometimes vindicated her rights', Hardy offers at once a less politic and more cynical observation: 'Love lives on propinquity but dies of contact.' Gibbon's remark strikes us as worldly; Hardy's, disillusioned. It is the remark of a man who apparently prefers the beloved in his vicinity, but not within his domain. Moments of crisis in Hardy's fiction generally transpire before closed doors (*The Return of the Native*, *The Woodlanders*), blocked entrances (Tess trapped in the tomb), or unscalable walls. These architectural and amatory figures of blockage, frustration, or indecision suggest that Hardy conceived of the benefits as well as the hazards of propinquity in structural and strategic terms. The part-title 'At Christminster' takes as one of its epigraphs Ovid's rendering of the beginning stages of the love between Pyramus and Thisbe, a myth that complements the Hardyesque vision of amorous destiny as one ruled by the figure of the wall: 'Notitiam primosque gradus vicinia fecit; / Tempore crevit amor' ('Contiguity caused their first acquaintance; / love grew with time'; *Metamorphosis*, bk 4, ll. 59–60). Initially that wall whose very existence denotes vicinity is the wall of Christminster itself, which encloses the promised land from which Jude is excluded: 'Only a wall divided him from those happy young contemporaries of his with whom he shared a common mental life ... Only a wall – but what a wall!' (p. 105). Through those condensations that permit Hardy to translate literal constructions into figures for the Spirit, the wall that impedes Jude's Christminster 'sentiment' is replaced, through an ingenious but inescapable series of metonymic associations, by the proper name that predicates Sue's sexual existence as a hymenal creature. Hardy, always a bold fabulator of names, denotes Sue as a 'bridehead', recalling Hymen's double existence as perforative wall and presiding spirit of marriage. Jude's erotolepsy and Sue's sexual inaccessibility are thus twin or mirror images of each other (as the language and acts of their exchanges intimate), and together reflect what we might call the ontology of virginity that in no way assumes an innate nor even a characteristic sexual innocence. Tess is a pure woman; Sue is a woman more variously compounded.

The ambiguous relationship that obtains between virginity and First Love can be more easily examined in a tale Hardy wrote in collaboration with Florence Henniker.[1] The story is titled 'The Spectre of the Real'. This title, I think, cryptically alludes to that presence that can never be pictured, that invisible but perforative wall, the hymen. The tale begins as a story of youthful sexual misadventure (the most common and unremarkable type of 'first love'), which both parties agree to have been pure folly. Years later the heroine, Rosalys, is about to marry a Lord Parkhurst, who has no knowledge or even suspicion of her earlier elopement. Hardy often satirises the romance of elopement, but in this story what is emphasised is the seemingly providential series of events which brings the heroine's former lover, presumed dead, home again. Although Rosalys is legally entitled to 'presume' her husband's death after seven years without word of him, she is less sure of her moral ground in proceeding with the nuptials. On the eve of her wedding, however, her former lover promises never to return or to contest his legal status as defunct. He drowns immediately after leaving Rosalys with these assurances, thus morally as well as legally absolving her of fraud or possible bigamy.

Hardy, as any of his narratives will testify, is unreasonably fond of such casuistical subtleties and often lets them dictate the finer moralities of his ironic tales. The 'rescued' heroine is, then, according to formula, safely married, and departs on her wedding-tour. On the brink of this channel (and narrative) crossing, the story takes an uncanny turn. The narrative shifts, almost brutally, to a newspaper report of Lord Parkhurst's suicide:

> We regret to announce that this distinguished nobleman and heroic naval officer, who arrived with Lady Parkhurst last evening at the Lord Chamberlain Hotel in this town, preparatory to their starting on their wedding-tour, entered his dressing-room very early this morning, and shot himself through the head with a revolver. The report was heard shortly after dawn, none of the inmates of the hotel being astir at the time. No reason can be assigned for the rash act.[2]

In the interval between evening arrival and morning departure, the aristocratic groom apparently encountered the spectre of the real. What other motive could be assigned for his suicidal act? What else could transform the bridal bed into a deathbed but firsthand proof of what Joyce sardonically termed the preordained frangibility of the hymen? In a letter to Henniker, Hardy insisted that 'the ending, good or bad, has the merit of being in exact keeping with Lord P.'s character'.[3] This is an odd remark, particularly since Lord P. has no character, only a title and its legacy of representative attitudes. A different merit attaches to this ending, which hints at, but never avers, the invisible but essential presence of the hymen in the sexual and social transaction known as marriage. Virginity is a spectre of the real; it can exist either with or without the physical evidence of its existence. Lord P. killed himself because he was a literalist, and wanted in body what his bride in fact offered him in spirit – the fruits of her first love.

Sue Bridehead's proper name, which defines her with an inspired if characteristically overdetermined linguistic precision, suggests that she is such an enigmatic figure precisely because she would both conceal and expose this partiality for maidenheads. Her name defines the logically untenable wish to be neither wife nor maiden, but to define a place or status between these two states. Sue cannot disclose this hidden desire, only point to it, as she does when, quoting Browning, she urges Jude to 'twitch the robe / From that blank lay-figure your fancy draped'. What Sue wants Jude to see is her own blankness as a lay figure who may consent to cross-dressing but not to sexual redressing. She chooses this moment to reveal that she consented to live with a man 'by letter', unconscious of his strict construction of terms: 'But when I joined him in London I found he meant a different thing from what I meant.' Sue's sense of contract, in which the spirit, not the letter, of cohabitation is fulfilled, proves victorious, yet even she confesses that a better woman would not have remained as she began.

Sue's actions are motivated by an antiliteralist logic which is, Hardy says, 'extraordinarily compounded, and seemed to maintain that before a thing was done it might be right to do, but that being done it became wrong' (p. 239). Her emotional logic, which directly contrasts with Jude's 'logic of first initiatives', is a hymenal logic of a necessarily perverse and, I believe, modern kind that dreads the consummation of the first principles it predicates. For Sue to act on her feelings is equivalent to cancelling or destroying them, a contradiction that Derrida explores in his double session on Mallarmé's *Mimique*, in which this hymenal logic is analysed as an obsession with fictionality. What seems pertinent to our understanding of Sue's nominal identity as 'bridehead' is Derrida's emphasis on the generative ambiguity of the hymen that 'sows confusion *between* opposites *and* stands *between* the opposites at once. What counts here is the *between*, the in-between-ness of the hymen.'[4] By virtue of its strategic placement, neither fully inside nor outside the female body, the hymen designates all the decided ambiguities of *entre* – inbetween-ness, and its homonym in French, *antre* – cave, natural grotto, or deep dark cavern. (Is this condensation what Hardy instinctively grasped in naming the mistress of the house where Sue lives with other maidens 'Miss Fontover'?) In Derrida's polymorphous play on *entre/antre*, which is more extensive than I have indicated here,[5] the hymen is prestigiously placed within the heart of the imaginary itself: as an impermeable but perforative membrane, the hymen is the oracular site ready to receive or disseminate the phallocentric Logos, desirous of cavities and caves.

Such a Derridean excursus, however, would eventually account for Sue's vacillations by positing the essential fictionality of the self. There is some truth, but not enough, in this understanding of her 'character'. Hardy himself diagnoses her neurosis as a historically conditioned and symptomatic 'abnormalism', a cautionary instance of 'modern nerves wed to primitive feelings fated to disaster'. Yet is not Hardy's psychologising marked by one of the four errors Nietzsche identified in his *Twilight of the Idols* – the error of mistaking the effect for the cause? For it is not the modern nerves of the pale bachelor girl that unsex her, but Sue's primitive feelings that unnerve her. Michael Millgate, who endorses as he explicates Hardy's reading of Sue's nervous sexuality, suggests that Sue's name roots her in anthropological ground. Bridehead, Millgate notes, is 'a Dorset place-name (for the source of the River Bride, near Little Bredy)'. Millgate then ventures that, as Hardy had been reading *The*

Golden Bough, 'it is perhaps worth noting that Frazer's discussion of the corn-spirit mentions that in parts of Scotland the last handful of standing corn at harvest-time was called "The maidenhead or the Head"'.[6] Whether it originates as a place-name or as a harvest name, *bride-* or *maidenhead* expresses the heathen concern with those forces or states that promote – or hinder and obstruct – fertility. Millgate's speculation thus complicates and deepens his more conventional interpretation of Sue as a woman 'fatally inhibited by the "head", by intellectuality and a revulsion from the physical'.[7] I will only propose, on the basis of Millgate's own source work, that Sue's compound name refers to a *specific* personal revulsion that is subject to communal taboo, the taboo, as Freud identifies it, of virginity.

Freud, still unrivalled in explaining the persistence of the archaic in the symptoms and symbols of modern thought, believed the taboo of virginity was originally linked to a complementary taboo against menstrual blood. These taboos in turn formed part of general prohibitions against murder and blood-lust that regulated primitive society. But he further recites an explanation I find useful in understanding Sue's final reversion to archaic thought. Freud associates the taboo of virginity with a 'perpetual lurking apprehensiveness' that appears most strongly 'on all occasions which differ in any way from the usual, which involve something new or unexpected, something not understood or uncanny'. Freud, in his canny way, locates the source of this apprehensiveness in the 'fear of first occurrences'.[8]

This fear of first occurrences governs the love story of *Jude the Obscure* and gives Hardy's familial and folk plot a startling anthropological clarity. Every 'new beginning' or 'turning point' that Jude undertakes in emotional obeisance to his logic of first initiatives occurs on the site of landmarks in danger of being obliterated, Hardy complains, by modern (and perishable) designs 'unfamiliar to English eyes'. In this novel, so concerned with acts of architectural restoration, Hardy's reparative imagination works to re-inspirit these sites by recalling to us those unquiet, indwelling spirits who once were controlled or appeased by honouring taboo. Violation of taboo leads to a curse transmitted across generations: in unconscious but prescient recognition of this fact, Jude and Sue first meet at the Spot of the Martyrdoms.

The Spot of the Martyrdoms seems to commemorate the two fears commingled in the taboo of virginity: the fear of first occurrences, itself an adumbration of the fear of blood. The narrative distribution of amorous episodes confirms this essential structure of sacrifice, which the novel's Christological imagery does more to obscure than to reinforce. The perforation of the hymen is traditionally the bloody act that signals the spiritual as well as literal (or legal) fulfilment of the marriage contract. Yet in her first marriage Sue clearly remains a 'Bride', as she confesses to Jude, and it is this abbreviation that is one of his pet or love names for her. The truncation already signals that impending catastrophe of defloration she dreads.

To whom or to what then can Sue, guardian of her own virginity, entrust the task of defloration, the first occurrence that will alter her nature – and confute her name – and make her at once a better and a diminished woman? This question is not rhetorical, but pointed, for Sue's conformation to the customs (if not delights) of the marital bed is the ethical dilemma confronting her. Her solution to this dilemma demonstrates her genius for adapting ancient practices to modern instances. Again, Freud will provide the relevant cases for us:

> The customs of primitive peoples seem to take account of this *motif* of the early sexual wish by handing over the task of defloration to an elder, priest or holy man, that is, to a substitute for the father. There seems to me to be a direct path leading from this custom to the highly vexed question of the *jus primae noctis* of the mediaeval lord of the manor. A. J. Storfer (1911) has put forward the same view and has in addition, as Jung (1909) had already done before him, interpreted the widespread tradition of the Tobias nights (the custom of continence during the first three nights of marriage) as an acknowledgment of the privilege of the patriarch. It agrees with our expectations, therefore, when we find the images of god included among the father-surrogates with defloration.[9]

This tradition of ceremonial defloration is revived in Sue's perverse request that Jude 'give her away' to Phillotson. 'You are "father", you know. That's what they call the man who gives you away' (p. 191). Sue is being conventionally minded in assigning Jude, the groom's former pupil, the paternal role of married relation. The reversal, read in Freudian terms, could suggest her wish that Jude be the one to deflower her, but Jude, so cruelly tormented by this novel revival of ancient custom, can only see that Phillotson's age gives him the literal qualifications for the role of 'father of the bride': 'Phillotson's age entitles him to be called that'. Two literal constructions compete with each other, and Sue, victimised by her own undecidable logic of virginity, seems doomed to remain perpetually confused on the question of who is her real husband and to whom – as Bride – she must surrender her virginity. She remains in a kind of ritual bondage to her 'fear of first occurrences', perhaps because she exists beyond the reach of a language or a logic – of an eroholeptic force – that would seize or transport her out of her in-between-ness and deliver her into a sexually and civically authorised place.

Freud suggests that the resistances accommodated by these taboos are of a psychological rather than sociological importance; they express the anger and resentment of the maiden whose 'frigidity' is symptomatic of her 'masculine protest' against castration. The pig's 'pizzle' is the manifest presence of this latent castration anxiety, but as a totemic object, it is associated, in broad folk humour, with an amorously determined Arabella. A more modern form of this protest, Freud rashly speculated, was 'clearly indicated in the strivings and in the literary productions of "emancipated" women'.[10] What interests me here is not the clinical truth but the psychological value of Freud's explanation in uncovering the archaism lurking in Hardy's portrait of Sue as the pale bachelor girl, already identifiable as a distinct modern type destined to revert to a 'fanatic prostitution' (p. 380). This projected catastrophe is as serious, if not as spectacular, as Jude's histrionic death on Remembrance Day. Sue's gradual involvement with Jude is marked by images or incidents of animal cruelty that dramatise mutilation anxieties. The lacerated leg of the rabbit caught in a gin is a literal instance of mutilation that is figuratively elaborated and incorporated in Jude's criticism of the 'artificial system of things': 'Is it that the women are to blame; or is it the artificial system of things, under which the normal sex-impulses are turned into devilish domestic gins and springes to noose and hold back those who want to progress?' (p. 238). All of Lawrence could be read as an extended answer to the unsettlements of this question. Hardy, I would venture, lets the question defeat him. He cannot bring himself to blame women, nor to exonerate them for the cruel fate of male erotolepsy. Hardy can dream of a future in which normal sex-impulses will abet rather than hinder 'those who want to progress', but he cannot envision a future that is anything but a reversion to the archaic forms and dead letters of the past. Like Sue's Voltairean redactions of the New Testament, Hardy's eroholeptic narratives, however progressive in spirit, are sex-tragedies transfixed by the spectacle of 'the dead limbs of gibbeted gods'.

Only once in the novel does the spirit reciprocate the letter in full and reconciling affection. The fateful exchange occurs as a drama of a kiss given in pledge of physical as well as spiritual surrender:

> They had stood parting in the silent highway, and their tense and passionate moods had led to bewildered inquiries of each other on how far their intimacy ought to go; till they had almost quarrelled, and she had said tearfully that it was hardly proper of him as a parson in embryo to think of such a thing as kissing her even in farewell, as he now wished to do. Then she had conceded that the fact of the kiss would be nothing: all would depend upon the spirit of it. If given in the spirit of a cousin and a friend she saw no objection; if in the spirit of a lover she could not permit it. 'Will you swear that it will not be in that spirit.'
> No: he would not.
>
> (p. 237)

Jude's refusal to submit to Sue's casuistical divorce of the spirit from the letter of the kiss leads to a look, simultaneously exchanged, that issues in a long and unpremeditated embrace in which these lovers 'kissed close and long'. The kiss, the narrator claims, 'was a turning-point in Jude's career'. It is hard to mobilise our suspicions against this erotic peripety which concludes with a unique Hardyesque auto-da-fé: Jude Fawley returning home to burn his books, the 'leaves, covers, and binding of Jeremy Taylor, Butler, Doddrige, Paley, Pusey, Newman and the rest ...' Again a woman conquers the Church fathers; once more Jude's erotolepsy triumphs over his love of divine letters. Yet this time Jude is liberated rather than trapped. His renunciation of the book frees him from a hated religious imposture: 'In his passion for Sue he could now stand as an ordinary sinner, and not as a whited sepulchre.' The replacement of Love for the Law ushers in a period of happiness, which has no history (the domain of scribes) and so goes unrecorded in the novel. We know of its existence only because it produces not books, but children, living proof of Sue's camaraderie.

What finally countermands and divides this Shelleyan union is what we could call the novel's rhetorical genetics. Darwinian logic might predict that the offspring of the substantial Arabella and the virile Jude would produce the child fittest to survive, but Hardy's cross-matchings are more sensitive to elective than to biological affinities. Sue and Jude's offspring are spiritually 'healthy'; that is, no pathological morbidity afflicts them. They appear to be the well-adjusted offspring of a spiritually compatible, if sexually tense, coupling. Oddly, it is the union of the idealistic dreamer and the substantial female animal that produces a figure of depressed consciousness – Little Father Time. Little Jude, both as diminished replica of his father and as harbinger of the coming universal wish not to live, is the necessary end term that gives decided, if morbid, direction to Hardy's sexual allegory of Unfulfilled Intention.[11] The child, once a rival of the book, becomes a bookish figure for the letter: that is, little Jude becomes Little Father Time, signalling his transformation from a biological or narrative figure (the child of human parents) into a rhetorical one.

This triumph of the letter over the spirit takes a specific literary form in Hardy's conscious parody of Wordsworthian childhood. Through a sardonic interpolation of the Intimations Ode, Hardy demonstrates how 'the inception of some glorious idea' gives rise in the transparent and susceptible natures of the young 'to the flattering fancy that heaven lies about them then' (p. 48). Wordsworth's intimation of a recuperable prophetic power is dismissed as the illusion of a 'milk-fed infancy'. But Hardy pays a price for these demystifications. He forgoes, in his repudiation of Wordsworthian childhood, the logic of Wordsworthian consolation. Wordsworth could acknowledge that 'nothing can bring back the hour' of childhood joy and yet still find 'Strength in what remains behind; / In the primal sympathy / Which having been must ever be' ('Ode: Intimations of Immortality', ll. 180–3). Hardy is not only grieved at what has been, but also dreads what is to come. His dark reasoning inverts Wordsworth's consoling proposition that the child is father to the man. The desponding 'Little Father Time' would not father a man, but would die a child. He is no child of joy, but a figure of age masquerading as juvenility.

The murder-suicide that represents Hardy's cathartic disavowal of Wordsworthian childhood represents the grisly cost of little Jude's hapless masquerade, and exposes it as an error of the literalist imagination. 'Done because we are too menny' – the testament of Father Time's motives – reflects the confusion of all allegorical figures in the presence of abundant but unaccommodated life, the life, that is, with which the novel, as secular narrative, is concerned. Father Time lacks the wisdom that not only gives life, but can interpret it charitably, that is, novelistically. His error, as any church doctor – good Lord, even his own father! – might have taught him, is to confuse the spiritual with the literal sense. He dies a victim of Sue's feminine instruction, mystified by the words of a woman who can neither fully explain nor fully conceal the material troubles that beset all living creatures. Perhaps he takes her words as a kind of indictment against his own existence as an allegorical figure whose meaning is fixed and delimited. His rejection of multiplied meanings and propagating life is not so much childish as precocious. His suicide is taken as the harbinger of a *universal* wish not to live, rather than a localised pathologic reaction to life. As a despondent figure and a beleaguered interpreter of modern conditions, Little Father Time presages the modernist crisis of representation, in which the will not to live takes the form of the refusal to narrate.

The coming of the universal wish not to narrate is the baleful dysangelism of this novel, which seems to welcome its own extinction once it discovers the flight of spirit from its verbal precincts. Hardy's narrative is structured in a way that suggests the crumbling of those metaphoric tenements that housed the Penates of the novel, its tutelary divinities and sanctities. The transformation of Christminster, the first object and site of Jude's desire, is the most spectacular instance of the frangibility of the walls that enclose us as well as separate us from the ideal life. Christminster, as many critics have noted, is first glimpsed as mirage, and yet as a place its existence is enduring. What is precarious is Jude's imaginative relation to the initial image of his First Love. Christminster undergoes a series of metaphoric substitutions that replicate but can never recapture the majesty of Jude's original eidolon. The mirage of Christminster is replaced by the actual institution; it is then reproduced in the miniature model Jude and Sue display in the itinerant exhibition where Jude and Arabella re-meet, thus building up the structure of reoccurrence so demoralising to a narrative so in love with first things and so fearful of repeated things. Finally Jude's 'Heavenly Jerusalem' is reincarnated as a perishable good, the Christminster cakes which Jude and Sue sell. This last metaphoric declension, in which a spiritual image is replaced by a material commodity, bitterly reflects the wisdom that man does not live by bread alone. The Rhadamanthine strictness of this degenerative process accounts for the remarkable folktale that seems to pertain to Jude and Sue's unauthorised love. On entering a church, they overhear a story about a satanic experiment in church 'restoration'; in the relettering of the Ten Commandments, all the *nots* were expunged. The Blakean inversion appears to counsel obedience to Instinct's imperatives – the body's *thou shalts*. But Hardy, like Phillotson, is a feeler rather than a reasoner about such revolutionary prescriptions. His belief in the possible realisation of desire in a Blakean utopia of the redeemed body is compounded in equal parts of sympathy and suspicion.

Eventually suspicion conquers sympathy and Hardy can only satirise, albeit regretfully, Jude's empowering belief in original acts. The novel that begins with a supreme contrast between a pig's pizzle and a young man's dreams concludes with a most bitter contrast between the hurrahs of strong-lunged young men and the whispers of the tubercular Jude, citing Job's lamentation: 'Let the day perish wherein I was born and the day it was said there was a manchild conceived.' To cite this text is to invoke authority for self-extinction. The coming universal wish not to live finds its most terrible expression in this wish to reach into the womb and annihilate life at its inception. It will find its most comic expression in Beckett's Neary, who curses the day he was born and then, in a bold flashback, the night he was conceived. Both curses are the inspirations of erotoleptics whose sexual transports find their natural end in a fatal dream of checked conception.

Nietzsche, in one of his skirmishes as a self-proclaimed untimely man, observed that 'in England one must rehabilitate oneself after every little emancipation from theology by showing in a veritably awe-inspiring manner what a moral fanatic one is. That is the penance one pays there.' Nietzsche was speaking of George Eliot and her strict adherence to Christian morality after she had dispensed with the Christian God. But it is Hardy's *Jude the Obscure* which provides a grim exemplification of the moral exactions that give to English fiction its 'consistency'. Hardy's last novel dramatises the recidivism of 'English' morality in the pitiable spectacle of a child's murder-suicide and a wife's fanatic prostitution. Yet it is not Sue, sacrificing herself to fulfil the letter of the marriage bed, but Jude, crying out against the fruit of the conjugal bed, whose moral fanaticism, like Job's, is identical to despair. Perhaps Hardy did not abandon narrative letters simply because of the public outcry against the antimarriage sentiments of his novel – he and others have survived obloquy of that sort – nor even because the spirit of the pale Galilean did in fact conquer his robust passion for his pagan idols – Venus and Apollo. For the worst may not be that the letter killeth. That epigram encapsulates the cathartic agency, not the tragic wisdom, of Hardy's fable. The worst may be that the letter cannot give life. A novelist cannot remain a novelist if he succumbs to the moral fanaticism of that creed. Was it the sterility rather than the murderousness of the letter that led an emancipated but desponding Hardy to compose out of the mythic materials of First Love his final drama of oblivion?

From Maria A. DiBattista, *First Love: The Affections of Modern Fiction* (Chicago, 1991), pp. 101–9.

NOTES

[This essay is taken from Maria DiBattista's examination of a number of modern narratives, *First Love: The Affections of Modern Fiction*. Her argument in the book is that the prevalence of narratives of first love in fiction reflects a cultural preoccupation with the revolutionary impulse – not necessarily in a political sense, but as 'some new feeling, force or individual capable of revolutionising the old, customary orders of life' (p. xi). It is in the adventure of first love, she argues, that there is a significant conjunction of what might be called the social and the subjective dimensions of individual life, social discourses like class and gender and subjectively experienced desires and creativities. The narrative of first love, then, gives structure to the myth of 'soul-creation' (p. 12), or transition into the actuality of selfhood.

Here, *Jude the Obscure* is explored as an 'erotoleptic narrative': that is, as 'a narrative which represents sexual transport as a literal as well as a figurative experience of erotic seizure' (p. 4). Ranging widely across philosophical, psychoanalytic and anthropological theories for her analytic concepts, DiBattista focuses on the centrality of myths of virginity and defloration as the traces of a desire to be first in the affections of the believed. A 'tragic triangulation' results from the inevitable, forced recognition that each beloved always possesses their own unique history of priority.

All quotations here are from the Macmillan edition of *Jude the Obscure* (London, 1974). References to other works of Hardy are designated by chapter numbers. Ed.]

1. Those interested in the personal aspects of this collaboration and in Hardy's talent for cultivating spiritual affinities will be interested in Robert Gitting's account of the Hardy–Henniker alliance, in *The Older Hardy* (London, 1978), and in the volume of their correspondence, *One Rare Fair Woman: Thomas Hardy's Letters to Florence Henniker, 1893–1922*, ed. Evelyn Hardy and F. B. Pinion (London, 1972).

2. Thomas Hardy and Florence Henniker, 'The Spectre of the Real', in *In Scarlet and Grey* (New York, 1977), pp. 209–10.

3. Thomas Hardy and Florence Henniker, *One Rare Fair Woman: Thomas Hardy's Letters to Florence Henniker, 1893–1922*, ed. Evelyn Hardy and F. B. Pinion (London, 1972), p. 33.

4. Jacques Derrida, *Dissemination*, trans. Barbara Johnson (Chicago, 1981), p. 212.

5. Derrida contends that *entre/antre* participates in as it recapitulates the double logic that governs the very edge of being:

At the edge of being, the medium of the hymen never becomes a mere mediation or work of the negative; it outwits and undoes all ontologies, all philosophemes, all manner of dialectics. It outwits them and – as a cloth, a tissue, a medium again – it envelops them, turns them over, and inscribes them. This nonpenetration, this nonperpetration (which is not simply negative but stands between the two), this suspense in the antre of per-penetration is, says Mallarmé, perpetual: '*This is how the Mime operates, whose act is confined to perpetual allusion without breaking the ice or the mirror: he thus sets up a medium, a pure medium, of fiction.*' (Ibid., p. 215).

The mime besotted with Hymen, who outwits all manner of ontologies and dialectics, is Pierrot, the erotoleptic clown whose mimes rehearse, as in Gautier's *Pierrot Posthume*, 'the supreme spasm of infinite masturbation'. The 'folly' of Jude's idealising love bears an uncomfortable, if poignant, resemblance to Pierrot's aspiration to a union with Colombine.

6. Michael Millgate, *Thomas Hardy: His Career as a Novelist* (New York, 1971), p. 410.

7. Ibid., p. 320.

8. Sigmund Freud, 'The Taboo of Virginity', in *The Standard Edition of the Complete Psychological Works of Sigmund Freud*, ed. James Strachey (London, 1953), vol. 11, p. 197.

9. Ibid., p. 204.

10. Ibid., p. 205.

11. [The term is Hardy's. See *The Woodlanders*, ch. 7. Ed.]

9

Jude the Obscure: What Does a Man Want?

MARJORIE GARSON

I

Jude Fawley wants; Jude Fawley is wanting. We know Jude through the rhythm of desire, repulsion, and renunciation which constitutes his inner life; we know him through those he wants, through Sue and Arabella and Christminster; and we know *them* in terms of their ability or inability to fulfil his desires. Jude is wanting: he is constituted in lack, defined from the first pages of the novel as 'a hungry soul in pursuit of a full soul' (p. 156). His emptiness is dramatised in the action – even in the part-titles – of the novel, as he moves from place to place in search of the fulfilment which continually eludes him. Jude's wanting provides the plot, the characters, and the emotional tone of the novel.

Jude wants Sue, and he wants a university education. Examination of Hardy's manuscripts has shown that the marriage problem was part of his conception of the novel from the very beginning, and that in his first draft it was Sue who was to have been the motivation for Jude's desire to visit Christminster.[1] Though Phillotson later replaced Sue in this capacity, there remain in the novel as it stands strong links between Jude's desire for Sue and his desire for Christminster. Sue is living in the city of his dreams, and reaching it involves discovering her. Desiring in her not only the woman but the cultivation she embodies – the kind of culture which exposure to Christminster has apparently already given to her – Jude attributes to her many of the values which he has attributed to the city, imagining them both as bodiless, visionary presences, as shining forms encircled by haloes of light.[2] Jude is temperamentally logocentric: he naïvely believes in the reality of the idealised images he has constructed from inherited materials. Christminster is to be the heavenly Jerusalem of Revelation, Sue is to be the haloed apparition in his aunt's photograph. However, both will remain hauntingly elusive: despite his obsession about staying close to the university and to Sue, Jude discovers that it does not necessarily help to be 'on the spot' (p. 100). For the truth is that both the desired woman and the desired city exist in their luminous purity only in Jude's imagination: by the very nature of his dreams, he is doomed to disappointment.

What particularly marks this novel, indeed, is the tone of what might be called 'logocentric wistfulness'. Like many of Hardy's heroes, Jude is a reader, but a reader of printed texts rather than of the signs of nature. The fact that it is the Bible which lies behind the language and imagery of the novel seems related to the stubbornness with which he insists upon a transcendent reality behind words and signs. And Jude's author shares his logocentric desire.[3] When Hardy presents his protagonist as a Christ-figure, there may be a degree of irony in the identification; but he treats Jude's analogous fantasies without disabling irony. Though we know from the beginning that Jude is going to be mistaken about Christminster and about Sue, we are to think more of him for his idealism, and less of those beings which fail to live up to his image of them. Christminster ought to be the City of Light, and if it is not, it is the city which is to blame; Sue ought to be 'worthy' of Jude's devotion. Both equally deserve his suggestively worded reproach to Sue: 'you are ... not so nice in your real presence as you are in your letters' (p. 197).

Indeed, what Jude wants is implicit in his view of language. As a child, Jude imagines that there is a key which will render the whole of language transparent – undo Babel.[4] When he finds that no such key exists, that he cannot master the whole, he starts to plug away at the parts. But his vision of identity is rather endorsed than otherwise, and the fantasy of wholeness underlies the text: the desire for magical translation into a state of pure presence, the desire to be lifted above competing voices, absorbed into a unified community. This dream seems to be presented as a legitimate desire, a vision betrayed by the social organisation of contemporary Oxford and by Victorian views of marriage.

Jude's Christminster is created for him by words, by printed books. Although the notion of a blessed place is suggested by Phillotson, the shape that place takes in his imagination derives from images which are essentially literary. Jude knows Christminster through the Bible, as the heavenly Jerusalem; through his study of Latin, as his 'Alma Mater' (p. 41); and through the written words of her sons, who speak to him of 'her ineffable charm' (p. 95) more kindly and clearly than Christminster ever speaks in person. These patriarchal texts testify with an authority which implies the reality of what they describe. But it is clear from the opening pages of the novel that the very terms in which Jude has conceived his desire preclude its fulfilment.

The famous opening to the second part of the novel, which has Jude listening to the 'ghostly presences' (p. 92) of Christminster, suggests why this is so. These voices of Oxford seem stilted, 'got up' by Hardy, but the very awkwardness of the passage is part of its meaning.[5] The episode raises in paradigmatic form some of the issues of autobiographical fiction, since the quotations Jude remembers have of course been culled from Hardy's own reading.[6] Hardy's awareness of their miscellaneous, even arbitrary character is reflected in the way the narrator accounts for them: they are supposed to be from 'a book or two [Jude] had brought with him concerning the sons of the University' (p. 94), evidently tourist-guide anthologies of 'purple passages'. The attribution suggests that Jude is not as well read as Hardy (the quotations are not collected by *him*) but on the other hand absolves Jude of the kind of jejune self-satisfaction implied by their assemblage. The passage dramatises the alienation it presents, its uneasy tone a perfectly accurate register of both the pride and the defensiveness of the autodidact. Its ironies make clear that print can provide no unmediated, unproblematical contact with culture as a whole or with the mind or spirit of the writers of the past.

Indeed, the episode raises the question of the relationship between the written and the spoken word, for though their resonant words seem 'spoken by them in muttering utterances' (p. 94), Jude has been introduced to the 'voices' through the printed pages 'he had just been conning' (p. 94), and their rhetoric (even that of Sir Robert Peel's Corn Law speech) is very much *écriture*. Jude dreams of appropriating what these voices represent, but they undo him even as they address him: as he listens to them, he begins to feel more ghostly, less substantial, than they. Each of these writers uses the first person pronoun; each one has a powerful ego and a confident, totalising vision of human experience. Yet, speaking together, the voices depict a Christminster which must remain incoherent, not only because (as Jude himself realises) it has always generated a wide range of conflicting opinions but also because it is constituted by the (inevitably) fragmentary reading of an (inevitably) partially educated individual. Jude seeks to be made whole, but it is clear that his very vision of Christminster must preclude the consummation he desires.

What Jude does for a living is relevant to these issues. A country stonemason who practises his craft 'holistically', he can turn his hand to a number of tasks, in contrast to the urban workers, who master one technique only. Jude's versatility recalls while it parodies Ruskin's vision of Gothic.[7] The values Ruskin imputes to the old architecture are seen as illusory, yet the presence in the novel of bastardised Victorian Gothic nevertheless implies *degrees* of authenticity and hints at a nostalgia for origin which the text at other times seems to debunk. (At times Hardy seems to suggest that Jude, in desiring a university education, is betraying a kind of Ruskinian vision of honest craftsmanship.) It is emblematic of this contradiction that Sue should dismiss the Gothic style as 'barbaric' (p. 369), and yet at the same time be 'sentimentally opposed to the horrors of overrestoration' (p. 361); it is not entirely clear whether this is supposed to be one of her many contradictions (as the narrator's adverb 'sentimentally' would seem to suggest) or whether the inconsistencies in Hardy's feelings shape her 'character' (for the noun 'horrors' may not be Sue's but the narrator's).[8]

For Hardy seems to endorse Jude's impulses by showing them as instinctively directed towards wholeness, while at the same time presenting that wholeness as an impossible dream. Is it because Jude is a working man, or simply because he is a human being, that he has to begin his apprenticeship laboriously and fragmentedly, by learning to shape one letter at a time? The process is analogous to the way he has to struggle with the heavy medium of the classical languages, alone and without help. The dream is of a whole which will at some moment add up to more than the sum of its parts, which will become monumental, permanent, resonant with interconnected meaning; which will make the individual whole, and unite him creatively with an organic community. But I would argue that the text is not entirely clear about whether it is Jude's class position which victimises him, or whether this dream is by definition a hopeless one.[9]

In my reading, the text is shaped even more radically by Hardy's feelings about the body than by his feelings about social class. It seems to me that Jude's desire – for a wholeness of a quasi-spiritual type, a wholeness which completely transcends the body, does not depend upon the body – is intrinsically unrealisable, and that the class theme in the novel is as much 'vehicle' as it is 'tenor'. Take for example Jude's occupation. The facts that he, like Hardy's father, is a stonemason and that his dusty working clothes make him invisible to the upper-class undergraduates who pass him on the street suggest that it is his class position which is decisive. On the other hand, there is something idiosyncratically Hardyan about the way Jude's craft is presented. It is suggestive that Jude is a worker in stone, the deadest and most intractable of materials, and that he sees himself as in the business of supplying dead bodies, helping to provide 'the carcasses that contained the scholar souls' (p. 37) – for while this ought to be a perfectly legitimate aim, and would be in Ruskin's terms, it is one which, in Hardy's world, cannot be achieved with impunity.

Embodiment means death; stone itself means death. His work chills Jude and makes him vulnerable to the lung infection which eventually kills him; the dust marks him and makes him invisible to those who look through his body as through a pane of glass. But these literal details only mask the deeper, figurative import of the stonemasonry. Its implications are crystallised in the famous moment when Jude cuts into a stone the word THITHER (p. 85) – an inscription which, we know, will remain to mock him. The act of embodying an aim in a word, and cutting that word in stone, is perfectly emblematic of Jude's logocentric desire. His aim is to make the word real – to ensure its fulfilment – by giving it a body. But in Hardy's world the opposite happens. When the word falls into matter, becomes incarnate in paper or stone, it partakes of the exigencies of material existence, and becomes sinister, mocking, dangerous. The common ('touch-wood') superstition that expressing satisfaction at a situation can reverse it is given an idiosyncratic slant by Hardy, who suggests that the real danger lies in inscribing the word, giving it a material body. The incarnate word takes the place of what it signifies, precludes its fulfilment. Incarnation means betrayal in this novel: to give or to take a body is to fall away from reality, to be involved in death.

II

Women give a man body; women betray the word and the spirit and lock a man into the flesh. The women in this novel thwart Jude by drawing him down into the body and then dismembering him – and this is as true of Sue as it is of Arabella. Though Mrs Oliphant's reaction to the novel is extreme, one of her sarcasms is well taken: 'it is the women who are the active agents ... the story is carried on, and life is represented as carried on, entirely by their means'.[10] This statement not only confirms a reader's impression of Jude's behaviour, as he dances to Sue's tune, but also echoes certain judgements of the narrator – 'if God disposed not, woman did' (p. 249) – and of Jude himself: 'strange that his first aspiration – towards academical proficiency – had been checked by a woman, and that his second aspiration – towards apostleship – had also been checked by a woman' (p. 261). Jude goes on to wonder whether 'the women are to blame; or is it the artificial system of things...?' (p. 261) – unable to imagine, evidently, any third alternative, assuming with Mrs Oliphant that 'men ... are quite incapable of holding their own against these remorseless ministers of destiny'.[11] For all its comments about the various weaknesses of woman (and there are a good many), the novel dramatises rather her fearsome strength. Even fragile Sue survives her male victims, while indestructible Arabella triumphs. There is an obvious structural similarity between *Jude* and *Tess*: in both novels, seduction by a sensual lover leaves the innocent protagonist vulnerable in a subsequent relationship with a 'spiritual' one.[12] In this novel, however, the victim is a man, and the destructive collaborators are women.

Through Arabella, Jude thinks he will achieve a new kind of wholeness:

> He had just inhaled a single breath from a new atmosphere, which had evidently been hanging round him everywhere he went, for he knew not how long, but had somehow been divided from his actual breathing as by a sheet of glass.
>
> (p. 45)

The pane-of-glass figure occurs three times in the novel, always to describe actual or potential alienation.[13] Here it is a fine and precise expression of the illusion of transfiguration by erotic love.[14] Jude translates himself instead of the Bible, and we know how he feels when he says that it is 'better to love a woman than to be a graduate, or a parson; ay, or a pope!' (p. 53). But we are never for a moment allowed to forget that he is wrong, and that this repossession of his body will lead to dispossession and dismemberment.

That Arabella is a castrating woman is all too obvious: Hardy relentlessly signals that she will dismember Jude as efficiently as she dismembers the pig – will cut up his schedule, derail his career, and disrupt his subsequent relationship with Sue. Though Jude cannot 'read' the overdetermined signs which characterise his mistress, Arabella – of the detachable pizzle and the detachable hair-piece – is presented as a fearsomely phallic figure. (There is an apparently unconscious aptness in the terms Jude uses to describe her – 'there was something lacking, and still more obviously something redundant, in the nature of this girl', p. 45). The link between Arabella's hair and her castrating power is made clear in the allusion to Samson and Delilah: Arabella will chop a man off and chop him up if she is given the chance. And she will do the same thing to the patriarchal text. Arabella is jealous of Jude's involvement with books. She has no use for his ambition, and resents the time he spends on study. The scene in which she mishandles his books, smearing them with pig-fat and finally flinging them about the room, dramatises her feeling of rivalrous contempt. As embodied male voices, books tend to become male bodies in this text – bodies which here are polluted and assaulted by the female touch.

But in the very act of assaulting the Word, Arabella also actualises it, for as Delilah, she is the word made flesh – a kind of incarnation. And this very fact qualifies Hardy's point. While the moral of the biblical allusion is clear – Arabella is the last of a long line of wicked temptresses, and Jude should have known better than to fall for her – the fact that it *is* an allusion also works against this moral, suggesting that the word has to stay word, remain on the page, remain a translation exercise, an exercise in culture, or a moral emblem reinforcing patriarchal prejudice, for Jude (and Hardy) to be satisfied with it. When Jude returns to his books and 'the capital letters on the title-page [regard] him with fixed reproach ... like the unclosed eyes of a dead man' (p. 53), we are meant to feel that Jude has betrayed male words, betrayed culture and religion, for a woman; indeed that he is a kind of murderer, and that Arabella is his accomplice. But this metaphor, too, has an excess of meaning which cuts against its moral: it evokes a male body so lifeless, so ghoulish, that its superiority to woman's body does not make itself felt as fully as it seems intended to do.[15] The paradoxical power of Hardy's figurative style lies in its tendency to deconstruct itself – here, to suggest that Arabella is a scapegoat even as it scapegoats her.

And it is clear that Arabella *is* a scapegoat.[16] We seem intended to see her as a kind of sensual monster and hold her responsible for much of Jude's bad luck. But an examination of the actual causality of the plot reveals that Arabella does less damage than the novel's rhetoric seems to suggest. It becomes increasingly clear that, even if he had never met Arabella, Jude could not have achieved his dream.[17] His premature marriage is not the decisive barrier to university entrance, which would have required a more thoroughgoing and pragmatic campaign than he could ever have mounted, even if he had remained single. Indeed, blaming Arabella dilutes the social criticism: *Jude the Obscure* is *not* really a coherent critique of the class system, because it conflates its condemnation of that system with condemnation of her.

Nor, even without Arabella, could Jude have mastered Sue. Jude shapes our interpretation of his story when he remarks that it is Arabella who has blighted his relationship with Sue; yet, although the way Arabella keeps turning up at crucial moments does suggest that she is some kind of avenging fury, pursuing her doomed victim, her influence is not as definitive as it seems to be. Sue apparently gives herself to Jude on the first occasion out of jealousy of Arabella; but are we to assume she would never otherwise have done so, or that Jude would have been better off if she had not? It is true that it is Jude's involvement with Arabella which apparently precipitates Sue's marriage to Phillotson; but Sue was already engaged to Phillotson before she ever heard of Arabella, and Jude cannot fully possess her even when both he and Sue are legally free of their respective spouses. Shedding Arabella is, indeed, anticlimactically easy: the novel is not a very good analysis of the divorce issue, if only because the divorces it depicts are so readily obtained. When the neighbours shun Jude and Sue, it is less because they were married to others than because they are suspected (quite correctly) of not being married to one another.[18] Although Hardy does what he can to implicate Arabella in Sue's return to Phillotson – by having her inform Phillotson that his divorce was obtained on grounds which were invalid at the time, and thus apparently preparing his mind to take his wife back – Sue's motives for fleeing Jude have nothing to do with her rival. What happens is that Arabella is often used to trigger, or to make seem fated , a course of action which was implicit in Sue's nature – to give Sue an excuse for administering pain which she was bound to administer eventually in any case. It is as though the two women, antipathetic to one another though they are, are at some level working together to destroy the protagonist.

I do not propose to deal in any detail with the question of Sue's sexual frigidity. It seems to me that her double nature is constituted by the male fantasies which shape her. Sue mirrors Jude – as the many references to their twinning and doubling make clear[19] – and she is what she has to be in order to arouse Jude and to thwart him. Jude creates her as a spiritual being before he ever sees her, and then expects her to satisfy him physically as well. Hardy creates her to play her part in the 'constant internal warfare between flesh and spirit' (p. 232) by which Jude will be defined and destroyed. My approach is not to treat her as a real person with an internal consistency which analysis can uncover, but frankly as a production of the text, a place where its needs intersect. For the purposes of this discussion, what is interesting is her relationship to the patriarchal Word.

Like Arabella, Sue sets herself up as a rival to the male texts Jude loves. If Arabella is a Delilah, Sue is an Eve who entices Jude from the realm of innocent logocentrism into experience, by manipulating sign-systems which are sacred to him.[20] In contrast to Jude, Sue works in design rather than construction, in paint and chalk rather than stone. Her cleverness consists in moving lightly among signs sacred to the dominant culture, in 'colouring' and manipulating words which have real value to other people. Jude's first glimpse of his cousin colouring ALLELUIA (p. 103) suggests to a reader her frankly opportunistic stance – though Jude sentimentally imagines an organic, Ruskinian relationship between what she is and what she does.

Having the word printed in Gothic characters emphasises its archaic visual decorativeness and recalls, while at the same time parodying, Jude's deeply felt THITHER.[21] It is characteristic of Sue that after making fun of the model of the city of Jerusalem, she is able to reproduce it exactly on the blackboard, for she is presented as a mere replicator and exploiter of discourse, echoing and playing with signs and concepts rather than internalising them.

The female voice is a sinister power in the novel. Male voices are spiritual, ghostly; they speak through print, are the pure 'presence' to which the written word points; they come out of the past as history, religion, culture; they are univocal, unequivocal, stand-taking, ordered, formally rhetorical; they project a sure sense of self.

Female voicing is more complex: it is oral rather than *écriture* (this is true even of Sue's notes, which are in the same distracting accents as her spoken word); it is of the body (involving clothing, gesture, body-language as well as actual speech); it is double, deceptive, contradictory; it involves mimicry, parroting, parody, role-playing; it is interactive, demanding and positing a response; it comes out of the past as legend, rumour, curse, or spell. None of these qualities is necessarily bad – indeed, they are the kind of things feminists are saying about women's language in general – but in this novel they are devastatingly and consistently destructive.[22]

Sue's dialogue has been criticised as stilted and unrealistic, but that is part of its point.[23] Her alienated, formal wording conveys perfectly the pert theoreticalness of everything she says. Like Jude, Sue is self-educated and half-educated: but where Jude's intellectual incoherence is seen as pathetic, Sue's seems wilful and aggressive: she uses her reading to rationalise her instinctual needs and desires. Her androgynous nature is relevant here: she 'tries on' male styles of thought as opportunistically as she dons Jude's clothing, or as she uses the arguments of the dead student whose lover she refused to become. Sue uses men against one another, and she uses men's ideas the same way. Less crudely but even more devastatingly than Arabella, she turns into 'missiles' the chopped-up bits and pieces of a male 'body'. There are two fragmenting processes which operate through Sue's words: female inconsequence and male analysis. Sue voices the conclusions of contemporary (male) criticism so as to undermine Jude's convictions intellectually, while her maddening ('female') inconsistency undoes him emotionally. The way Hardy describes Sue's behaviour during her last breakfast with Phillotson – 'she talked vaguely and indiscriminately to prevent his talking pertinently' (p. 271) – neatly captures the aggressively scatterbrained quality of her chatter throughout the novel, even when what she is saying seems to have some intellectual content. The moment when she quotes Mill against Phillotson is untypically comic, but it otherwise epitomises her technique throughout.

Jude wants Sue to help him preserve his logocentric virginity: he flees to her in horror after reciting the creed in Latin on a bet. But she does the opposite. In Sue's nervous chatter, the patriarchal Word becomes text, and the text falls apart. When Sue quotes Swinburne to the effect that the Christian saints are 'dead limbs of gibbeted Gods' (p. 180), when her Higher-Critical stance dissolves the biblical text into separable headings, chapters, and editions, when she offers to prepare Jude a new New Testament by dismembering the traditional one and reassembling its parts in 'chronological order as written' (p. 182), we are in the presence of an antisacramental *sparagmos*: the metaphor acquires shocking force in the context of Hardy's imagery, and prefigures the scene in which Jude dismembers and burns his own books, 'the leaves, covers, and binding of Jeremy Taylor, Butler, Doddridge, Paley, Pusey, Newman' (p. 262): a mass-murder, as well as suicide. Sue's irresponsible babble dismantles the text and undoes Jude.[24]

This is not to say, of course, that Hardy is consciously hostile to most of Sue's opinions, or even to the way she expresses them. Like Jude's 'voices', Sue's quotations are really Hardy's, gleanings from his own reading, often quotations from his favourite authors. But by reproducing 'familiar quotations' in two modes – the Jude-mode of phenomenological reverence and the Sue-mode of opportunistic *bricolage* – the text suspends their message somewhere in the gap between, relativises it. And by making Sue both an intellectual mentor and a sexual tease, Hardy problematises Jude's conversion to her 'modern' point of view.

Jude loses his faith for emotional as much as intellectual reasons, as he becomes more depressed and less hopeful in his private life; and since Sue is responsible for his hopelessness, she is also responsible not only for his scepticism but for the link between scepticism and hopelessness.[25] It is paradoxical that even though Jude *progresses* towards the beliefs which Hardy himself holds and towards an apparently liberating unconventionality which the text endorses, his maturing point of view seems to reflect not so much intellectual energy and independence as lassitude and collapse. A Jude who can ask Sue what edition of the Apocrypha she recommends (p. 244) is a man who has surrendered, been at once seduced and emasculated by her opinions.

I would argue, however, that Hardy is scapegoating Sue just as he is scapegoating Arabella. Sue uses signs the only way one can in the post-Christian age posited by Hardy – to define, express, and defend herself rather than to transcend herself – and because she does this she is made to bear the weight of the ontological crisis. The novel knows that there is no truth behind signs, yet makes Woman culpable for pointing this out: it dramatises as female scattiness the breakdown of logocentric security. Hardy's characterisation of Sue enables him at once to depict woman as unable to 'master' male thought, and to blur male responsibility for the fragmenting force of that thought by having its *content* voiced by a woman.

Sue's scepticism makes her into the rival of the male 'voices' Jude has loved. Indeed, she effectually destroys his relationship with the voices of the patriarchy, which she mocks, undercuts, and dismembers. She emasculates him not only by denying him her body but by destroying his dream of cultural solidarity with the great men of the past and present. Though it is clearly not in any literal sense Sue's fault that a Christminster education is beyond Jude, her mockery of what such an education would have stood for implicates her in his bitter disappointment. The collapse of his university dreams makes Jude pathetically dependent upon Sue. Her ghost replaces the ghosts of Christminster; indeed, when Jude declares that he will not be divided from her by 'things present nor things to come' (p. 290), he implies that she has replaced God himself.

Indeed, Jude's obsession with Sue – or is it his obsession with Christminster? – isolates him from all his fellow *men*. Although Jude works with men, drinks with them, and apparently feels a vocation to teach them (he is even said to have led a working-men's reading group, which is, however, mentioned only at the moment when it expels him!), the narrative never dramatises his putative capacity for male comradeship. There are indeed only two male friendships in the novel: Jude's original passion for Phillotson, and Phillotson's friendship with Gillingham: these two, and the relationship between them, I shall return to in a moment. There is no group of tolerant rustics in this novel to provide a sense of male community; Jude feels only justified contempt for the group represented by Tinker Taylor, with whom he occasionally drowns his sorrows – and whose generic name suggests a dismissiveness on the part of the author himself. The dream of inclusion in an idyllic community of scholars seems to have stood in the way of ordinary friendships with ordinary men, the relationship with Sue to have absorbed Jude's emotional energy when that dream falls apart. There is something downright claustrophobic about Hardy's picture of Jude's life with Sue.[26] While it seems appealing that their relationship is conceived as a friendship as well as a love affair, that Sue is his 'comrade' and companion as well as his life-partner, it also points to a vacuum in Jude's life. Sue fills the gap left by the dream of male fellowship, and that dream – not Arabella – is her real rival.

It is worth noting how the rivalry between Sue and Christminster contributes to the startling conclusion of the novel. The despair which causes Little Father Time to kill himself and murder his little siblings can be traced directly to Jude's behaviour on Remembrance

Day – behaviour which by any ordinary standards can only be described as self-indulgent and irresponsible.[27] By insisting on standing in the rain until he has seen the procession, Jude not only makes himself ill, he makes it impossible to get an adequate room for the night. In effect, he deserts Sue, leaving her alone with the children. Her singularly ill-timed frankness to the landlady, when she admits that, although visibly pregnant, she has no husband, is so gratuitous that it might seem to be a bitter reflection on Jude's behaviour – if any such motive could be attributed to Sue, who at this point in the novel has become almost saintly in her endurance and uncritical devotion. In any event, the end result of Jude's fecklessness is the death of the children, and Sue's return to Phillotson. Jude sacrifices Sue's welfare to his obsession with Christminster, and then – though the novel establishes no *direct* link between the events – loses her to the rival who had imbued him with that obsession.

Why are women presented as rivals to the dream? Why are Christminster and Sue conceived as in some way interchangeable? How is the question of education connected with the marriage question? Indeed, what precisely is it that Jude wants in wanting Christminster?

III

The evidence is inconsistent, even somewhat contradictory. There is the sense that the bookish life is a last resort, since Jude is no good for anything else.[28] Yet it is never entirely clear whether Jude loves reading as an end in itself. Certain passages seem to suggest that he does: that he has been inspired by the hymn to Diana, or the passages from the Christminster writers which are apparently supposed to be lodged in his memory. But most of his study seems to be less joyful discovery than painful toil; and reading loses some of its charm for him when every working man is doing it.

Indeed, it is also suggested that Jude's main motive is ambition, a wish to distinguish himself from other people. The young Jude dreams of becoming 'even a bishop' (p. 40) and looking 'down on the world' through the windows of 'those palaces of light and leading' (pp. 100–1). He remembers Phillotson telling him that 'a degree was the necessary hall-mark of one who wanted to do anything as a theologian or teacher' (p. 119), and later admits, in renouncing it, that his motive had been 'social success' (p. 148). It is only when he realises that he can never be an ordained clergyman that Jude lights on the 'new idea': to 'preach and do good to his fellow-creatures' (p. 153). At that point he confesses that his former scheme had been motivated by 'mundane ambition', 'a social unrest which had no foundation in the nobler instincts' (p. 153); but he is in a penitential mood, and part of the appeal of the new scheme is that it is a properly 'purgatorial course worthy of being followed by a remorseful man' (p. 153).

Jude's desire, then, is overdetermined: none of these motives is fully dramatised in the novel, and the very fact that all of them can be invoked makes all of them seem somewhat theoretical. Something deeper and more consistent is needed to account for Jude's fanatic and ultimately suicidal obsession. What about the positive reasons, the details which convey the depth of his desire – the erotic motives for Jude's fascination with Christminster?

His first impulse towards Christminster is simply presented as a yearning to join Phillotson. The power of this motive is startlingly suggested by the intensity with which Jude '[parts] his lips as he [faces] the north-east, and [draws] in the wind as if it were a sweet liquor' when he realises that it was 'in Christminster city between one and two hours ago ... touching Mr Phillotson's face, being breathed by him' (pp. 21–2). The wind is the spirit not of God but of the only other Father he has known. Yet this father is described with lover-like intensity – even in a topos borrowed from Petrarchan love-poetry. And for good reason: this passage was originally written to describe Jude's feelings not for Phillotson, who was added at a later stage of the composition to bolster the education theme, but for Sue herself.[29] That Hardy felt able to retain the paragraph, essentially changing only the pronouns, is a remarkable testimony to the ambiguity of the erotic impulse of this fable.

As Jude grows older his desire becomes less personal but no less intense. His desire for Christminster is a desire for a transfigured state of being. Outside the walls of Christminster, experience is fragmented, he is alienated from his fellow men, and the world is brown, grey, dark, and gloomy (the word 'gloom' recurs frequently, to denote both emotional and physical states). He wants transfiguration, he wants to be swept out of this fallen world, translated, illuminated, penetrated, 'imbued with the *genius loci*' (p. 136). The transformation involves being contained within the walls of the mystical city. 'Only a wall' divides him from the communion he desires – 'Only a wall – but what a wall!' (p. 100).

Christminster the cultural centre is a kind of Great Barn of English thought,[30] 'the intellectual and spiritual granary of this country' (p. 133), and, like the Great Barn in *Far from the Madding Crowd*, a metaphorically female body. Christminster the university is the welcoming mother, and Jude 'her beloved son, in whom she shall be well pleased' (p. 41);[31] Christminster the city is Jerusalem the heavenly bride – before whose image, for a moment, he forgets Bridehead (p. 126). Seduced by her 'romantic charms' (p. 37), Jude longs 'to reach the heart of the place' (p. 91), to '[penetrate] to dark corners which no lamplight reached' (p. 91), 'to be encircled as it were with the breath and sentiment of the venerable city' (p. 91). But in her 'ineffable charm' (p. 95), 'so lovely, so unravaged' (p. 94), Christminster remains, like Sue, tantalising but inaccessible; and the gates are shut against him. It is a premonitory image, for Jude's fate is to remain 'outside the gates of everything' (p. 100). Hardy's protagonist is always being denied access to a female body which would make him whole, and it is always the fault of a woman.

The misquotation of Matthew 3: 17 is significant: in imagining himself 'her beloved son, in whom she shall be well pleased', Jude has changed the pronoun of the biblical text and the gender of the complacent parent. Father becomes Mother: the fusion is significant, for there is a paradoxical element to Jude's desire. The sheltering body is metaphorically female, but the community contained within her walls is a community of men, of spiritual fathers and brothers; a dream-world where there are no distracting Arabellas and Sues, except as 'gorgeous nosegays of feminine beauty' rendered harmless by distance, 'fashionably arrayed in green, pink, blue, and white' (p. 490); an enclosed community where Jude could be at one with 'those happy young contemporaries of his with whom he shared a common mental life' (p. 100). Jude wants to be taken into the body of a woman who can make him a man among men. The problem is that this wholeness is a fiction in the first place, 'a very imaginary production' (p. 125), as Sue says of the model of Jerusalem. Instead of acknowledging this, and condemning Jude for his wishful thinking, the novel blames the various female figures who fail to fulfil his impossible desires.

Jude's grievances against women go back a generation. His mother deserted his father – and Jude. His foster-mother, Aunt Drusilla, is a cold, rejecting woman who transforms family accidents into family myth: she displaces his mother, and then tells him he can never have a wife. Indeed Drusilla, 'opposed to marriage, from first to last' (p. 251), is a kind of witch. Though the text allows the myth of the family curse to be understood as an ignorant woman's primitive superstition, whatever Drusilla predicts comes true, as if, in repeating it, she had willed it. Drusilla tells Jude on the day of his marriage to Arabella that it would have been better if he had died at birth, and he eventually comes to feel the same way. It is significant that her 'good' counterpart, Mrs Edlin, who professes to be more positive about marriage, has an equally negative impact on Jude's marital career. It does seem somewhat grotesque for her to relate, on the eve of Jude's planned marriage to Sue, the (possibly untrue) story of his and Sue's ancestor, gibbeted in a sort of corpse custody case. Since Sue has consented to the wedding because of her desire to provide an orthodox home for Arabella's child, the anecdote has a peculiar relevance to their situation; and although she herself is not shown taking account of this relevance, the effect of the gruesome tale is to make her call off the marriage. It is interesting that when she does, Mrs Edlin expresses her disappointment by complaining that they have 'spoiled' the saying 'marry in haste and repent at leisure' (p. 346)! The doubling of Drusilla and Mrs Edlin reveals the deep structure of the mythic subtext. Women tend to work together in Hardy, however far apart they believe themselves to be.

Sue and Arabella also work with Drusilla to make her curses come true.[32] Even though Drusilla as a character is steadfastly opposed to Jude's relationship with both women, they both play into her script and actualise her dire and spiteful predictions, taking over her role of demonic mother and completing the destruction she has foretold. The text knows that because what Jude seeks is given in an illusory way by the (m)Other, no actual woman can ever provide it. So it creates a dual mother in Sue and Arabella, both of whom go through the motions of nurturing him but who really kill him.

Arabella is a mother out of nightmare. Her sheer size and physical vigour are intimidating, her immense bosom particularly threatening. She first appears less than a page after Jude's fantasy of the Alma Mater; she seduces him by playing games with the egg she is hatching between her prodigious breasts, and traps him into marriage by pretended maternity. She tends to reduce Jude to infantile helplessness, her presence in the bar at one point destroying 'his momentary taste for strong liquor as completely as if it had whisked him back to his milk-fed infancy' (p. 217). In the final sequence, as Jude lies dying, Arabella denies him the care he needs to survive.

Sue is the very opposite physically: the narrator explicitly contrasts 'the small, tight, apple-like convexities of her bodice' with 'Arabella's amplitudes' (p. 225). But the mother's curse nevertheless also operates through Sue, whose own mother was a shrew and who, unlike Jude, re-enacts the role of her abusive parent. Jude flees to Sue in the first place for maternal comfort and guidance, 'under the influence of a childlike yearning for the one being in the world to whom it seemed possible to fly' (p. 145). His visionary image of her as haloed guide, counsellor, comforter, and friend makes it appropriate that one of her names is Mary.[33] And Hardy assigns to her at the end of the novel a speech which rewords the fatalistic conception of his own mother: 'There is something external to us which says "You shan't"' (p. 407).[34] But what definitively places Sue in the position of a mother to Jude is that she marries, and eventually deserts Jude for, the man who initially served as a father to him – and that the children she mothers indirectly send her into this man's arms.

On the other hand, Sue's role as a mother and a stepmother to these real children is not entirely plausible. Her instant interest in and sympathy with young Jude – even in the face of her distress that 'half' of him 'is' Arabella – seems no more credible than her repeated pregnancies, which in view of her sexual skittishness and her intact and immaculate body-image are hard to visualise. Sue has some peculiar ideas about procreation which might seem to militate against successful maternity. Her fantasy, expressed in her complaint to Phillotson, that, if Eve had not fallen, 'some harmless mode of vegetation might have peopled Paradise' (p. 271), is more startling, not to say unorthodox, than it seems intended to be in context. The text apparently sympathises with Sue's objection to marrying, on the grounds that marriage involves bringing forth, in Shelley's words, 'Shapes like our own selves hideously multiplied' (p. 345) – even though the context makes the argument illogical, since Sue and Jude find themselves quite able to bring forth such shapes even in an unmarried state. And yet the narrator endorses as one of 'man's finer emotions' (p. 212) Jude's wish that Sue's children should be her clones, containing nothing of Phillotson – 'shapes like her own self', precisely.[35]

Such fantasies might suggest that the children in the novel are less likely to be believable individuals, characters in their own right, than figures for or mirrors of the main characters – 'shapes like their own selves' in one way or another. And indeed this turns out to be the case. The children are more vivid as the grotesquely undifferentiated trail of corpses, or as the little bundles of empty clothing hanging on the pegs, than they are when alive; and Sue as a mother and step-mother turns out to be as grotesquely destructive as they are unreal.

The figure through whom Sue operates is Little Father Time, less a child than 'an enslaved and dwarfed Divinity' (p. 332) – a *deus ex machina*, that is, enslaved to the exigencies of Hardy's plot.[36] It is impossible to respond to him as to a real child, a character in his own right: the only way of getting at his function in the novel is to look at the connections he forms among the other characters.

Through this child, Sue and Arabella are linked in motherhood. The two women's relationship to young Jude parodies their rela-tionship to his father: Arabella's connection is physical only; Sue ex-presses idealised affection for both Judes, but she lets them both down in the end, so that they die of despair. It takes the two women to finish the child off – as it takes both of them to kill Jude, and both Alec and Angel to destroy Tess. As in *Tess of the d'Urbervilles*, it is the more 'spiritual' and idealistic one of the pair who does the more damage. Like Drusilla, Sue gives her foster son the message that it would have been better for him to die young; and Little Father Time, already predisposed to agree, acts out her suggestion.[37] What precisely he brings about when he does so is made clear by looking at his relationship with his 'mother' and father, and with the other 'mothers' and 'fathers' in the novel.

Jude's father is dead before the book begins, and seems to have left his son no legacy – indeed to have made no impression upon him at all.[38] Although it was his abusive behaviour which drove Jude's mother away, Jude's feelings about him are never mentioned, except in a generalised way, as an aspect of the family problem with marriage. It is perhaps worth noting that Jude, when he deals with women, takes the very opposite tack: far from abusing his women, he allows them to abuse him – yet he loses them all the same. There is no suggestion that Jude's behaviour is a deliberate response to his father's, that (like Joe for example in *Great Expectations*) Jude has chosen to abjure his father's bullying stance; but there is a sense that the father, for whatever reason, has left his son wounded and de-fenceless. The novel opens with Jude's loss of a substitute father. Jude's first love, apparently, is Phillotson, but Christminster and then Sue take this father/lover away from him. Seeing Phillotson as occupying the place of the father makes some patterns in the novel emerge more clearly. The shape of the plot – with the four main characters changing partners – releases meanings which go beyond facile irony.

The romantic plot of the novel emphasises how Phillotson takes Sue away from Jude, but it is equally true that Sue takes Phillotson away from Jude. Indeed, Sue meets Jude precisely at the point when it is made clear to Jude that Phillotson never had the emotional investment in Jude that Jude had in him. The older man's brutally insensitive remark – 'I don't remember you in the least' (p. 118) – is underemphasised by the narrative: Jude scarcely seems to notice it. In view of the place Phillotson had held in Jude's imagination, Jude's obliviousness to the rudeness is as disconcerting as the remark itself. Indeed, there seems to be a 'loop' in the sequence at this point: Phillotson loses his 'halo' (p. 118) for Jude just *before* he speaks, because of his unimpressive physical appearance. But Phillotson's callous comment is a much more plausible trigger for Jude's sudden disenchantment than his faded looks, which might have depressed an ardent idealist like Jude but should scarcely have lessened his interest and sympathy. Once again, as in the motivation of Mrs Charmond's hostility in *The Woodlanders*, a lesser motive seems to be substituted for a greater, and the substitution alerts the reader to a covert level of meaning. It is important that it is at this moment in the novel that Phillotson suddenly becomes physically unattractive, that his repulsive exterior is from this point on a constant feature of his character notation, and that this unattractiveness acquires a specifically sexual dimension. There seems to be some displacement going on here, and the ground shifts under the reader's feet as the characters, not only of Phillotson but of Jude himself, suddenly seem to change.

Sue replaces Phillotson as the focus of Jude's interest in Christminster; she also replaces Jude as Phillotson's student and protégée. It is more than just a neat 'ironical clinch' (p. 129) that Jude hastens to introduce Sue to the man who will take her from him: it is a clue to their structural interchangeability. The loss Jude suffers in Phillotson is re-enacted again and again in various parodic and sometimes gratuitous ways. Jude's idealism is betrayed by Tetuphenay and later by the composer Highridge. Even Vilbert becomes involved in the pattern. When Arabella marries him at the end of the novel, Vilbert becomes linked structurally to Phillotson (a parallel reinforced by Vilbert's lie, when he refers to Jude as 'a pupil of mine, you know', p. 355), in that Jude has finally lost both his women to the two men who seemed to father him in the opening pages. The text makes clear that Jude will never get what he wants from a man. Indeed, he could say of any of the men in his life what he says of Sue: 'you are not worth a man's love' (p. 470).

Jude's relationship to his son is no more fruitful than his relationship to his 'fathers'. In a naturalistic novel the root of their alienation might well be biological: Jude could easily be shown as unable to sympathise with the 'half' of young Jude which comes from Arabella. What Hardy actually does with the figure shows that his method is less naturalistic than symbolic. For in spite of the fact that Sue's words foreground the question of genetic connection, Little Father Time is not like his mother at all. He is, indeed, the little clone Sue and Jude have both desired, a parodic epitome of both the authors of his being – both Jude and Hardy. A precocious infant, he seems to have possessed from birth the secret they did not glimpse until the age of 11.[39] Jude names the 'little hungry heart' (p. 335) after himself, identifies with him, and projects on to him his own ambitions and his own reflections, imputing to him the sentiment – 'Let the day perish ...' (p. 330) – which he later uses as his own epitaph (p. 188). Little Father Time is less Jude's child than his dwarfish double – a parodic mirror-image, created to punish him. One's sense of what sin Jude is being punished for depends upon one's reading of what it is that the child accomplishes.

Little Father Time is less a character than an awkward plot device, but one which reveals the *origin* of the plot itself. Or rather, of one of the plots; for two are needed to deliver Sue into the hands of Phillotson. The first of these is the Sue–Jude–Arabella triangle, a familiar fictional pattern Hardy has already worked out in *Tess*. The second is the Sue–Jude–Phillotson triangle, which looks more and more like a Freudian family romance. Standing in for his father and namesake Jude, Little Father Time – both child and father, in a parodically unWordsworthian way – acts out the child's desire to block the union between Mother and Father, as well as his suspicion that such opposition is suicidal, that Father is going to win in the end. He has advised against the marriage of his parents, and goes on to break up their relationship. But he dies in the process, and succeeds only in delivering his 'mother' over to the original 'father', and to the patriarchal order with which that father has recently renewed his connection.

For Phillotson has suddenly lined up with Gillingham. Indeed, Phillotson's 'character' shifts according to the needs of the plot and the symbolic structure. Callously tactless when Jude attempts to renew acquaintance with him, smoothly courteous to Arabella in the same situation (p. 382); articulately sensitive to Jude and Sue's Shelleyan oneness while obtuse and even vulgar in his emotional intercourse with his wife; gallant, even heroic in giving Sue up in the first place; finely independent of Gillingham then, cravenly suggestible in the end – Phillotson is not really the consistent figure invented by Lawrence.[40] Rather, he seems to be a counter manipulated by a text in pursuit of certain patterns of meaning, his character necessarily sacrificed to his multiple functions. Although himself excluded from Christminster, Phillotson now becomes, when he possesses Sue, one of the excluders. The unworthy world of men who love women defeats Jude in the end.

Yet while he robs Jude, Phillotson also acts for Jude. The text has spoken of revenge upon Sue – revenge which it now takes. The text, through little Jude, hands Sue over to a father who will torment her. Sue, like her own mother, has abused her 'husband'. Jude, unlike his real father, has never retaliated. But he has played father – taken Phillotson's part in the wedding rehearsal Sue sadistically insisted he enact. And he has, like Sue's student lover, warned her that she could play her 'game' once too often (p. 313). It is easy to see Sue's fate as retribution for the way she has acted to Jude – retribution which Jude himself cannot be allowed to think of taking. The way the text dwells on her shrinking white body has, however, a certain sadistic relish. Jude had spoken of the 'utter contempt' a man might feel for a tease after she was dead and gone (p. 313). That after Jude himself is dead and gone Phillotson remains to enact his revenge is an irony the text cannot openly acknowledge.

Instead, it must end with the assertion that Jude, even in death, remains the object of both women's desire. In the last line of the novel Arabella suddenly speaks for Sue, in heightened language which recalls Marty South's envoi to *The Woodlanders*:

> 'She may swear that [she's found peace] on her knees to the holy cross upon her necklace till she's hoarse, but it won't be true … She's never found peace since she left his arms, and never will again till she's as he is now!'
>
> (p. 494)

Arabella's words seem validated by their portentous placement. But her sudden elevation into choric commentator is as disconcerting as her assertion is implausible: Sue was never very consistent in her desire to be in Jude's arms, and if she has suddenly become so, it is less, one might feel, because he is the only man for her than because she has finally lost him. But Arabella's rhetoric does not seem intended to leave the reader with any such cynical reflection.[41]

What gives Arabella the authority to speak for Sue? Why do women suddenly unite like this in Hardy? The unexpected ending seems to express once again Hardy's intuition that women are somehow united in a way men cannot understand. Something more is going on in this particular novel, however, where Arabella's words always acquire a peculiar authority (and an attractiveness for certain critics) whenever she is testifying to Jude's desirability.[42] If the text has blamed women for denying Jude wholeness, it has also implied that a man can get wholeness through a woman. Whatever Jude lacks in his own eyes or in the eyes of the reader, he must not lack in the eyes of Woman; however disparate the natures and needs of Sue and Arabella, they must agree in their desire for him. Arabella's sudden oracular status owes less to her 'character' than to the needs of the text. The magical power of the word is lent to the woman so that it can be borrowed back by Hardy to confirm his male protagonist.

From Marjorie Garson, *Hardy's Fables of Integrity: Woman, Body, Text* (Oxford, 1991), p. 152–78.

NOTES

[In her book, Garson reads seven of Hardy's novels as 'fables about the constitution of self and about its inevitable dissolution' (p. 1). She argues that Hardy's fiction is permeated by what she calls 'somatic anxiety' (p. 1), in which fear about the nature of the self and its mortality is expressed through anxiety about bodily integrity and imagined threats to it. This, for Garson, is what lies behind certain notable recurrences in her writing: images of bodily fragmentation and dismembered body parts, for example, or the use of 'humanoid' figures which combine the human and the mechanical. Drawing on feminist theories and on the psychoanalytic theory of Jacques Lacan, she argues that anxieties about bodily wholeness in Hardy take a particular, gendered form: they convey a strong sense of maleness under threat from women. Although her critical method is focused on the fictional characters, she regards them, not as the equivalent of real people in the world, but as structures and functions in a recurrent fable.

In this chapter, for example, Garson highlights the fact that, however differently the *content* of the characters of Arabella and Sue may be portrayed, their structural function makes them more alike than different. With a theoretical eclecticism that brings together elements of structuralist, feminist, psychoanalytic, and deconstructive theory, she analyses the narrative power and energy that derive from the intersection of private myth and wider cultural anxieties.

All quotations in the text are from the Wessex Edition of *Jude the Obscure* (London, 1912). Ed.]

1. Patricia Ingham, 'The Evolution of *Jude the Obscure*', *Review of English Studies*, 27 (1976), 27–37, 159–69 demonstrates that the marriage question was always central and that the education theme was repeatedly expanded in revision. John Bayley, *An Essay on Hardy* (Cambridge, 1978), p. 203, argues that the two subjects are not convincingly related.

2. For the parallel between Sue and Christminster, see A. Alvarez, 'Afterword', in Thomas Hardy, *Jude the Obscure* (New York, 1961; reprinted in Albert J. Guerard [ed.], *Hardy: A Collection of Critical Essays* [Englewood Cliffs, NJ, 1963], p. 114); also Ramón Saldívar, *Jude the Obscure*: Reading and the Spirit of the Law', *ELH*, 50 (1983), 611. [Reprinted in this volume – see pp. 32–52. Ed.] J. Hillis Miller, *Thomas Hardy: Distance and Desire* (Cambridge, MA, 1970), p. 185, traces the image of the halo or nimbus in Hardy's poetry and fiction.

3. I am assuming a degree of identification between Hardy and his protagonist. Hardy himself repeatedly denied that the novel was autobiographical (Florence Emily Hardy, *The Later Years of Thomas Hardy 1892–1928* [London, 1930], pp. 44, 196), referring oddly to Jude on one occasion as 'that fictitious person. If there ever was such a person' (p. 233). But the novel contains an episode also recorded in the *Life*: see Ian Gregor's fine analysis of the moment in which young Jude looks through his straw hat and is 'seized by a sort of shuddering' (*The Great Web: The Form of Hardy's Major Fiction* [London, 1974], pp. 1–2; cf. Florence Emily Hardy, *The Early Life of Thomas Hardy 1840–1891* [London, 1928], pp. 19–20). On the link between narrator and author see also John Bayley, *An Essay on Hardy* (Cambridge, 1978), p. 195, and William Morgan, 'The Novel as Risk and Compromise, Poetry as Safe Haven: Hardy and the Victorian Reading Public', *Victorian Newsletter*, 69 (1986), 3.

4. For a discussion of this fantasy see Ramón Saldívar's analysis of 'natural law' as an illusionary construct in '*Jude the Obscure*: Reading and the Spirit of the Law', *ELH*, 50 (1983).

5. Patricia Ingham, 'The Evolution of *Jude the Obscure*', *Review of English Studies*, 27 (1976), 169, notes that 'At the proof stage of the first book edition the Christminster voices were still being added to' for the purpose of expanding the education theme.

6. Michael Millgate, *Thomas Hardy: A Biography* (New York, 1982), p. 68, suggests, as an influence on the structure of this passage, Horace Moule's 1858 lecture for the Working Man's Mutual Improvement Society of Dorset on 'Oxford and the Middle Class Examinations'.

7. For Hardy's interest in Ruskin, see Lennart A Björk (ed.), *The Literary Notebooks of Thomas Hardy* (London, 1985), vol. I. *passim*; Harold Orel (ed.), *Thomas Hardy's Personal Writings: Prefaces, Literary Opinions, Reminiscences* (Wichita, KS, 1966), pp. 154, 274 n.; J. B. Bullen, *The Expressive Eye: Fiction and Perception in the Work of Thomas Hardy* (Oxford, 1986), *passim*. Michael Millgate, *Thomas Hardy: A Biography* (New York, 1982), p. 346, observes that Hardy's involvement in the restoration of a local church coincided with the writing of *Jude* and notes the relevance of the poem which came out of this experience: the lament of 'The Young Glass-Stainer', who, 'loving the Hellenic norm', is obliged to work in the 'crude', 'abnormal' Gothic style.

8. In his suggestive reading of the novel, Goode seems to eliminate these ambiguities, asserting that Jude himself realises that the 'mechanistic bits of reproduced masonry are probably no more factitious than the weather-worn originals' ('The Decadent Writer as Producer', in Ian Fletcher [ed.], *Decadence and the 1890s* [London, 1979], p. 122). I feel that the text is more ambivalent than Goode allows about some of its 'decadent' enthusiasms, including the taste for the Gothic. Hardy in his non-fiction prose continued to make a sharp distinction between restored or imitation Gothic and the original. See Florence Emily Hardy, *The Early Life of Thomas Hardy 1840–1891* (London, 1928), pp. 40–1, 145; and *The Later Years of Thomas Hardy 1892–1928* (London, 1930), pp. 71, 78–9, 145 (where an old building is compared to 'a unique manuscript'), pp. 150–1, and 'Memories of Church Restoration', 1906 (Harold Orel [ed.], *Thomas Hardy's Personal Writings: Prefaces, Literary Opinions, Reminiscences* [Wichita, KS, 1966], pp. 203–27); Lennart A Björk (ed.), *The Literary Notebooks of Thomas Hardy* (London, 1985), vol. i, item 809. J. B. Bullen, *The Expressive Eye: Fiction and Perception in the Work of Thomas Hardy* (Oxford, 1986), pp. 126–8, summarises the evidence about Hardy's growing disenchantment with Gothic revival and restoration.

9. Michael E. Hassett, 'Compromised Romanticism in *Jude the Obscure*', *Nineteenth-Century Fiction*, 20 (1971), 432–43, sees Jude and Sue as Romantics whose imaginative vision of life is intrinsically unrealisable; see also David Lodge, *Jude the Obscure*: Pessimism and Fictional Form', in Dale Kramer (ed.), *Critical Approaches to the Fiction of Thomas Hardy* (London, 1979), pp. 193–201.

10. Margaret Oliphant, 'The Anti-Marriage League', *Blackwood's Magazine*, 159 (1896), 140.

11. Ibid.

12. D. H. Lawrence, 'Study of Thomas Hardy', in *Phoenix: The Posthumous Papers of D. H. Lawrence*, ed. E. D. McDonald (1936; reprinted London, 1961), p. 488, points out the structural parallel between Tess–Angel–Alec and Jude–Sue–Arabella.

13. In the schoolroom episode, Phillotson literally watches Sue through a pane of glass (p. 271); Jude feels separated from the undergraduates at Christminster, who 'saw through him as through a pane of glass' (p. 100). The same image is used in the *Life*, where Hardy is described as 'seeing through' individuals who condescended to him 'as though they were glass' (Florence Emily Hardy, *The Later Years of Thomas Hardy 1892–1928* [London, 1930], p. 179).

14. John Bayley, *An Essay on Hardy* (Cambridge, 1978), p. 211, points out that 'Jude's courtship of Arabella is more essentially Shelleyan than his relation with Sue'.

15. Robert C. Slack, 'The Text of Hardy's *Jude the Obscure*', in *Nineteenth-Century Fiction*, 11 (1957), 268, notes that the 1895 edition of the novel has Jude closing his book before he goes out; for the 1903 Macmillan edition, Hardy eliminates this inconsistency and saves the simile.

16. D. H. Lawrence, 'Study of Thomas Hardy', in *Phoenix: The Posthumous Papers of D. H. Lawrence*, ed. E. D. McDonald (1936; reprinted London, 1961), pp. 488–95, complains that Hardy inartistically vilifies both Alec d'Urberville and Arabella, who actually strengthens rather than harms Jude; see also A. Alvarez, 'Afterword' in Thomas Hardy, *Jude the Obscure* (New York, 1961; reprinted in Albert J. Guerard [ed.], *Hardy: A Collection of Critical Essays* [Englewood Cliffs, NJ, 1963], pp. 116–17).

17. This point is made by Terry Eagleton, Introduction to the New Wessex Edition of *Jude the Obscure* (London, 1974; reprinted in Harold Bloom [ed.], *Thomas Hardy's Jude the Obscure* [New York, 1987], pp. 61–71). See also John Bayley, *An Essay on Hardy* (Cambridge, 1978), p. 214, on the 'false causal link' which vitiates the novel.

18. Patricia Ingham, 'The Evolution of *Jude the Obscure*', *Review of English Studies*, 27 (1976), noting the 'remarkable ease' with which the divorces are obtained, decides that by 'the marriage question' Hardy must have meant 'whether marriage is a satisfactory and rational institution' rather than 'the stringency of the marriage laws' (p. 164). See also David Lodge, '*Jude the Obscure*: Pessimism and Fictional Form', in Dale Kramer (ed.), *Critical Approaches to the Fiction of Thomas Hardy* (London, 1979), p. 194, and John Bayley, *An Essay on Hardy* (Cambridge, 1978), pp. 208–9, who argues that it is not marriage which is the problem, but simply 'a free and emancipated sexual relation' after the glamour has worn off.

19. For example, the episode in which Sue puts on Jude's clothing (pp. 172–84). Lacan's insights about 'hommosexual' love are relevant here: see Jacques Lacan, *Feminine Sexuality: Jacques Lacan and the Ecole freudienne*, ed. Juliet Mitchell and Jacqueline Rose (New York,

1982), p. 155; Juliet Flower MacCannell, *Figuring Lacan: Criticism and the Cultural Unconscious* (London and Lincoln, NE, 1986), pp. 44, 71–2, 107. Readers who see Sue's sexual attitudes as a projection of Hardy's and/or Jude's attitudes or conflicts include Michael Steig, 'Fantasy and Mimesis in Literary Character: Shelley, Hardy, and Lawrence', *English Studies in Canada*, 1 (1975), 167; John Goode, 'Sue Bridehead and the New Woman', in Mary Jacobus (ed.), *Women Writing and Writing About Women* (London and Totowa, NJ, 1979), pp. 102–4; A. Alvarez, 'Afterword' in Thomas Hardy, *Jude the Obscure* (New York, 1961; reprinted in Albert J. Guerard [ed.], *Hardy: A Collection of Critical Essays* [Englewood Cliffs, NJ, 1963], pp. 115–17); Ramón Saldívar, '*Jude the Obscure*: Reading and the Spirit of the Law', *ELH*, 50 (1983), 611–12. Those on the other hand who treat her as a coherent character include D. H. Lawrence, 'Study of Thomas Hardy', in *Phoenix: The Posthumous Papers of D. H. Lawrence*, ed. E. D. McDonald (1936; reprinted London, 1961), pp. 398–516, whose 'strong misreading' of the novel is brilliantly suggestive; Robert B. Heilman, 'Hardy's Sue Bridehead', *Nineteenth-Century Fiction*, 20 (1966), 307–23; Michael Steig, 'Sue Bridehead', *Novel*, 1 (1968), 260–6; Albert J. Guerard, *Thomas Hardy: The Novels and Stories* (Cambridge, MA, 1949), pp. 109–14; A. Alvarez, 'Afterword' in Thomas Hardy, *Jude the Obscure* (New York, 1961; reprinted in Albert J. Guerard [ed.], *Hardy: A Collection of Critical Essays* [Englewood Cliffs, NJ, 1963], pp. 118–19); Irving Howe, *Thomas Hardy* (New York, 1967), pp. 141–3; Ian Gregor, *The Great Web: The Form of Hardy's Major Fiction* (London, 1974), pp. 215–22; Mary Jacobus, 'Sue the Obscure', *Essays in Criticism*, 25 (1975), 304–28; and Penny Boumelha, *Thomas Hardy and Women: Sexual Ideology and Narrative Form* (Brighton, 1982) [Reprinted in this volume – see pp. 53–74. Ed.]. Sue's link with feminism and with the New Women of the 1890s is explored by A. R. Cunningham, 'The "New Woman Fiction" of the 1890s', *Victorian Studies*, 17 (1973), 177–86, Boumelha (pp. 63–97), and Kathleen Blake, 'Sue Bridehead, "The Woman of the Feminist Movement"', *Studies in English Literature*, 18 (1978), 703–26 (reprinted in Harold Bloom [ed.], *Thomas Hardy's Jude the Obscure* [New York, 1987], pp. 81–102); see also note 25. For biographical material which contributed to the figure of Sue, see Michael Millgate, *Thomas Hardy: A Biography* (New York, 1982), pp. 350–5.

20. Lawrence's discussion of Sue's need for the Male and for the Word is suggestive in relation to her greedy appropriation of these texts ('Study of Thomas Hardy', in *Phoenix: The Posthumous Papers of D. H. Lawrence*, ed. E. D. McDonald [1936; reprinted London, 1961], p. 496).

21. Hardy's use of unusual typography is discussed by William Harmon, 'Only a Man: Notes on Thomas Hardy', *Parnassus*, 14/2 (1988), 309.

22. See Patricia Meyer Spacks, *Gossip* (New York, 1985); Luce Irigaray, *This Sex Which Is Not One*, trans. Catherine Porter and Carolyn Burke (Ithaca, NY, 1985), pp. 134–7, 111–13, and *passim*; Toril Moi, *Sexual/Textual Politics: Feminist Literary Theory* (London, 1985), pp. 140–7.

23. See A. Alvarez, 'Afterword' in Thomas Hardy, *Jude the Obscure* (New York, 1961; reprinted in Albert J. Guerard [ed.], *Hardy: A Collection of Critical Essays* [Englewood Cliffs, NJ, 1963] p. 119); J. I. M. Stewart, *Thomas Hardy: A Critical Biography* (London, 1971), p. 190; John Bayley, *An Essay on Hardy* (Cambridge and New York, 1978), pp. 201–2; Paul Pickrel, '*Jude the Obscure* and the Fall of Phaeton', *Hudson Review*, 39 (1988), 248.

24. Mary Childers, 'Thomas Hardy: The Man Who "Liked" Women', *Criticism*, 23 (1981), 322, comments on meekness, silence, and irrelevant chatter as women's weapons in Hardy's fiction.

25. For the historical placing of their clash of opinion, see Robert Gittings, *Young Thomas Hardy* (London, 1975), pp. 93–5, who argues that Sue's loss of religious faith and her Positivism are anachronistic for the New Woman of the 1890s and that she is rather 'The Girl of the Period' of the 1860s.

26. Sue, too, is curiously isolated, without friends of her own sex. Michael Millgate, *Thomas Hardy: A Biography* (New York, 1982), pp. 351–2, notes the oddness of this, considering that Sue attends a training college and that her experience there is to some extent based on that of Hardy's sisters Kate and Mary, who did have warm friendships. The idea of such friendships, moreover, intrigued Hardy: see his journal entry on the 'mother–daughter' pairings at Stockwell Training College (Florence Emily Hardy, *The Early Life of Thomas Hardy 1840–1891* [London, 1928], p. 310). Hardy was anxious to protect Sue against the suspicion of lesbianism: he insisted to Gosse that there was 'nothing perverted or depraved in Sue's nature. The abnormalism consists in disproportion, not in inversion': see Millgate, p. 354. (Hardy alludes to Sappho in his epigraph to Part III of the novel: see Lennart A. Björk [ed.], *The Literary Notebooks of Thomas Hardy* [London, 1985], vol. I, items 522, 524, for other references to Sappho.) John Bayley, *An Essay on Hardy* (Cambridge and New York, 1978), p. 205, comments on the 'judicious' tone of the letter – 'as if Hardy had just learned to talk like that (perhaps from Gosse and Ibsen)'. Richard Dellamora, *A Study of Masculine Desire* (Chapel Hill, NC, 1989), p. 215, notes the lack of the same-sex bonding for both Jude and Sue. Analysing the formalisation of gender roles in the 1890s, Dellamora also points out where Hardy 'learned to talk like that', noting that the word 'inversion' is the language of the new sexology, and that Hardy's defensiveness about Sue's 'abnormalism' lines him up with the sexologists in an essentially conservative view of 'natural' sexuality. My

feeling is that the emphatic foregrounding of Sue's problems with sexuality and gender may serve to repress similar problems of Jude's. Sue's and Jude's isolation from the community is discussed by Robert B. Heilman, 'Hardy's Sue Bridehead', *Nineteenth-Century Fiction*, 20 (1966), 322–3, and Ian Gregor, *The Great Web: The Form of Hardy's Major Fiction* (London, 1974), pp. 219–28. On the theoreticalness of their 'comradeship' see Bayley, p. 212.

27. Michael Millgate, *Thomas Hardy: His Career as a Novelist* (London, 1971), p. 329, and John Bayley, *An Essay on Hardy* (Cambridge and New York, 1978), p. 210, note Jude's responsibility for the deaths of the children.

28. Hardy makes a similar point about himself: 'Everybody said that Tommy would have to be a parson, being obviously no good for any practical pursuit' (Florence Emily Hardy, *The Early Life of Thomas Hardy 1840–1891* [London, 1928], p. 19). The emphasis is changed in a later statement: 'As a child, to be a parson had been his dream' (Florence Emily Hardy, *The Later Years of Thomas Hardy 1892–1928* [London, 1930], p. 176). The two statements, taken together, seem to register an ambivalence similar to the novel's.

29. See Patricia Ingham, 'The Evolution of *Jude the Obscure*', *Review of English Studies*, 27 (1976), 166. John Paterson, 'The Genesis of *Jude the Obscure*', *Studies in Philology*, 57 (1960), 90, prints the passage with its revisions. Michael Millgate, *Thomas Hardy: A Biography* (New York, 1982), p. 351, suggests that one of the models for Phillotson was Horace Moule. Hardy's journal entry for 20 June 1873 describes his last visit to Moule, in a context which recalls the imagery of *Jude*: 'we could see Ely Cathedral gleaming in the distant sunlight. A never-to-be forgotten morning. H. M. M. saw me off for London. His last smile' (Florence Emily Hardy, *The Early Life of Thomas Hardy 1840–1891* [London, 1928], p. 123). On Hardy's relationship with Moule, see Millgate, pp. 155–6 and *passim*.

30. For another comparison between Christminster and the Great Barn, see George Wotton, *Thomas Hardy: Towards a Materialist Criticism* (Dublin and Totowa, NJ, 1985), p. 105. Douglas Brown, *Thomas Hardy: The Mayor of Casterbridge* (London, 1962), p. 13, and Andrew Enstice, *Thomas Hardy: Landscapes of the Mind* (London, 1979), p. 6, have noted the similarity between Christminster and Casterbridge.

31. See David Lodge, '*Jude the Obscure*: Pessimism and Fictional Form', in Dale Kramer (ed.), *Critical Approaches to the Fiction of Thomas Hardy* (London, 1979), p. 200, on the parodic baptism which follows this statement.

32. Lascelles Abercrombie, *Thomas Hardy: A Critical Study* (London, 1912; reprinted New York, 1964), pp. 160–1, observes the two

women's 'kinship in Jude's destruction'. The doubling of characters is noted by A. Fischler, 'An Affinity For Birds: Kindness in Hardy's *Jude the Obscure*', *Studies in the Novel*, 13 (1981), 250–65 and 'Gins and Spirits: the Letter's Edge in *Jude the Obscure*', *Studies in the Novel*, 16 (1984), 1–19; Terry Eagleton, Introduction to the New Wessex Edition of *Jude the Obscure* (London, 1974; reprinted in Harold Bloom [ed.], *Thomas Hardy's Jude the Obscure* [New York, 1987], p. 69); Paul Pickrel, '*Jude the Obscure* and the Fall of Phaeton', *Hudson Review*, 39 (1988), 246–50. A number of discussions of Hardy's misogyny deal with this novel: see Kathleen Rogers, 'Women in Thomas Hardy', *Centennial Review*, 19 (1975), 249–58; Mary Childers, 'Thomas Hardy: The Man Who "Liked" Women', *Criticism*, 23 (1981), 317–34; Elizabeth Langland, 'A Perspective of One's Own: Thomas Hardy and the Elusive Sue Bridehead', *Studies in the Novel*, 12 (1980), 12–28. Mary Jacobus, 'Sue the Obscure', *Essays in Criticism*, 25 (1975), 304–28, on the other hand, argues that Hardy presents Sue sympathetically, allowing us to see her side of the story. Eagleton, who sums up the case against Sue, suggests that she is a '"representative" character in the great tradition of nineteenth century realism ... and her elusive complexity points beyond herself, to a confused and ambiguous structure of feeling which belongs to the period in general', p. 68.

33. Michael Millgate, *Thomas Hardy: A Biography* (New York, 1982), pp. 350–3, suggests biographical sources for Sue's names. 'Bridehead' is also the name of one of the 'old-fashioned psalm-tunes associated with Dorsetshire' (Florence Emily Hardy, *The Later Years of Thomas Hardy 1892–1928* [London, 1930], p. 127).

34. Michael Millgate, *Thomas Hardy: A Biography* (New York, 1982), p. 21.

35. Cf. the central fantasy of *The Well-Beloved*.

36. Dissatisfaction with this figure has been general: see Lascelles Abercrombie, *Thomas Hardy: A Critical Study* (London, 1912; reprinted New York, 1964), pp. 164–6; Albert J. Guerard, *Thomas Hardy: The Novels and Stories* (Cambridge, MA, 1949), p. 69; A. Alvarez, 'Afterword' in Thomas Hardy, *Jude the Obscure* (New York, 1961; reprinted in Albert J. Guerard [ed.], *Hardy: A Collection of Critical Essays* [Englewood Cliffs, NJ, 1963], p. 121); Irving Howe, *Thomas Hardy* (New York, 1967), pp. 145–6; John Bayley, *An Essay on Hardy* (Cambridge and New York, 1978), pp. 203–4.

37. Robert B. Heilman's 'Hardy's Sue Bridehead', *Nineteenth-Century Fiction*, 20 (1966), 313, 318, suggests that Sue 'provides the psychological occasion, if not the cause' of the deaths and also comes 'close to husband murder'. See also Ian Gregor, *The Great Web: The Form of Hardy's Major Fiction* (London, 1974), p. 226.

38. The process of designing a tombstone for his own father, who died in July 1892, perhaps suggested to Hardy the trade of his protagonist (Florence Emily Hardy, *The Latter Years of Thomas Hardy 1892–1928* [London, 1930], p. 15).

39. See Florence Emily Hardy, *The Early Life of Thomas Hardy 1840–1891* (London, 1928), p. 19–20, and the poem 'Childhood among the Ferns'.

40. D. H. Lawrence, 'Study of Thomas Hardy', in *Phoenix: The Posthumous Papers of D. H. Lawrence*, ed. E. D. McDonald (1936; reprinted London, 1961), pp. 501–2.

41. Arabella's choric role invites commentary: see Michael Millgate, *Thomas Hardy: His Career as a Novelist* (London, 1971), p. 324; Ian Gregor, *The Great Web: The Form of Hardy's Major Fiction* (London, 1974), p. 232; John Bayley, *An Essay on Hardy* (Cambridge and New York, 1978), pp. 212–13; Penny Boumelha, *Thomas Hardy and Women: Sexual Ideology and Narrative Form* (Brighton, 1982), p. 150.

42. See A. Alvarez, 'Afterword' in Thomas Hardy, *Jude the Obscure* (New York, 1961; reprinted in Albert J. Guerard [ed.], *Hardy: A Collection of Critical Essays* [Englewood Cliffs, NJ, 1963], p. 118); Paul Pickrel, '*Jude the Obscure* and the Fall of Phaeton', *Hudson Review*, 39 (1988), 249.

10

Jude Fawley and the New Man

TIM DOLIN

I begin with a commonplace: that sexual ideology is reproduced in literary forms, but also in critical practices; and that gender criticism is effective and necessary because it is always a double critique, refracting its focus on texts from other times and places onto the time and place and gender of its own writing. As Mary Jacobus has written, '*engagée* perforce, feminist criticism calls neutrality in question, like other avowedly political analyses of literature'.[1] I therefore want to situate the following discussion of *Jude the Obscure* within two distinct sexual contexts, the first constituted by ideologies of masculinity and femininity in late nineteenth-century English culture, and in the narrative discourses on which the novel draws; and the second constituted by my own time and place, by the novel's recent critical history, and by my participation in the politics of gender criticism. In this I am allowing *Jude the Obscure* to transgress what we might conventionally understand as its contextual boundaries and encroach upon the space that I occupy. I also want to suggest a reading practice which can transgress category boundaries, those that separate a gendered phenomenology of reading from a textual dynamics of gender relations, and those that protect the abstract from the personal.

If these preliminary images of boundary, encroachment and occupation betray a man's concern with property and trespass, it is a concern that also surfaces in *Jude*'s critique of hermeneutics and masculinity, its drama of a man 'outside the gates of everything'

(p. 106). If thinking and writing about this novel has caused me to reflect upon the very activity of writing criticism as a man, it has done so exactly because, in the exchange between novel and criticism which I will be exploring here, I find myself interrogating *and* reproducing tropes that the novel interrogates and reproduces in its theme of the fortress of scholarship. Further, this image of an academic stronghold, while it suggests a latent antagonism not to men like Jude but to women in the academy, announces too a self-consciousness (on my part, and more broadly) about the place, or otherwise, of men in feminist criticism. Thus, I also mean to address this antagonism and defensiveness through the following reading of *Jude*.

When a male critic positions himself within a text and an inter-pretive structure, he also in one sense finds himself already there, in his choice of a congenial period, author, and approach, and in his emphases and exclusions. But in another sense he also finds himself absent, or only furtively present, there. For what exactly *is* 'literary masculinity'? How is it possible, without reverting to some sort of canon of manliness, to identify, let alone study, 'maleness', even in the texts of a powerful and visible male culture such as that in Victorian England – a maleness, that is to say, which remains dis-tinct from, though wholly determined by, patriarchy?[2] What form does the analysis of a 'narrative masculinity' take?

In the first place, I would argue that masculinities in realist narra-tives are not exclusively or even chiefly to be found in attributes of character, but in narrative forms themselves.[3] If the issue of manhood is less obvious in *Jude the Obscure* than in *The Mayor of Casterbridge*, for instance, then that is surely in part because of our conception of masculinity against an index of manliness, and hence wholly in terms of character. Against Henchard the manly, Jude the feeble may at first seem irrelevant to my subject, even though male heterosexuality and its discontents are as crucial to *Jude the Obscure* as female sexuality and its mysteries. Henchard is so obligingly the Lear of the earlier piece, commanded to tragic folly by his physic-ally, psychologically, and socially consuming manhood, that we forget how Jude, Arabella's 'tender-hearted fool' (p. 84), is likewise the victim of his gender, and we ignore other novelistic elements through which masculinities may be declared. If the Victorian novel is a patriarchal form – a form which reproduces and entrenches the power that men exercise over women – what does it mean to suggest that it is a masculine form? In his study of masculinity and reason, Victor Seidler questions the assumed continuity between a dominant language which 'encodes and validates a particular masculinist version of reality' and 'men's experience of the world'.[4] This is also one of the central problems entered upon in *Jude the Obscure*: what happens when a man's life does not coincide with the stories of men? Is it true to say that the specific cultural conformations of patriarchy always represent the experience of men in that culture? When Bathsheba Everdene claims (in *Far from the Madding Crowd* [ch. LI]) that it "'is difficult for a woman to define her feelings in language which is chiefly made by men to express theirs"', do we ask whether men could likewise be victimised by the language they make to express themselves and consolidate their ascendancy? As Seidler observes, if 'we live in a "man's world" it is not a world that has been built upon the needs or nourishment of men. Rather it is a social world of power and subordination in which men have been forced to compete if we want to benefit from our inherited masculinity.'[5] If the Victorian engagement (by men and women) with the language of men makes possible subversive feminine subtexts, is it imaginable that, again in writing by men or women, there is space for masculine subtexts, or is the act of writing and reading *man* only capable of complicity with, or at best unwitting acquiescence in, the linguistic institutionalisation of male power? *Jude the Obscure*, with its unrelenting anatomy of masculine narrative formulation, tests the possibilities of alternative narrative structures of masculinity in its exploration of the consequences of patriarchy's very *resistance* to such a project.

In what follows, therefore, I will refer not to masculinity but to historical masculinities.[6] To do otherwise would be to suppose that what is masculine were not 'continuously subject to a process of reinterpretation',[7] that it signifies always and everywhere the same qualities of reason, aggression, competition, ambition, insensitivity, and so forth. Arthur Brittan has named this form of essentialist thinking 'masculinism', and argued that it is an ideology which 'gives primacy to the belief that gender is not negotiable'.[8] Not only does such a belief dangerously foreclose the issue of sexual violence, it implicitly rejects the possibility of feminist intervention, constructs homosexuality as deviance, and forbids the possibility that men – who *are* the rapists, violent criminals, and gay-bashers – can change.

In what follows I want to argue that in the novels of Thomas Hardy, and especially in *Jude*, stable definitions of masculinity are undermined. It is a tentative gesture, to be sure, and one which is never fully conscious of its intentions. But because the challenge to a social order presided over by male heterosexual desire comes, throughout the nineteenth century, from women and not men – because it is the woman who comes into view as the paradigm of gender – it is not immediately obvious that these changes also effected changes to (that is, brought into focus) the social specificity of masculinity.

Hardy's novel takes as its starting point the question: how is it possible for men to alter the courses of lives already determined by class and character? I would like to take as my starting point a slightly different question: how is it possible for men to recognise, let alone alter, their masculinity? This raises further questions. What is the relationship between masculinity and male sexualities? How is a novel to structure the process of changing what a culture identifies as masculinity if the very notion of change in that culture is figured, validated, and preserved in terms of entrenched masculinities? How, that is to say, can a character like Jude Fawley adapt to the radical and menacing socio-sexual revolution instituted by the new woman – how can he change into a new man – with recourse only to myths of transformation that follow and elaborate rites of masculinity? Thus, Jude sets himself the ultimately hopeless task of improving his social standing via a set of rules of conduct appropriated by the Victorian middle classes and collected under the epithet *mobility*, but he is also set the painful challenge of transforming something that falls outside that realm of transformation: his own masculinity.

For the first task Jude must invoke and perpetuate a number of specific cultural traditions which reinforce his forlorn belief that advancement is the right of the man who labours hard: the working-class ideal of useful knowledge, which originated in the bourgeois philanthropy of earlier decades; biblical myths of exile and return, the test of faith, and the typologically informed belief in a new Jerusalem and a new man of learning presiding over a new enlightenment; and an Evangelical Christian 'vision of life as a perpetual struggle in which one's ability to resist temptation and overcome obstacles needed to be subject to constant scrutiny'.[9] Jude values these myths because of his misplaced faith in what it is possible for a man to become, and when Sue demands that he become a different sort of man, he is faced with a conversion for which there is no *mythos*. Jude conceives the necessity for this change as an urgent need to reform himself as a sexual being: it is his libido and not his masculinity that is so irksome. Significantly, though, the moment of his acceptance of Sue's demand is the moment that the narrative ceases to be able to tell, and can only proceed by visiting upon Jude a consumptive end. As Christine Brooke-Rose asks, why 'the remarkable occultation' of the two and a half year period of Jude's and Sue's happiness?[10] The only course open to the novel, I would argue in response, is that which reinstalls its hero within a readable model of transformation, in which even the utter failure to effect change is admitted not as a negation of transformative myths but as their regulation by an oppressive class, Sue's '"something external ... which says, 'You shan't!'"' (p. 357). The novel has, of course, throughout subjected these myths to the blackest scepticism – indeed, as I argue below, they are at odds with Hardy's project of exposing the limitations of Victorian fiction – but it is nevertheless compelled to retreat to them in the panic of the unnarratable. The dark irony that Jude's death recalls Christ's does not strike out the effect that the failure of one man may help to secure the redemption of others: Jude's defeat does nothing to cancel a man's right to reform himself. Even an ending utterly destitute of optimism, a complete debacle – and this is critical – is explicable in terms of myths of dispossession and loss (the story of Job), and the forsaking of the father (the passion of Christ), both of which are rendered the more tragic by the value of the cultural property that is sacrificed. Like Job's trial, Jude's is a successive taking-away of the things he most prizes. In such myths the substitution of a heroine, who has nothing so valuable to lose, is simply unimaginable. Sue cannot curse the moment a woman-child is born, because such an event is never, in terms of myths of cultural change, ever a moment for rejoicing.

The fate of Sue, then, which deliberately parallels that of Jude, is not legible in the same mythic terms. Jude's vagrancy is affixed, as it were, to a mythic homelessness which is an exclusively masculine discourse, and which guarantees a measure of meaning and coherence to his plight which is unavailable to Sue, as it has been to Tess Durbeyfield. The 'phases' of Tess's life are meant to be as inexorable, and, discursively, almost as unnegotiable, as the phases of the moon, but this part-structure is also a grim commentary on the implication of development and progress in her fate. Their titles emphasise how terribly the determinative may be compressed into a few terse words, as though her doom could be spoken into existence by a phrase: maiden no more, the consequence, the woman pays, fulfilment. Tess's response is likewise muted, a far cry from Jude's verbose and grandiose contextualisations of *his* decline. J. Hillis Miller, looking to parallel Henchard's mythological heritage and

Tess's, finds that hers is also part of a venerable cultural history, but it is a history which is exclusively of Hardy's invention: while 'Henchard's life repeats the experiences of Cain, Job, Saul, or Lear', Miller writes, 'Tess is one of a long line of similar victims of the Immanent Will stretching before or after her own life.'[11] In the same way, Jude's tormented rambling is recuperated by Job, but Sue's is explicable only in terms of polarities of hysteria and frigidity, radicalism and conventionality. The loosening of a woman from conventions (and plots) of marriage, however, loosens her altogether, and she scrambles for the safety of the formalities of marriage and home she so abhors. Sue's dispossession and Jude's, then, are represented as quite different states of being, with quite different consequences, and urging quite different narrative solutions.

Hardy proposes for Jude a number of such solutions, none of which is finally satisfactory. If Jude struggles from town to town, displacing, or being displaced by, one master narrative after another, then his author is no less troubled by gender in his effort to shape his hero's peregrinations into a meaningful design. The ideal of realist narrative development, which is analogous to the myths of change the novel is ambivalently endorsing on other levels (in the symbolic narratives to which Jude turns, as I argue above), is clearly far from satisfactory. *Jude* is, we are always reminded, Hardy's last word on the novel. As Terry Eagleton argues, it stands as an 'imaginative resolution' of a problem about 'the limits of art',[12] and it is certainly deeply concerned with what the novel could not be or do. Indeed, it is the very anti-type of the Victorian fictions to which it adverts in its thematic emphases and narrative organisation. *Jude* abandons as untrue – and this is the source of its characters' misery – each of several versions of the book of life typically invoked by Victorian fiction. This abandonment takes the form of a gradual process of disillusionment and disavowal which lends the plot its unremitting pathos. Like its hero, the novel invokes and finds untenable precisely those narratives which seek to reproduce most closely the shape of human existence: the spiritual journey; the story of individual vocation and education; the marriage plot. Its organisation into curiously self-contained parts, a sort of episodic form writ large, follows the arrangement of Jude's life into distinct phases, each of which is overseen by an informing myth or masterplot. Thus, the ideal of Christminster overlaps with and is then succeeded by the ideal of manual labour, which gives way to the governing idea of the devotional life, and so on until the final trope of sacrifice is invoked by Jude to impose form and meaning upon his otherwise totally meaningless end. Few novels so powerfully evoke in their structure the tension of discontinuity against a hankering after coherence and sequence. Well may Phillotson moan about the quiet life.

Jude is an ironic *Pilgrim's Progress*, which 'makes grisly fun of its predecessors';[13] in its often tiresome wordiness and its unclear polemic it is almost a negation of the fiction of ideas and the novel of earnest discussion; it represents an interrogation of the role the novel plays in reform; and it is a bitter addendum to the new-woman fiction of the 1880s and 90s. But it is also more. As Penny Boumelha has argued,[14] it is a mutation of the narrative formulation that dominated European culture during this century and which encodes the supremacy in England of male middle-class aspiration: the *Bildungsroman* and its formal cognates – novels of youth and apprenticeship, self-culture and social accommodation. Of most interest to my reading of the novel is the role of the *Bildungsroman* in formulating a particular ideology of middle class masculinity. The form, which crossed from Germany into France and England after the publication of Goethe's *Wilhelm Meisters Lehrjahre* in 1795, developed culturally specific variants in each country, bringing into question the aptness of the single covering term.[15] However, what *is* common to them – and even, or especially, to those like *Jane Eyre* which instate a woman in the hero-apprentice's place – is that they plot a middle-class man's labour to prove himself. That is to say, they are stories of a boy's initiation into manhood, and they are rituals of masculine identity. The final proof of the male self is a sort of assiduous accumulation of the products of this identity: material wealth, class integration, education, family. Yet, as Franco Moretti has asserted of the English *Bildungsroman*, its 'insipid' middle-class heroes – innocent, sincere, orthodox – need only to prove the self that they have always shared with the dominant class to which they belong, and it is duly restored to them as their rightful inheritance. When David Copperfield speculates whether he will turn out to be the hero of his own life, he is questioning whether he can prove himself to be what he indubitably already is. In this, the conflict between self-determination and socialisation is never internalised in the hero, as it is in the Continental *Bildungsroman*, but is played out between already socially valorised heroes, and the monsters and villains that impose transgression from beyond. Thus, the ceremony of proof is a kind of initiation that does *not* require transformation. Moretti excludes all forms of becoming from the English novel, seeing their narratives as merely protracted processes of inheritance. The English middle classes, he avers, found narrativity threatening because of its potential lawlessness, and thus they instituted only narratives in which the *fabula* invariably triumphed over a phantom *sjuzet*, as a kind of triumph of 'the culture of justice'.[16] The primacy of democratic process over revolutionary impetus in English bourgeois society is preoccupied, in this argument, with restoring narrative events to order, establishing, as in a trial, the true sequence. The Victorians were perhaps the first real consumers of narrative, and the ascendancy of part-publication indicates the significance to them of instituting a ritual drama of becoming which was, in fact, merely the rehearsal of sedition through the prolongation of narrative suspense. The span of youth is a dangerous and unwished-for interlude between childhood and the arrival at a point at which one is recognised not for what one has become but for what one has always been.

The irony of *Jude*'s revision of the English *Bildungsroman* lies in its renovation in the form of a working-class hero of this 'insipid protagonist' of the middle-class novel. For Jude also becomes only what he has always been, a poor rural artisan. Framed as a *Bildungsroman* ('the concept of *Bildung*,' as Jeffrey Sammons points out, 'is intensely bourgeois'[17]), *Jude* supplies a commentary on the ideological bias of the notion of individual change operating within societal stability, Moretti's balancing equation of the terms *self-determination* and *socialisation*.[18] The fundamental lie that constitutes the formulation of the Victorian novel of self-development is, as Boumelha has shown, the lie of class mobility.[19] When a working man strives to better himself, in the tradition of Victorian labour movements such as the Society for the Diffusion of Useful Knowledge, he strives upward and out of his own class. But if Moretti is correct in his assessment of the English *Bildungsroman*, Jude, as a working-class incarnation of David and Pip, gets what he deserves: work. *Jude the Obscure* also recalls a specific tradition of Victorian working-class autobiography, again one virtually exclusively male. Henry Broadhurst's *The Story of his Life from Stonemason's Bench to Treasury Bench. Told by Himself* (1901), and William Lovett's *Life and Struggles of William Lovett in Pursuit of Bread, Knowledge and Freedom* (1876), among hundreds of others, explore, as David Vincent has shown, the relationships between manual labour, book knowledge, and independence which provided the prototype of the new working man – the self-educated artisan.[20]

Mythologised manhood, then, informs the structuring of novelistic plots across class, a structuring which many critics agree is under review in *Jude*. I want now to indicate how masculinity also enters the critique of that process. Peter Brooks, in *Reading for the Plot: Design and Intention in Narrative* (1984), apparently unconcerned about the implications for sexual difference of a thesis in which the primacy of masculine sexuality is wholly determinative of plot, sets out a detailed 'textual erotics'.[21] The equation of narrative desire and psycho-dynamics (Brooks writes that 'life in the text of the modern is nearly a thermo-dynamic process; plot is, most aptly, a steam engine'[22]) posits a desiring-interpreting subject that is a man. Plot is driven by an energy which simultaneously imposes sequence through a desire for possession and mastery. This model of narrative impetus and order is ahistorical, in spite of Brooks's claim to an explanation of modernity, and it would be easy to endorse its evasion of history by describing it simply as masculine and leaving the matter there. What is at issue, however, is once again precisely the historical and heterosexual specificity of the masculinity he engages. Against the historicist notion that masculinities are being constantly revised and redefined, however imperceptibly, Brooks sets the established masterplots of Western man – sacred plots, and plots of cultural initiation, inheritance, loss, and death – authoritative stories of beginnings, middles and endings, but more: authoritative accounts of *acts* of beginning, continuance, and ending. More telling still, Brooks installs an ahistorical interpreter:

> If plots seem frequently to be about investments of desire and the effort to bind and master intensive levels of energy, this corresponds on the one hand to narratives thematically oriented toward ambition, possession, mastery of the erotic object and of the world, and on the other hand to a certain experience of reading narrative, itself a process of reaching for possession and mastery.[23]

In *Jude the Obscure* anxieties about interpretive mastery and male heterosexual desire converge in the figure of the hero and his struggle against the academy. Critical accounts of *Jude the Obscure*, the numberless acts of interpretation consequent upon Jude's ruin (including this one), stand in special relation to the text: they serve as a corrective and a recompense for Jude himself, whose tragedy, after all, is pre-eminently one of incoherence. Disillusionment, consistently an ironical agent of change in the novel, is principally exegetic disillusionment. Jude moves 'purblind' from one interpretive authority to the next, but the coherent plot of his decline can be explained again and again within different 'authoritative' interpretive systems. The irony, that systems of interpretation both destroy Jude (in the text) and reconstitute him (in aftertexts), is important here. Ramón Saldívar, in an astute analysis of Jude's tragic delusions, comments that Hardy's hero is 'beguiled by his desire for order'. Jude suffers, Saldívar writes, because 'for his own sporadically controlled, partially understood world, he substitutes the image of a unified, stable, and understandable one'.[24] But critics of the novel, Tetuphenays all, finally come to stand in for the Christminster that walls itself in against all but its own internally authorised incoherence, and that recognises how Jude would have 'a much better chance of success in life' by submitting to the tyranny of their separate spheres (p. 137). The Master of Biblioll casts his advice in terms which suggest Jude might as well be a woman, and so, in keeping with the rest of the book, intrudes questions of gender into questions of class. Paradoxically, though, the critical act as Brooks explains it must also inevitably originate in the critic reproducing Jude's debilitating desire. Again, it is Jude's very failure, his repeated failure, that continually reinstates desire as the source of the novel's impetus and the energy that it can derive, as I suggested above, from the vast cultural resources of masculine transformative myths.[25] That endlessly thwarted desire finds its clearest expression in the matter of Jude's libido.

Interpretive mastery, denied Jude because of his class, is allied to the sexual mastery – both in the sense of being a husband and in the sense of being master of his own sexual drives – which Jude is also denied by what Hardy conceives as a tragic flaw in his character. Like Henchard, Jude is a victim of his masculinity. Surely, though, Hardy, in creating a man who, as Irving Howe puts it, is 'racked by drives he cannot control, drives he barely understands',[26] signals the difficulty of representing in the same terms the sexualities of *both* women and men in the fiction of the period. Women in Hardy are explicable (and inexplicable) as sexual beings because they represent the problem of their own representation: that is, they are part of a process on Hardy's part and on the part of the culture as a whole through which men make sense of women and (coercively) make women legible to themselves. George Wotton goes so far as to claim that 'there is no other writing in English which elaborates a more profound contemplation of women than Hardy's'.[27] Gender comes into focus as *the* subject of the novel, but whether it does so equally transparently in relation to masculinity is another question. Though Jude complains that men's sexual identities are equally the products of socialisation, it is very noticeable that male sexuality is frequently explained in the novel in terms of physiology. Against the sexual complexity of the 'lovely conundrum' (p. 156), against Sue's inconsistency and illegibility, we are offered the all-too consistent, all-too legible, drives of Jude the sexual male. Yet beneath this explanation is the question of the direct effect upon men of feminist campaigns for women's rights and subsequent changes to laws relating to divorce and the property of married women. The figure of the man challenged by a strong wife is drawn in the popular imagination as the harridan and the hen-pecked husband – most often a difference of physical constitution – and the first English productions of Ibsen's *A Doll's House*, for instance, only served to accentuate the caricature. Numerous drawings and parodies of 'Ibsenity' in *Punch* in 1891 show the burlesque of the harrowed man hounded and abandoned by the strong woman. In Hardy, and particularly in those novels written after *The Mayor of Casterbridge* – *The Woodlanders*, *Tess of the d'Urbervilles*, and *Jude the Obscure* – legislative reform invites a concomitant shift in the social constitution of the masculine, informs the endemic vacillations and inconsistencies of men in their relationships with women, and suggests a potentiality for cultural, and more specifically narrative, revision. Yet Hardy's is a most frangible revisionism, indeed is scarcely revisionist at all, because, as I suggested earlier, the new man created by the new woman simply had no stories of his own.

I have already indicated how in *Jude the Obscure* fiction is silenced by this redefinition of masculinity which must itself then be silenced in order to reanimate and successfully conclude proceedings. I want to take this hypothesis further and suggest, following what I have just been arguing, that in this novel Hardy was attempting to represent the social forces that construct sexual difference, but only had clear imaginative access to the processes which were actively and visibly intervening in and contesting the redefinition of femininity. What I mean by this – and *Jude the Obscure*, with its close treatment of the woman question, is especially eloquent here – is precisely that man is not an obvious question, for Victorian culture or, for that matter, for either Moretti or Brooks. Desire and plot, progress and history, are all agents of a supreme desiring, plotting, historically advancing subject that is nevertheless rendered invisible as a gendered subject by its monolithic hegemony. For

Brooks, masculine desire goes without saying: it is beyond question. The masculinity that is central to *The Mayor of Casterbridge*, the story of the unmanning of a man of character,[28] is counterpointed by the undoing of Hardy's pure woman Tess; and this pair, I would argue, are in turn balanced by *Jude*'s double exploration of a man and a woman. But it is femininity in the novel that is seen as the more expressive, the shifting sign of the modern: Sue is the woman who does (though, now she is more often characterised as the woman who doesn't); Jude is simply the man who wants to but can't.[29] In the same way, and this is germane to the crossovers between this essay and *Jude*, 'it is feminism ... that has put the critical study of men and masculinities on to the agenda'.[30] It needs to be stressed again that I can only write about men in the way I am doing because of the context feminism has provided for that discussion. As Jude is obscured by his very masculinity, so masculinity in the novel (and in my criticism) is present only in the light of its new woman.

If the incomprehensibility of women is necessary for their reconfiguration, this suggests one reason why the new man has such trouble surfacing. Jude is so powerfully constituted as the novel's master subject by the primacy of his desire and the primacy of narrative desire – both masculine – that the question of his own comprehensibility or otherwise is itself incomprehensible. The illegibility which, as Goode puts it, 'constitutes the novel's effect'[31] is offered as Sue, and Sue exists as an element in Jude's interpretive education. One difficulty I have with Goode's argument is that it does not ask *why* we cannot conceive of Jude himself as an unreadable element in a world otherwise dominated by the unreadable. Hardy organises the materials of Jude's tragedy so exclusively through the consciousness of his hero, that Jude himself is simply unavailable to the incertitude he witnesses, and is so preserved as a relic of a unified subject deserted by a unified voice. Certainly, as Goode writes, 'we don't ever ask what is happening to Sue; because it is rather a question of Sue happening to Jude'.[32] Conversely, though, when the novel 'takes reality apart'[33] it does so before Jude's eyes as it were, while he remains with his desire intact. Hardy dismantles the representational novel, and while Jude is victimised by this dismantling, he is not dismantled by it.

Like Jude himself, therefore, *Jude the Obscure* is so tirelessly intent on interrogating the feminine psyche (a defensive and dogged masculine enterprise itself) that the context created by feminism for a speculative masculinity goes unnoticed. Womanhood is its central mystery and manhood, it seems, its central fact. Frustration is Jude's lot as an intellectually ambitious labourer, certainly, but it is also his biological destiny. The whole question of 'manhood' only inevitably reminds us of the penis that it euphemistically represents. Hardy wrote that 'the best tragedy – highest tragedy in short – is that of the WORTHY encompassed by the INEVITABLE',[34] and Jude's sexual inheritance is the agent of tragedy because it is unchangeable and asocial. Thus, when Jude gets smacked on the ear by his animal manhood, in the form of a pig's pizzle, it literally rouses him from his daydream of intellectual advancement and social eminence, where 'he had become entirely lost to his bodily situation' (p. 43). Even the images of his attraction to Arabella are masculine: the 'predestinate Jude' (p. 64), 'in commonplace obedience from conjunctive orders from headquarters' (p. 59), is compelled by an 'arm of extraordinary muscular power' (p. 64). Thus, the chiselled pointing hand that had 'embodied his aspirations' thither in Christminster (p. 94) becomes in this context ironically phallic, and suggests that we might read *Jude*'s project ironically almost from the start. The very regularity with which Jude's sexuality points him towards Arabella undermines his loftily cerebral ambition with what is, in the end, the sublimation of an altogether different kind of impulse. So it is that Arabella comes to represent a debasement of this intersection of Jude's sexuality and ambition, a debasement that is consistently overwritten by an authorised and elevated desire, a desire that can legitimately be embodied as both sexual and intellectual, in Sue. Though Jude's relationship with Sue must be kept from public view, then, his relationship with Arabella he must keep almost out his *own* sight. The interpretation of the hand of fate as a pointing penis (later modestly covered), is, like Arabella herself, suggested only to be rejected.

Jude is betrayed into obscurity, then, not only by language but by his body. Yet abstraction, framed as the renunciation of the body, also comes to taunt his repressed instinctual life. The idea of Jude's infatuation with Christminster curiously conflates the bodily activities of physical work and his studies, which are also described consistently in terms of labour. Though Jude sways between 'the intellectual and emulative life' and 'the ecclesiastical and altruistic life' (p. 148), it is really only ever the material and subsisting life that he attains. But the fraternity of scholarship causes him to imagine his lonely studies as part of a tradition of collective labour in which he works as a fellow artisan. Jude also thinks of learning as his inheritance (the addressees of Jude's invocations and the sources of his quotations are his forefathers), and that Christminster is both God the father and mother to his Christ: "'Yes, Christminster shall be my Alma Mater; and I'll be her beloved son, in whom she shall be well pleased'" (p. 58). Hardy omits from *Jude* the explicit homo-eroticism which had marked the Henchard–Farfrae liaison, but in the plot's identification of Jude's sexual passion and his passion for Christminster, we can see a confusion of patrimony and homosocial desire. In Jude's cross-dressing of Sue, likewise, we are offered an image of their 'two-in-oneness' (p. 357), a version of the manly love so notorious in Victorian literature. Sue's relationship with the undergraduate, "'like two men almost'" (p. 168), is revisited upon Jude (who is also likened to Phillotson), and he does attain his ideal of a community of like-minded men, only with a woman – "'O my comrade'" (p. 357). Thus, Jude's careful discrimination of the life of the mind (fellowship with men) and the body (spiritual and sexual communion with a woman), a regime under which he keeps distinct that which purifies and that which defiles him, is defeated from the start. Likewise, the persistent characterisation of Sue as a bodiless ideal, an incarnation of the incorporeal, an embodiment of the abstraction so treacherous to Jude – like 'the shabby trick played him by the dead languages' (p. 51) – commits her and 'her liquid, untranslatable eyes' (p. 109) bodily, as it were, to Jude's frustrated enterprise of translation.

What am I to conclude from all this? The title of the Sixth Phase of *Tess of the d'Urbervilles* intimates what (little) promise there is for change in the men in that book. 'The Convert' of the piece is Angel Clare.[35] He flees to Brazil 'to escape from his past existence' (ch. VI), and there is befriended by a 'large-minded' stranger, 'also an Englishman', but with a cosmopolitan mind to which 'such deviations from the social norm [as Tess's], so immense to domesticity, were no more than are the irregularities of vale and mountain-chain to the whole terrestrial curve'. The words of this stranger inspire in Angel a dramatic and complete change of mind, but it is a change which must be enacted outside the bounds of England, discovered like an ark in the South American hinterland. The exoticism of this transformation is necessary because Angel's parochialism is precisely the parochialism of domesticity, that is to say, the parochialism of a predominantly domestic form, the Victorian novel. This brief episode eloquently points up the difficulties that are at the heart of *Jude the Obscure*'s struggle to shape within this same narrative form the sexual *new*. *Jude*, after all, is structured around a number of futile attempts to avert, or subvert, the pressure of parochialism.[36]

John Goode has remarked of *Jude the Obscure* that 'the textual allegiances of this novel are apocryphal',[37] but the relationship it maintains between apocryphal and cardinal texts is surely uneasy. Certainly, when Sue provokes Jude with her confession of cutting up and rearranging into chronological order the books of the New Testament, it reminds us of her heretical temperament but also of her own and Jude's slavish conformity to sequence, a slavishness that recalls Moretti's formulation of English bourgeois narrative. As Robert Alter notes, the word *Bible* derives from the Greek *ta biblia*, 'the books',[38] and that, in one sense, describes *Jude* precisely: its arrangement into parts is like a collection of separate volumes, each with its new beginning. Jude, too, finally tears his books apart to burn them, and even, when the household goods are sold for the last time, Sue and Jude sit above and listen to tales of their past selves randomly passed around the gathering, as though they are attending an auction of their own histories, sold not as a seamless story but as narrative lots. This bazaar of identity recalls all too well the schizophrenia of gender criticism, attempting to reclaim the gendered identity of the critic in the midst of what seems to be a *donnée* disavowal of the unified subject. But, as *Jude* tries to say, feminism is surely the site both of the dissembling and the reclamation of identities which are fixed, and threaten again and again to be re-fixed, by the power relations of gender.

More important than Jude's failure, then, is the novel's failure to accommodate stories of men seamlessly to the life of one man. Gone is Brooks's conception of a possessive, mastering agent of plot, and gone too is Moretti's final triumphant *fabula*. *Jude* is so overburdened with assorted plots of doomed self-education and social improvement – plots of a man's transformation – that it finally succeeds, ironically enough, in making 'man' a question: it opens itself to a narrativity that is dangerous, lawless, unresolved. *Jude the Obscure* does manage to subvert the sign of masculinity because it invokes a space, however confined and however obscured, in which to imagine other stories about men, and hence to imagine other men. But it also revokes that space in its persistent refusal of a secure lodging. Through its hermeneutic pessimism and its doomed interpreter-hero, it reclaims the flaws that separate houses, narrative incidents, and books and readers, flaws through which other meanings can issue; and finally it makes present for critique the masculinities that inform world, text, and critic.

NOTES

[This essay was specially commissioned for this collection, but Tim Dolin has also published *Mistress of the House* (London, 1997), on the relationship between Victorian fiction, law, and social change, and edited several of Hardy's novels for Penguin Classics.

Ranging across feminist criticism, masculinity studies and genre criticism, Dolin explores the conventions of narrated masculinity, in a kind of companion-piece to the feminist analyses represented elsewhere in this collection. He identifies a range of narrative forms identified specifically with the construction of maleness; chief, but by no means exclusive, among them is the *Bildungsroman*, or novel of becoming, that dominated nineteenth-century European narrative.

Dolin's reading of *Jude* is a significant contribution in its demonstration that criticism focused on masculinity does not need to be masculinist-triumphalist; by exploring ideological constructions of gender and their determinations upon the possibilities of narrative form, Dolin is able to place Jude once more at the centre of the novel that bears his name without in the process marginalising the novel's radicalism.

Quotations from *Jude the Obscure* in this essay are from the paperback New Wessex edition of his novel, ed. P. N. Furbank (London, 1974). References to others of Hardy's works are designated by Roman chapter or book numbers. Ed.]

1. Mary Jacobus, *Reading Woman: Essays in Feminist Criticism* (London, 1987), p. 67.

2. For examples of this type of reading, see George J. Worth, 'Of Muscles and Manliness: Some Reflections on Thomas Hughes', in *Victorian Literature and Society: Essays Presented to Richard D. Altick*, ed. James R. Kincaid and Albert J. Kuhn (Cleveland, OH, 1984), pp. 300–14, and *Manliness and Morality: Middle-Class Masculinity in Britain and America, 1800–1940*, ed. J. A. Mangan and James Walvin (Manchester, 1987).

3. I mean by this that a novel's ideologies of masculinity are not borne by the *men* in fiction but by novels' hierarchies of discourse. In this, as in my general approach to Hardy's fiction (indeed, to all fiction), I acknowledge Penny Boumelha's *Thomas Hardy and Women: Sexual Ideology and Narrative Form* (Brighton, 1982). Thus, p. 6: 'The text does not "express"ideology; rather, it produces, re-produces and transforms elements of ideology into its own literary effects. The "history"of the text is not a reflection or a doubling of real history, but it represents an ideologically constituted experience of real history. In this will consist

the ideological project of the work (which may or may not have some correspondence with the views and intentions of its writer).'

4. Victor Seidler, *Rediscovering Masculinity: Reason, Language and Sexuality* (London and New York, 1989), p. 8.

5. Ibid., p. 21.

6. See Michael Roper and John Tosh, 'Historians and the Politics of Masculinity', in *Manful Assertions: Masculinities in Britain Since 1800* (London and New York, 1991), pp. 1–24.

7. Arthur Brittan, *Masculinity and Power* (Oxford, 1989), p. 1.

8. Ibid., p. 4.

9. Stefan Collini, *Public Moralists: Political Thought and Intellectual Life in Britain 1850–1930* (Oxford, 1991), p. 105.

10. Christine Brooke-Rose, 'Ill Wit and Sick Tragedy: *Jude the Obscure*', in *Alternative Hardy*, ed. Lance St John Butler (London, 1989), pp. 36–7. [Reprinted in this volume – see pp. 122–44. Ed.]

11. J. Hillis Miller, *Thomas Hardy: Distance and Desire* (Cambridge, MA, 1970), p. xi.

12. Terry Eagleton, 'Introduction', *Jude the Obscure*, ed. P. N. Furbank (London, 1974), p. 10.

13. Barry Qualls, *The Secular Pilgrims of Victorian Fiction: The Novel as Book of Life* (Cambridge, 1982), p. 193. See also Vincent Newey, 'The Disinherited Pilgrim: *Jude the Obscure* and *The Pilgrim's Progress*', *Durham University Journal*, 80: 1 (1987), 59–61.

14. 'It is in *Jude the Obscure* that Hardy most directly confronts [the *Bildungsroman*] and its ideological underpinnings': Penny Boumelha, '"A Complicated Position for a Woman": *The Hand of Ethelberta*', in *The Sense of Sex: Feminist Perspectives on Hardy*, ed. Margaret Higonnet (Urbana and Chicago, 1993), p. 243.

15. This problem is discussed exhaustively in James N. Hardin, *Reflection and Action: Essays on the* Bildungsroman (Columbia, OH, 1991).

16. Franco Moretti, *The Way of the World: The* Bildungsroman *in European Culture* (London, 1987), especially pp. 207–11.

17. Jeffrey Sammons, 'The *Bildungsroman* for Nonspecialists: An Attempt at a Clarification', in James N. Hardin, *Reflection and Action: Essays on the* Bildungsroman (Columbia, OH, 1991), p. 42.

18. Moretti explores this equation variously as adultery and marriage, Europe and England, narrativity and its suppression, transgressive mobility (change) and final stable identity, freedom and happiness, youth and maturity, and metamorphosis and security.

19. Penny Boumelha, '"A Complicated Position for a Woman": *The Hand of Ethelberta*', in *The Sense of Sex: Feminist Perspectives on Hardy*, ed. Margaret Higonnet (Urbana and Chicago, 1993), pp. 242–4.

20. David Vincent in *Bread, Knowledge, and Freedom: A Study of Nineteenth-Century Working Class Autobiography* (London, 1981), studies 144 autobiographies. See also Keith McClelland, 'Masculinity and the "Representative Artisan" in Britain, 1850–80', in Michael Roper and John Tosh, *Manful Assertions: Masculinities in Britain Since 1800* (London and New York, 1991), pp. 74–91.

21. Peter Brooks, *Reading for the Plot: Design and Intention in Narrative* (New York, 1984), p. 37.

22. Ibid., p. 44. Susan Winnett argues that 'Brooks's articulation of what are ultimately the oedipal dynamics that structure and determine traditional fictional narratives and psychoanalytic paradigms is brilliant ... [but] it seems clear that a narratology based on the oedipal model would have to be profoundly and vulnerably male in its assumptions about what constitutes pleasure and, more insidiously, what this pleasure looks like': 'Coming Unstrung: Women, Men, Narrative, and Principles of Pleasure', *PMLA*, 105 (1990), 506.

23. Peter Brooks, *Reading for the Plot: Design and Intention in Narrative* (New York, 1984), p. 143.

24. Ramón Saldívar, *Figural Language in the Novel: The Flowers of Speech From Cervantes to Joyce* (Princeton, NJ, 1984), p. 160.

25. Christine Brooke-Rose argues that 'what matters to Hardy is desire (male), while marriage is death ... desire is by definition for something absent. The equally obvious fact that it is sometimes not so, that some rare people have the ludic "art" of love, another form of "knowledge", does not interest Hardy, or indeed most novelists, since narrative is based on desire, yet for this of all relationships, where so much depends on that mysterious quality called companionship (which is what Sue wanted), the imaginative effort should have been made', 'Ill Wit and Sick Tragedy: *Jude the Obscure*', in *Alternative Hardy*, ed. Lance St John Butler (London, 1989), pp. 37–8.

26. Irving Howe, *Thomas Hardy* (New York, 1967), p. 141.

27. George Wotton, *Thomas Hardy: Towards a Materialist Criticism* (Totowa, NJ, 1985), p. 122.

28. See Elaine Showalter, 'The Unmanning of the Mayor of Casterbridge', in *Critical Approaches to the Fiction of Thomas Hardy*, ed. Dale Kramer (London, 1979; reprinted in *Thomas Hardy's* The Mayor of Casterbridge, ed. Harold Bloom, Modern Critical Interpretations (New York, 1988), pp. 53–68.

29. The new woman provoked as much misogynistic as pro-feminist fiction. Indeed, Sue recalls only too well the motif of the killer woman: see Fraser Harrison, *The Dark Angel: Aspects of Victorian Sexuality* (New York, 1978), ch. 7 and especially pp. 130–3. Of course, the climate of socio-sexual change in the era of the New Woman appalled a great many men. It could be argued that, during the period in which *Jude* appears, masculinity is in fact more than ever deeply entrenched as asocial. The key is precisely the conspicuousness of that entrenchment in masculinities of all classes. The period in which the situation of women in England changed most publicly – let us say the years between 1857 (Matrimonial Causes Act) and 1928 (Women's Suffrage) – was also a period in which separatist masculine ideologies and groups flourished. One has only to recall the public school and the Boy's Own Paper; the working man and the empire man; the Boy Scouts and the Polar explorers, the Salvation Army and the MCC and the Great War; Sherlock Holmes and James Barrie and Rudyard Kipling and Rider Haggard and Lawrence of Arabia; but also Richard Jefferies, Henry Williamson, Wyndham Lewis, Ezra Pound, and so on and on. The decade from the mid-eighties to the mid-nineties, moreover, introduced Londoners not only to Jude Fawley, but to Dr Jekyll and Mr Hyde, Svengali, Jack the Ripper, Ayesha, and Count Dracula.

30. David H. J. Morgan, *Discovering Men* (London and New York, 1992), p. 2.

31. John Goode, 'Sue Bridehead and the New Woman', in *Women Writing and Writing About Women*, ed. Mary Jacobus (London, 1979), p. 108.

32. Ibid., p. 104.

33. Ibid., p. 100.

34. Thomas Hardy (with Florence Hardy), *The Life and Work of Thomas Hardy*, ed. Michael Millgate (London, 1984), p. 265.

35. 'The Convert' suggests manifold contexts of male conversion in Victorian fiction, in the religio-melodramatic tradition of the penitent villain, and the tradition – also invoked in Alec – of the phoney reform of the rake.

36. So too the reformed parochialism of the new man in feminist criticism takes something from the image of the convert, and from the cosmopolitanism of the stranger in the strange land. However, it is conspicuously the man on whom the privilege of a new insight is bestowed, a privilege again predicated upon Angel's mobility.

37. John Goode, *Thomas Hardy: The Offensive Truth* (Oxford, 1988), p. 143.

38. *The Literary guide to the Bible*, ed. Robert Alter and Frank Kermode (Cambridge, MA, 1987), p. 11.

Further Reading

The volume of critical and scholarly writing on Hardy, and on *Jude the Obscure*, is quite enormous. I have not attempted here to give a comprehensive analysis. Rather, I have suggested some starting-points in biography and editions, and then given references that will enable the reader to follow up particular areas of interest arising from the essays and Introduction in this volume. Not all are cited as examples of the best criticism to be found. I have not included the works from which the essays reprinted above are drawn, nor all works cited in my Introduction. I repeat from there the comment that works of criticism do not fall neatly into distinct boxes, and that some of the recommended further reading could easily be included in more than one section. All entries are listed in order of the date of publication within each category.

THOMAS HARDY

Those wanting to know more about Thomas Hardy and his career as a novelist could well begin with the classic biography by Michael Millgate, *Thomas Hardy: A Biography* (Oxford: Oxford University Press, 1982). Also interesting and readable is Martin Seymour-Smith, *Hardy* (New York: St Martin's Press, 1994).

The Literary Notebooks of Thomas Hardy have been very well edited by Lennart A. Björk (2 vols, London and Basingstoke: Macmillan, 1985), and Patricia Gallivan has explored the notebook entries during the period of composition of *Jude the Obscure*, in her essay 'Science and Art in *Jude the Obscure*', in *The Novels of Thomas Hardy*, ed. Anne Smith (London: Vision Press, 1979), pp. 126–44. Hardy's *Collected Letters*, ed. Richard Little Purdy and Michael Millgate (7 vols, Oxford: Clarendon Press, 1978–98) are not as revealing as some researchers might hope.

Thomas Hardy's Personal Writings: Prefaces, Literary Opinions, Reminiscences, ed. Harold Orel (London: Macmillan, 1967), brings together a number of Hardy's essays and prefaces.

THE TEXT AND COMPOSITION OF *JUDE THE OBSCURE*

There is no standard modern edition of *Jude the Obscure*. Hardy's own Wessex edition (London, 1912–31) remains a commonly used standard text. Among notable modern editions, either for the editorial content or for their introductions, are:

Jude the Obscure, with an Afterword by A. Alvarez (New York: New American Library, 1961).
——, ed. with an Introduction by I. Howe, Riverside Edition (Boston: Houghton Miflin, 1965).
——, Introduction by Terry Eagleton, with notes by P. N. Furbank, New Wessex Edition (London: Macmillan, 1975).
——, ed. by Norman Page, Norton Critical Edition (New York: Norton, 1978).
——, ed. with an Introduction by Patricia Ingham, The World's Classics (Oxford: Oxford University Press, 1985).

On the composition and publication of *Jude the Obscure*, the following may be useful:

Robert C. Slack, 'The Text of Hardy's *Jude the Obscure*', *Nineteenth-Century Fiction*, 11 (1957), 261–75.
Patricia Ingham, 'The Evolution of *Jude the Obscure*', *Review of English Studies*, 27 (1976), 27–37, 159–69.
Arlene M. Jackson, *Illustration and the Novels of Thomas Hardy* (London: Macmillan, 1982).
James M. Harding, 'The Signification of Arabella's Missile: Feminine Sexuality, Masculine Anxiety and Revision in *Jude the Obscure*', *Journal of Narrative Technique*, 26 (1996), 85–111.
Simon Gatrell, *Hardy, the Creator: A Textual Biography* (Oxford: Clarendon Press, 1998).

EARLY RESPONSES

There have been a number of useful collections of early reviews and responses to Hardy's writing. R. G. Cox (ed.), *Thomas Hardy: The Critical Heritage* (London: Routledge and Kegan Paul, 1970) is an accessible collection, while *Thomas Hardy: Critical Assessments*, ed. Graham Clarke (4 vols, Mountfield, Sussex: Helm Information, 1993) is more comprehensive. Among the most interesting early responses are:

Havelock Ellis, 'Concerning *Jude the Obscure*', *Savoy*, 6 (October 1896), 35–49; reprinted as *Concerning Jude the Obscure* (London: Ulysses Bookshop, 1931).
D. H. Lawrence, 'Study of Thomas Hardy', in *Phoenix: The Posthumous Papers of D. H. Lawrence*, ed. Edward D. McDonald (London: Heinemann, 1936, reprinted 1961), pp. 398–516.

GENERAL CRITICISM

Most of the critical studies listed here are included as very good examples of criticism that is not based on any of the theoretical starting-points or areas of concern categorised below. For this reason, most – though not all – predate the 'theoretical turn' of the 1980s. Also included here are collections of essays that may range across a wide variety of critical perspectives.

Albert J. Guerard, *Thomas Hardy: The Novels and Stories* (Cambridge, MA: Harvard University Press, 1949). An influential early account of Hardy as 'anti-realist'.

Roy Morrell, *Thomas Hardy: The Will and The Way* (Kuala Lumpur: University of Malaysia Press, 1965). This study was important in shifting critical attention away from notions of fate and pessimism, by its focus on an existentialist understanding of the characters' choices.

J. Hillis Miller, *Thomas Hardy: Distance and Desire* (Cambridge, MA: Harvard University Press, 1970). One of the very best of the older critical studies, influenced by phenomenology, and giving a persuasive account of the roles of observation and distance in the novels.

Penelope Vigar, *The Novels of Thomas Hardy: Illusion and Reality* (London: University of London: Athlone Press, 1974). A lively and acute discussion of a persistent thematic contrast in Hardy's writing.

John Bayley, *An Essay on Hardy* (Cambridge: Cambridge University Press, 1978). A brilliant, meditative critical overview, including (on pp. 191–218) a particularly good discussion of Hardy's use of Shelleyan themes and allusions.

J. B. Bullen, *The Expressive Eye: Fiction and Perception in the Work of Thomas Hardy* (Oxford: Oxford University Press, 1986). Detailed and interesting account of Hardy's strong visual orientation and his allusions to the visual arts.

Harold Bloom (ed.), *Thomas Hardy's* Jude the Obscure: *Modern Critical Interpretations* (New York: Chelsea House, 1987). Some influential and well-known essays included.

Dale Kramer (ed.), *Critical Essays on Thomas Hardy: The Novels* (Boston, MA: G. K. Hall, 1990). Some significant essays and a very useful critical introduction.

HARDY AND CLASS

Included here are some significant early contributions and good recent work on this topic.

Arnold Kettle, *Hardy the Novelist: A Reconsideration* (Swansea: University College of Swansea, 1966). Established Jude as 'the first working-class hero' (p. 12).

Terry Eagleton, 'Introduction', in Thomas Hardy, *Jude the Obscure*, New Wessex edn (London: Macmillan, 1975), pp. 13–23. Reprinted in Harold Bloom (ed.), *Thomas Hardy's* Jude the Obscure: *Modern Critical Interpretations* (New York: Chelsea House, 1987), pp. 61–71. Vigorous argument for the centrality of class to the novel's educational theme in particular.

George Wotton, *Thomas Hardy: Towards a Materialist Criticism* (Dublin: Gill and Macmillan; Totowa, NJ: Barnes and Noble, 1985). Marxist study, also taking up issues of gender.

Ruth Danon, *Work in the English Novel: The Myth of Vocation* (London: Croom Helm; Totowa, NJ: Barnes and Noble, 1985), pp. 156–98. Deals with the importance of class, work and vocation in *Jude*.

Peter Widdowson, *Hardy in History: A Study in Literary Sociology* (London: Routledge, 1989). Study focused on the critical formation of a Hardy canon.

Joe Fisher, *The Hidden Hardy* (Basingstoke: Macmillan, 1992). Succinct and vigorous account of the novel's radicalism.

HARDY AND GENDER

Included here are some influential early contributions on this topic and some interesting recent work.

Kate Millett, *Sexual Politics* (London: Rupert Hart Davis, 1971), pp. 130–4. Pioneering, if rather inaccurate, feminist reading of the novel.

Mary Jacobus, 'Sue the Obscure', *Essays in Criticism*, 25 (1975), 304–28. Firmly places Sue Bridehead at the centre of the critical agenda.

John Goode, 'Sue Bridehead and the New Woman', in *Women Writing and Writing about Women*, ed. Mary Jacobus (London: Croom Helm in association with Oxford University Women's Studies Committee; Totowa, NJ: Barnes and Noble, 1979), pp. 100–13. One of the first accounts of the novel to focus on the figure of Sue Bridehead in relation to late nineteenth-century feminism.

Adrian Poole, '"Men's Words" and Hardy's Women', *Essays in Criticism*, 31 (1981), 328–45. Introduces an important area of interest, the linguistic alienation of Hardy's female characters.

Rosemarie Morgan, *Woman and Sexuality in the Novels of Thomas Hardy* (London: Routledge and Kegan Paul, 1988). Detailed and extensive feminist reading.

Patricia Ingham, *Thomas Hardy* (New York and London: Harvester Wheatsheaf, 1989). Structuralist-influenced study of Hardy's 'narrative syntax' and of his 'women as signs'.

Phillip Mallett, 'Sexual Ideology and Narrative Form in *Jude the Obscure*', *English*, 38 (1989), 211–24. Examines the novel's form as a dramatisation of its heroine's predicament.

T. R. Wright, *Hardy and the Erotic* (London: Macmillan, 1989). Opens up some important areas of concern, but is not altogether coherent critically.

Margaret R. Higonnet (ed.), *The Sense of Sex: Feminist Perspectives on Hardy* (Urbana and Chicago: University of Illinois Press, 1993). A strong collection, with a notable essay on masculinity in *Jude* by Elizabeth Langland and a controversial account of the novel's relation to sadism by James R. Kincaid.

Laura Green, '"Strange [In]difference of Sex": Thomas Hardy, the Victorian Man of Letters, and the Temptations of Androgyny', *Victorian Studies*, 38 (1995), 523–49. Fine examination of Hardy's concern with ideals of androgyny and determinations of gender.

HARDY AND TEXTUALITY

Included here are critical and scholarly studies focused on Hardy's language and style, as well as discussions of his allusions.

John Sutherland, 'A Note on the Teasing Narrator in *Jude the Obscure*', *English Literature in Transition*, 17 (1974), 159–62. Brief but helpful account of the narrative manipulation of knowledge through allusion and withholding.

Marlene Springer, *Hardy's Use of Allusion* (London and Basingstoke: Macmillan, 1983). Usefully details and categorises Hardy's allusions, but does not offer a very sophisticated critical perspective.

Ralph W. V. Elliott, *Thomas Hardy's English* (Oxford: Basil Blackwell, 1984). Linguistic study of Hardy's writing.

Dennis Taylor, *Hardy's Literary Language and Victorian Philology* (Oxford: Clarendon Press, 1993). A more specialised study of 'the awkwardness of Hardy's literary language' (p. 1) and its significances.

Listed here are critical accounts of the novel, earlier and recent, drawing on various theoretical perspectives and on formalist criticism, but concerned with its textuality.

Frank R. Giordano, Jr, '*Jude the Obscure* and the *Bildungsroman*', *Studies in the Novel*, 4 (1972), 580–91. Reads *Jude* as a parodic invocation of the generic conventions of the nineteenth-century *Bildungsroman*.

Ian Gregor, *The Great Web: The Form of Hardy's Major Fiction* (London: Faber, 1974). Argues for Hardy as an experimenter with fictional form, using *Jude* as a key example of 'a conflict between a kind of fiction which he had exhausted and a kind of fiction which instinctively he discerned as meeting his need, but which, imaginatively, he had no access to' (p. 209).

Dale Kramer, *Thomas Hardy: The Forms of Tragedy* (Detroit: Wayne State University Press, 1975). Reads *Jude* in relation to the generic conventions of tragedy.

Vincent Newey, '*Jude the Obscure*: Hardy and the Forms of Making', *Proceedings of the English Association, North*, 1 (1985), 29–52. Analyses *Jude* as a novel which draws attention to its own status and modes as a text.

Patricia Alden, *Social Mobility in the English* Bildungsroman*: Gissing, Hardy, Bennett and Lawrence* (Ann Arbor: University of Michigan Press, 1986). Historically informed genre-based account.

Jan B. Gordon, 'Gossip and the Letter: Ideologies of "Restoration" in *Jude the Obscure*', *Lore and Language*, 8 (1989), 45–80. A theoretically sophisticated examination both of Hardy's process of textual revision and of the linguistic theme of the novel.

HARDY AND THE USES OF MYTH

Ruth A. Firor, *Folkways in Thomas Hardy* (New York: Russell and Russell, 1931). The first and most comprehensive exploration of the importance of folklore in Hardy's writing, although it is not always reliable.

Jean R. Brooks, *Thomas Hardy: The Poetic Structure* (London: Elek, 1971). Explores Hardy's use of archetypes to convey a pre-Freudian understanding of motivation.

Janet Burstein, 'The Journey Beyond Myth in *Jude the Obscure*', *Texas Studies in Literature and Language*, 15 (1973–4), 499–515. Lucid argument that *Jude* constitutes Hardy's rejection of mythic structures.

Gayla R. Steel, *Sexual Tyranny in Wessex: Hardy's Witches and Demons of Folklore* (New York: Peter Lang, 1993). Argues for the importance of the figures of the witch and the demon in Hardy's representation of conflict between the sexes.

Shirley A. Stave, *The Decline of the Goddess: Nature, Culture, and Women in Thomas Hardy's Fiction* (Westport, CT: Greenwood Press, 1995). A reading employing feminist archetypes.

HARDY AND PSYCHOANALYSIS

Perry Meisel, *Thomas Hardy: The Return of the Repressed* (New Haven, CT: Yale University Press, 1972). Classic Freudian study.

Rosemary Sumner, *Thomas Hardy: Psychological Novelist* (London: Macmillan, 1981). Argues that Hardy anticipated in his fictional writing the theoretical insights of Freud, Jung, and other twentieth-century psychoanalysts.

Jeffrey Berman, 'Infanticide and Object Loss in *Jude the Obscure*', in *Compromise Formations: Current Directions in Psychoanalytic Criticism*, ed. Vera J. Camden (Kent, OH: Kent State University Press, 1989), pp. 155–81. Suggests that the figure of Little Father Time betrays a particular form of depressive relation to the world.

Notes on Contributors

Penny Boumelha is the Jury Professor of English Language and Literature and Deputy Vice-Chancellor (Education) at the University of Adelaide. Her publications include *Thomas Hardy and Women: Sexual Ideology and Narrative Form* (Brighton, 1982), *Charlotte Brontë* (Brighton, 1990), and articles on nineteenth-century fiction, realism, and eighteenth-century literary manuscripts. She is currently working on gender and nationality in late nineteenth-century Irish writing and writing about Ireland. She is the editor of this Casebook and is currently editing Charlotte Brontë's *Shirley*.

Christine Brooke-Rose is an English experimental novelist who lives in Provence, France. Until she retired in 1988 she was Professor of English and American Literature at the University of Paris VIII. Her publications include *A Grammar of Metaphor* (London, 1958), *A ZBC of Ezra Pound* (London, 1971), *A Rhetoric of the Unreal: Studies in Narrative and Structure, Especially of the Fantastic* (Cambridge, 1981), and *Stories, Theories and Things* (Cambridge, 1991). The collected *"Utterly Other Discourse": The Texts of Christine Brooke-Rose*, ed. Ellen G. Friedman and Richard Martin, was published by Dalkey Archive Press in 1995.

Richard Dellamora teaches in the departments of English and Cultural Studies at Trent University, Ontario. He is the author of *Masculine Desire: The Sexual Politics of Victorian Aestheticism* (Chapel Hill, NC, 1990), *Apocalyptic Overtures: Sexual Politics and the Sense of an Ending* (New Brunswick, NJ, 1994) and *Postmodern Apocalypse: Theory and Cultural Practice at the End* (University of Pennsylvania Press, 1995). He has recently compiled *Work of the Opera: Genre, Nationhood, and Sexual Difference*, ed. Daniel Fischlin (Columbia University Press, 1997).

Maria DiBattista is Professor of English and Comparative Literature at Princeton University. She is the author of *Virginia Woolf's Major Novels: The Fables of Anon* (New York, 1980) and *First Love: The Affections of Modern Fiction* (Chicago, 1991). She has also jointly edited, with Lucy McDiarmid, *High and Low Moderns: Literature and Culture, 1889–1939* (Oxford, 1996).

Tim Dolin is Lecturer in English at the University of Newcastle in Australia. He has published *Mistress of the House* (London, 1997), on the relationship between Victorian fiction, law and social change, and has edited Hardy's *The Hand of Ethelberta* for the Penguin Classics Series (1997).

Marjorie Garson is Associate Professor of English at the University of Toronto. She is the author of *Hardy's Fables of Integrity: Woman, Body, Text* (Oxford, 1991).

John Goode was formerly Professor of English Language and Literature at the University of Keele. He is the author of *George Gissing: Ideology and Fiction* (London, 1978) and *Thomas Hardy: The Offensive Truth* (Oxford, 1988). He edited *The Air of Reality: New Essays on Henry James* (London, 1972) and George Gissing's *New Grub Street* for The World's Classics Series (Oxford, 1993). John Goode died in 1994. *The Collected Essays of John Goode*, ed. Charles Swann, was published by Keele University Press in 1995.

Patricia Ingham is Fellow in English at St Anne's College, Oxford, and Times Lecturer in English Language. Her recent publications include *Thomas Hardy: A Feminist Reading* (New York, 1989), *Dickens, Women, and Language* (1992) and *The Language of Gender and Class: Transformation in the Victorian Novel* (London, 1996). She has also edited Hardy's *Jude the Obscure* (The World's Classics, Oxford, 1985) and *The Pursuit of the Well-Beloved and The Well-Beloved* (Penguin Classics, 1997), and Elizabeth Gaskell's *North and South* (Penguin, 1996); and written an Introduction to *Tess of the D'Urbervilles* (Everyman Classics, 1991).

Carla L. Peterson is an Associate Professor of Comparative Literature and English at the University of Maryland, College Park. She is the author of *The Determined Reader: Gender and Culture in the Novel From Napoleon to Victoria* (New Brunswick, NJ, 1986) and *Doers of the Word: African-American Women Speakers and Writers in the North (1830–1880)* (Oxford, 1995), and has published essays in *American Literary History: Frederick Douglass: New Literary and Historical Essays*, ed. Eric Sundquist (Cambridge, 1990), and *The (Other) American Traditions*, ed. Joyce Warren (New Brunswick, NJ, 1993).

Ramón Saldívar is Professor of English and Comparative Literature at Stanford University. He is the author of *Figural Language in the Novel: The Flowers of Speech from Cervantes to Joyce* (Princeton, NJ, 1984); *Chicano Narrative: The Dialects of Difference* (Madison, WI, 1990); and *The Borderlands of Culture: Modernity, the Nation, and Chicano Subject Formation* (forthcoming).

Index